DISCOVERING CALIFORNIA

A selection of articles and photographs
from *Pacific Discovery* magazine
in facsimile reprint

Edited by Bruce Finson

California Academy of Sciences
San Francisco

California Academy of Sciences
Golden Gate Park
San Francisco, California 94118

Edited by Bruce Finson
Editorial assistant — Patricia Jackson
Production coordinator — Ku, Fu-sheng
Typesetter (front matter) — Regent Street Type and Design, Berkeley, CA
Printed in Chelsea, Michigan by BookCrafters Inc.

Distributed to the book trade by Strawberry Hill Press, San Francisco

Manufactured in the United States of America

Library of Congress Cataloging in Publication Data
Main entry under title:

Discovering California.

    1. California—Description and travel—Addresses, essays, lectures. 2. Indians of North America—California—Addresses, essays, lectures.
3. California—History—Addresses, essays, lectures.
4. Natural history—California—Addresses, essays, lectures. I. Finson, Bruce, 1932–   . II. Pacific Discovery.
F861.5.D57   1983   979.4   83-7671
ISBN 0-940228-13-0
ISBN 0-940228-12-2 (pbk.)

CONTENTS

PUBLISHED BY THE CALIFORNIA ACADEMY OF SCIENCES · SAN FRANCISCO

IN THIS ISSUE: *William Beebe*

Olaus J. Murie · Robert T. Orr · Robert Cunningham Miller

Earle G. Linsley · A. Starker Leopold

VOLUME I · NUMBER I

January-February 1948

FIFTY CENTS

A JOURNAL OF NATURE AND MAN IN THE PACIFIC WORLD

Cover of the first issue of *Pacific Discovery*, January-February, 1948.

INTRODUCTION

California has been discovered again and again—by poppies and redwoods, grizzly bears and wolves, wandering Toltecs, exploring Europeans . . . and vactioning Americans. You can discover California for yourself, not only in journeys through parks and forests, but also in the pages of this book of discovery. Selected from *Pacific Discovery* magazine, these articles about the golden state will help you re-discover even places you have seen and known. For they will help you look at the landscape with understanding as well as delight.

A popular magazine of natural history and human ecology, *Pacific Discovery* is published by the California Academy of Sciences. The articles selected from the magazine will show you, in enjoyable prose and an abundance of photos, how your state looks from the point of view of the naturalist-observer. In the articles included here, you will learn about California's native inhabitants, its European explorers, its abundant wildlife, its varied greenery, and its mountain, seaside, desert, and forest landscapes.

Since its founding in 1948, and during the tenures of its first two editors—Don Kelley and Bruce Finson— *Pacific Discovery* has published about 1000 articles, and perhaps 10,000 photographs about man and nature and their interrelation. May you delight in the landscapes and inhabitants of your state as revealed by the writers, photographers, artists, and editors who have produced this magazine—and may you go on from this book to the pages of the magazine itself, available to members of the Academy and to all those who wish to subscribe to "A Journal of Nature and Man in the Pacific World."

BRUCE FINSON
Editor

PREFACE

On a spring day in 1853 seven San Franciscans met in an office on Kearny Street. Their common bond was an interest in the natural sciences and they were convinced that California offered "a field of richer promise in the department of natural history in all its variety than has previously been discovered."

In a period of high gold fever, with the infant State of California not yet three years old and San Francisco itself boasting only two paved streets, these men of vision founded an academy, the California Academy of Sciences, to explore the riches of the natural history of the state.

This exploration is still going on today. The academy has widened its field beyond California, but even here hundreds of new species have yet to be discovered and named, and the history of the nature of California's plants and animals, rocks and fossils, is still slowly being unfolded.

Over the years, scientists and explorers from the Academy and other institutions have explained their findings through the medium of *Pacific Discovery*, the Academy's natural history magazine. Many of the articles are classic descriptive statements, as valid now as when they were written. Editor Bruce Finson therefore proposed that the best of them should be published in the form of a book on California.

Personal exploration is a necessity for each new generation. All of us, native born or immigrant, need to learn about our surroundings, and the more we can learn to understand what we see of the origin of coast and estuary, mountain and plain, and the patterns of animal and plant life, the more we enrich our enjoyment of our environment. To understand is also necessary if we are to preserve what is good.

Mr. Jeffery W. Meyer, vice-chairman of the board of trustees of the Academy, helped make the concept of this book a reality, and this volume is due to his enthusiasm and his support.

I hope that this book helps many, both young and old, to a fuller understanding of the varied and fascinating state of California.

FRANK H TALBOT
Director

THE FIRST CALIFORNIANS

The European conquest of North America was justified, in part, by the claim that the Native Americans were inferior, perhaps even subhuman, beings. And in the region of North America considered to be the most desirable—perhaps because of its climatic resemblance to the Holy Land—the Indians were referred to in the most scathing fashion. Their capability of living off the land without farming or herding, but by harvesting its abundant natural yield, was derogated by the term "diggers." Even after the Native American Rebellion of the sixties, which earned a more nearly rightful place in history for most of the tribes, the now-almost-extinct Indians of California were still looked upon as having been less noble than the other savages. In the pages of *Pacific Discovery* an abundance of articles has helped present the true stature of these people and their culture.

The Chumash tribe occupied the coast around what is now Santa Barbara, from San Luis Obispo to Los Angeles, and east to Bakersfield. Their extraordinarily rich artistic culture has been reconstructed by teams of archaeologists, and their murals, still in part preserved on rock formations in the forest, have been recorded. In "The Chumash Indians of California" (1977), the story of their material culture is presented by two California archaeologists. At the time this article was written, Allen Pastron was Assistant Professor of Anthropology at the University of Santa Clara. He has since done extensive fieldwork among the Tarahumara Indians of Mexico. C.W. Clewlow has been Chief Archaeologist of the UCLA Archaeological Survey, has studied the early Olmec culture of Mexico, and has co-authored a book on prehistoric rock art of California.

Much of the Native American's skill at harvesting wild food plants and preparing delicious recipes from them still remains among surviving California Indians. Many of them have supplied extensive wild-food information to people who wished to learn how to live in a more direct relation to the land, and have also allowed their food-preparation techniques to be documented photographically. In "Food Plants of the California Indians" (1971), Robert L. Hoover, Assistant Professor of Anthropology at California State Polytechnic College in San Luis Obispo, presents an overview of these food plants, and of the methods of using them still practiced.

As European penetration into the backwoods of North America became geographic and cultural dominance, many upheavals occurred among the Native American tribes caught between the two cultures. Tribes were moved from place to place to suit the Europeans' need for land or labor, frequently being pushed onto one another's territory, often with violent results. One of the strangest incidents occurred on the offshore island of San Nicolas, when a group of Aleuts left by a whaling captain killed all the native Nicoleno Indians but one. The story of the last woman of the Nicoleno, who lived alone on the island for eighteen years, has been a source for fictional treatments. In "Desert San Nicolas and the Last Nicoleno" (1960), the factual details are presented by Robert M. Norris, geologist at the University of California in Santa Barbara, who visited the island several times to collect anthropological and geological data.

When the Indians of the mainland were pushed further back into the forests and canyons and rocky areas unsuited for European life-styles, their way of life changed from peaceful occupance of the land, through warlike ferocity in defence of their world, to cautious hiding as they tried to survive any way they could. Remnant bands were hunted down by white settlers eager to rid what was now their land of these natives-become-intruders. One of these Indians, the last survivor of the massacre of the Yahi tribe, finally gave himself up. He came to live in San Francisco, where he demonstrated the hunting and fishing techniques of his lost culture. The story of Ishi has been made known through several books, notably by Theodora Kroeber, but one of the earliest accounts, prior to the books, was presented in "The Haunted Canyon" (1948), by biologist Joel Hedgpeth, who has explored the region around Deer Creek Canyon where Ishi and the last of his fellow tribesmen lived.

One more-recent result of the resurgence of Indian consciousness has been the informal banding-together of Indians from several tribes within a region, in order to share their culture, maintain social contacts, and continue aspects of their lifeway in the midst of the modern world they have adapted to. At Grinding Rock State Park, where acorn-grinding stones with over 1000 mortar-holes have been preserved, a number of Miwok and related central California groups have constructed a replica of an Indian village. Once a year, during the Indian holiday gathering known as BigTime, Indians gather here as of old to celebrate the acorn harvest with songs, dances, and ritual games. In "BigTime at *Chaw'se*" (1982), the annual celebration is presented in words and pictures by ecological and anthropological writer Elizabeth Leite.

THE CHUMASH INDIANS OF CALIFORNIA

Allen G. Pastron and C. W. Clewlow, Jr.

IN OCTOBER of 1542 the Spanish adventurer Juan Cabrillo, exploring the legend-shrouded coast of Alta California, sailed into the calm, sun-washed waters of the Santa Barbara Channel. He hoped to discover gold and add to the dominions of his king. He found no treasure but did, somewhat to his surprise, encounter a remarkably prosperous and vigorous native society. This tribe, whom the Spaniards called Chumash, numbered between 10,000 and 15,000 individuals. As such, they constituted one of the largest groups of Indians anywhere in western North America. Their territory was correspondingly vast and diverse, encompassing some 6500 square miles of coastline and adjacent hinterlands between present-day San Luis Obispo and Malibu. The centrally-located Santa Barbara region was the geographic and cultural heart of the Chumash world, and contained the largest, most densely populated settlements.

The Spanish explorer was impressed by the Chumash, who received him in a friendly, yet dignified, self-assured manner. He noted that their populous villages were the largest he had seen outside Mexico. The climate of their country was mild, the environment bountiful. The technology which the Indians employed to exploit the resources of their habitat was both ingenious and efficient. Cabrillo, a devout Catholic, could not help but take a special, almost morbid, interest in Chumash religious life. He found their spiritual beliefs and customs to be complex and intricate yet at the same time frightening, incomprehensible, and bizarre. All in all, Cabrillo, like most later Spanish explorers who encountered the Chumash, came to the conclusion that these Indians were, in terms of both their material and social culture, by far the most sophisticated of all native Californians.

Today the Chumash, once so numerous and widespread, have vanished. Cabrillo's visit was for the Indians the first step on what was to be a long, weary trail leading to oblivion. Three centuries of unremitting hardship, disease, and exploitation, visited upon them first by Spanish missionaries and

Above, Chumash Indians dancing at Mission San Jose, 1806, their bodies colorfully and elaborately painted (from "Bemerkunden auf einer Reise um die Welt in den Jahren 1803 bis 1807," by G. H. von Langsdorff. Courtesy, The Bancroft Library).

7

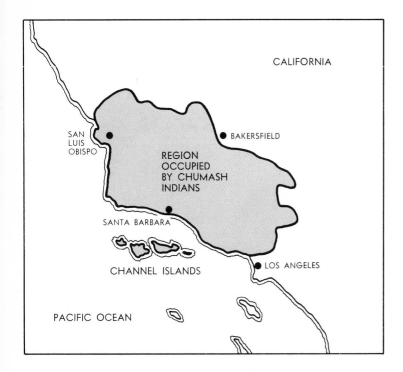

Top, map of Chumash territory. Above, Chumash house (from "The Rock Paintings of the Chumash" by Campbell Grant, University of California Press, 1965). Right, interior of a Chumash house (from "Personal Narrative of Explorations in Texas, New Mexico, California, Sonora and Chihuahua," by J. R. Bartless, Appleton, 1854).

soldiers, later by Mexican ranchers, and finally by American miners and settlers, brought about the total extinction of the Chumash Indians and their way of life.

Considering how large and important a tribe the Chumash were, surprisingly little is known about them and their culture. They left no written testament to tell of themselves, and whatever fragmentary oral tradition may have somehow survived into the twentieth century passed forever beyond recovery with the death of the last full-blooded Chumash in 1952. Even the Spanish chroniclers, who observed Chumash culture in its full flower, wrote mainly in terms of sweeping generalities, based on their often clearly prejudiced impressions. They recorded few useful, unbiased facts about the specific workings of the aboriginal social, economic, and religious systems. What we are left with are the remains of the now silent, buried villages, and the broken, discarded tools and other cultural remnants they contain. Any story of the Chumash must now be reconstructed through the medium of archaeology. Only by the tedious probings of the archaeologist's trowel can we hope to give the memory of these remarkable people a future.

The contemporary American public is almost totally ignorant of the Chumash. While many tribes of American Indians, particularly those with large extant communities such as the Sioux and Navajo, have captured the popular imagination,

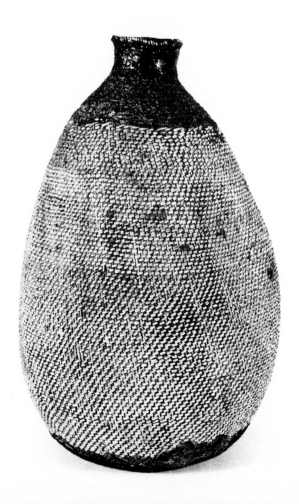

Left, the Chumash had no pottery, but made baskets watertight by lining them with asphaltum obtained from seeps. The baskets were lined by coating a hot rock with asphaltum and rolling it about the interior. Asphaltum was also used as a trade item with other tribes. Above, cooking vessel made of steatite quarried on Catalina. Steatite was easily carved and heat-resistant. Below, vegetable foods, especially acorns, were ground in stone metates. The profusion of metates reflects the importance of acorns and seeds in the Chumash diet.

the Chumash, along with many other groups of native Californians, remain virtually unknown. What little general information exists is mainly negative in nature, since the California Indians have been among the most maligned and misrepresented of all Native Americans. As a result of the ignorant and self-serving writings originating with the mid-nineteenth century gold rush, many people still picture aboriginal Californians as rude, debased "diggers"—insensitive savages totally devoid of culture.

No characterization could be further from the truth. All cultures are well worthy of respect and serious consideration since each, in its own way, formulates unique and ingenious strategies to cope with the universal problems of making a living and passing on its knowledge to the next generation. Every society possesses art, religion, music, and other forms of philosophical and intellectual expression. That some cultures are technologically simple while others are complex does not make one better or more worthy of respect than another.

The Chumash, in many ways different from ourselves, nevertheless enjoyed the benefits of a thriving society, one which clearly merits our unfortunately belated attention and understanding. Possessing a highly adaptive economy, they tapped their country's subsistence potential to the fullest. Their political organization was well developed and complex; their spiritual notions abstract and well developed. They had a rich artistic heritage in both painting and sculpture. Some of the Chumash painted caves are world-famous and rank among the finest examples of North American Indian rock art. Like the well-known paleolithic cave art of France and Spain, Chumash picto-

Left above, U.C.L.A. Archaeological Survey at work on a Chumash village (photograph by Allen G. Pastron). Left, Chumash baskets were woven in highly formalized decorative patterns (from Lowie Museum of Anthropology, Berkeley, California). Right, a Chumash canoe, with Mission Santa Barbara and Presidio in the distance (from "A History of Upper and Lower California, north of Mexico" by A. Forbes, Smith and Elder, London, 1839). Right above, a Samala Chumash in ceremonial costume of a shaman (photograph by Leon de Cessac, 1879, collection, Musee de l'Homme, Paris).

graphs were far more than simple decorations. They had deep symbolic significance, and were intimately linked to religious beliefs, portraying aspects of the supernatural world.

The Chumash, like most other groups of native Californians, made their entire living by hunting, and collecting wild foodstuffs. They did not farm or domesticate livestock. Yet in opposition to the popular conception of the eternally hungry, culturally impoverished hunter, the Chumash did not suffer economic want.

The prosperity and stability of Chumash culture can be seen in the remains of their large coastal villages. Many of these settlements were permanently occupied and contained over 1000 inhabitants. The Chumash house, circular in shape and often exceeding twenty-five feet in diameter, provided comfortable shelter for as many as thirty people. The frame was of poles, supported by a number of thick posts near the center. The roof was thatched with surf grass. The door was constructed of two whale ribs placed to form an arch.

Each village contained at least one large *temescal*, or sweat house, probably the most universal institution in aboriginal California. Both men and women retired daily to the *temescal* for physical and spiritual rejuvenation as well as relaxation.

Productive as it was, the economic system that supported these large settlements was, in most respects, no different from that of other hunting and collecting societies. Like other California Indians, the Chumash made extensive use of wild plants for food. The great accumulations of ground and pecked stone mortars and pestles, grinding slabs *(metates)* and grinding stones or

mullers *(manos)* attest to the great importance of vegetable foods in the aboriginal diet. Seeds, roots, tubers, fruits, and nuts were, in their respective seasons, regularly collected by Indian women. Acorns constituted the most important plant food, since large quantities could be stored and kept in reserve as insurance against lean times.

The Chumash hunted deer, black bear, rabbits, and other game in the inland reaches of their territory, and collected numerous species of marine animals along the coast. The large quantities of shellfish remains in all Chumash sites indicates how heavily the people relied upon abalone, crabs, clams, mussels, and other marine invertebrates for regular and predictable sources of food.

What differentiated the Chumash economy from those of other California Indians was the possession of one specialized item of material culture that allowed the Chumash to exploit an entire sphere of the ecosystem that was beyond the reach of other peoples. The seagoing plank canoe, the *tomol,* was the glory of Chumash technology. It opened up the vast resources of the ocean to the Indians and assured them of a virtually inexhaustible supply of food. In their plank canoes, the Chumash fished the rich kelp beds just off their beaches year-round, catching anchovies, bonita, yellowtail, skipjack, and sea bass in incredible numbers. The largest fishes were harpooned, while most species were taken with baited shell hooks attached to lines made from plant fibers. The small fish running in schools were caught in nets and seines fashioned out of twisted yucca or some other equally suitable vegetable fiber.

The remarkable Chumash *tomol* was unique in native North America. Fashioned with meticulous, time-consuming care out of pine or some other coniferous tree, canoes ranged from 12 to over 25 feet in length, with an average beam of between three and four feet. The planks, laboriously shaped by razor-like chisels of sharpened shell or flint, were sewn together at the seams with strong thread. The joints were then covered with pitch. Finally, the entire craft was painted red with hematite.

The *tomol* was extremely light (two men could carry even a large one with ease), yet durable and infinitely more seaworthy than the heavier, bulkier, dugout canoes utilized by some Native American peoples. In these vessels, Chumash sailors, armed with detailed knowledge of local currents, winds, and surf conditions, braved the open ocean to explore and colonize many of the offshore islands.

The conquest of the Santa Barbara Channel

The Chumash used stone in many ways. Above, top to bottom, leatherworking and bead-making drills, arrowshaft straighteners, digging-stick weights, steatite pipes for smoking botanicals such as datura, and fishnet sinkers (from Lowie Museum of Anthropology).

enriched the lives of the Chumash in numerous ways. Indians living offshore maintained regular social and commercial contacts with those on the mainland, supplying them with chipped stone tools, baskets, and beadwork for seeds, acorns, and wooden implements. The Chumash commonly made the 100-mile or more round trip to Santa Catalina Island to quarry the highly prized steatite, a soft, pliable, heat-resistant stone from which cooking vessels, bowls, beads, and even pieces of sculpture were carved. Even the farthest island, San Nicolas, some 65 miles from the mainland, was not beyond the range of Chumash seamen, who regularly landed there in search of rich fishing grounds or some of the other locally abundant resources.

The relative economic and material affluence enjoyed by the Chumash gave them time to develop a correspondingly high level of social complexity and sophistication. Politically, the Chumash were organized into a number of autonomous or semi-autonomous village units. Each village possessed its own jealously-guarded hunting and collecting preserves, and was led by a hereditary chieftian. Alone among the people, the chief had the right to wed more than one spouse. Political leaders were usually men, but Spanish explorers reported having seen female chiefs in some settlements. The common people paid homage to their leaders by bringing them tributary offerings of food and shell money.

Some villages banded together in political and military alliances with one another, usually under the leadership of one powerful, dominant leader. The formation of these federations was not always peaceful. Some village chiefs with expansionist intentions subordinated their militarily weaker neighbors. Early Spanish accounts comment upon the frequency and ferocity of inter-village warfare. Chumash burial grounds often contain the remains of individuals who died by other than natural causes. Some skeletons have projectile points embedded in the bones; others have crushed ribs, broken limbs, or smashed skulls. Yet such chaos and social disruption should not be interpreted entirely negatively, for in these disorderly events can be seen the emergent beginnings of a type of political centralization and unity that characterizes all of the world's civilizations including our own.

Relations between the Chumash and neighboring tribes were, for the most part, peaceful and primarily concerned with commerce. The mainland Chumash regularly traded with the Salinans to the north, the San Joaquin Valley Yokuts and Kern River Tubatulabal to the east, and the Shoshonean-speaking Gabrieleno of the Los Angeles

The glory of Chumash culture was its elaborately beautiful and colorful paintings on cave walls. There are dozens of them in various stages of preservation, and they constitute one of the major art treasures of Native Americans. (Photograph by Allen G. Pastron.)

basin to the south. The Chumash provided their inland neighbors with the products of the sea, and in return received animal pelts, obsidian, piñon nuts, and other commodities commonly found in the Central Valley and foothills of the Sierra Nevada. Through trading activities the Chumash became acquainted with such distant peoples as the Mojave Indians of the Colorado River region, whose homeland was located over 400 arduous miles from the beaches of Santa Barbara.

About the religious beliefs of the Chumash, next to nothing is known. Fragmentary Spanish sources indicate that aboriginal spiritual activities were well organized and complex. Every village had an enclosed plaza where the people occasionally congregated to dance and worship. Spanish accounts also mention secret shrines, hidden deep in the most inaccessible reaches of the mountains. Large numbers of Indians would sometimes make pilgrimages to these mysterious places in order to leave offerings and participate in religious ceremonies. Perhaps these shrines were located in those places where today we find rock art. It is unfortunate that today no one can state with certainty what particular aspects of native religious beliefs are represented by the designs preserved on the walls of these caves and rock shelters.

Grave goods found in association with burials often give intimate glimpses into the spiritual world of the people who deposited these offerings of farewell. In addition to shell beads and the like, many Chumash burials contain numerous examples of the so-called fish effigies, small pieces of steatite carved in the shapes of whales or other marine creatures. While we do not know the specific significance of these funerary artifacts, we can nonetheless see in them the unparalleled impact of the sea upon the Chumash mind.

The Chumash knew a pristine California of which many of us today dream, but can never possibly know. They knew their environment well and were better adapted to it than we. They attained a balance with their habitat which eludes modern man. They achieved prosperity without detrimentally altering the face of the land or despoiling the earth of its treasures. Far from being the miserable "diggers" they have often been characterized to be, the Chumash achieved much of value that would be well worth our while to take the time to understand. We share a common homeland with the Chumash and other native Californians and, therefore, to a certain extent, a common heritage as well. We would be totally incorrect and ignorant to blithely assume that California history begins with the sixteenth-century Spanish explorations. For while European acquaintance with California spans some four centuries, the Chumash and their predecessors had been here for more than 10,000 years. No history of California would be complete without a lengthy treatment of such native peoples as the Chumash, and the cultural heritage they have bequeathed to all of us. ✢

Chumash sweathouse (Forbes, 1839).

FOOD PLANTS OF THE CALIFORNIA INDIANS

Robert L. Hoover

TODAY, Californians often overlook the great variety of environmental niches within the boundaries of their state as they rush from one spot to another on their high-speed freeways. Industrial man has created his own standardized environment which is much the same in Tahoe City or El Centro. His shelters are similar and contain artificial temperature controls. His mass-produced clothing and widely accepted standards of food are nearly identical everywhere. The California Indians, with a simpler technology at their command, were not able to insulate themselves from their environment with such efficient thoroughness. They had to adapt to their immediate environment and become experts in its exploitation in order to survive. By the time of the first Spanish explorers, the Indians had become quite good at the business of survival. Though the state accounts for only one per cent of the total area of North America, its rich environment supported ten to fifteen per cent of the continent's population. This proportion of California aborigines to North Americans is, interestingly, about the same today.

The California Indians utilized most plants at one time or another for various purposes, but certain plants served as food staples or were used for special gastronomic purposes. The acorn was the

Steps in preparing acorns for use as food:
Left, after gathering, acorns are stored until
needed in a cache on a wooden platform.
Above, cracking acorns for the day's use.

major plant staple in the valleys and coastal ranges of California. Coast live oak or encino *(Quercus agrifolia)*, valley oak or Roble *(Quercus lobata)*, tanbark oak *(Lithocarpus densiflora)*, canyon oak *(Quercus chrysolepis)*, and black oak *(Quercus kellogii)* were preferred, depending upon local availability. The acorns were harvested when they turned a ripe brown in the fall. Over 500 pounds of acorns might be required to feed an Indian family for a year. The harvested acorns were slowly dried in the sun.

Acorns were stored whole or in cracked condition in special large acorn storage baskets, bins, or hollow tree trunks. The Miwok Indians of Tuolumne County constructed outdoor acorn bins of four stout posts supporting a deep basin of twigs and brush. The structures were covered with thatched roofs as protection from the rain. The bins were about one yard in diameter and up to six feet tall. Such containers provided good protection against the elements but were useless against the incursions of squirrels and chipmunks. The Maidu Indians of the eastern Sacramento Valley stored their acorns in special baskets on shelves around the edges of their pit houses.

The Indians ground a portion of their stored acorns into flour when they were ready to use it. The pulverization process took place in bedrock mortars, portable stone bowls, or hopper mortars. The hopper consisted of a basket-like frame with

no bottom. It was placed over a stone slab and was secured with tar in southern California or was simply held down with the legs in northern California. A few acorns at a time were poured into one of these containers and were reduced to meal by women using elongated handstones or pestles. The meal was sifted in a circular basket, and the coarser particles were reground until satisfactory.

Unprocessed acorn meal contains large quantities of bitter tannic acid which the California Indians removed by a lengthy leaching process. The details of this process varied with the particular Indian group. Many northern tribes spread the acorn meal directly in a basin of fine sand on a river bank. Water was slowly and repeatedly poured over the meal, carrying the tannic acid away with it into the sand. The Indian women tasted the meal periodically and, when the bitterness was gone, sometimes only after a full day, the leaching process was complete. Some central California groups lined their sand basins with fir or cedar leaves and, farther south, open-work baskets were similarly lined and used for leaching.

Acorn meal is, at best, a bland substance after leaching. Pulverized berries, cedar bark flavoring, or iron-rich clay were sometimes added by the Indians to improve the taste. Atole, a thick gruel of acorn meal and water, was heated in special watertight mush boiling baskets by dropping heated stones into the mixture. This indirect me-

After cracking and grinding, the acorn meal is leached to rid it of tannic acid, above. Right, the boiling the acorn mush in a basket with heated stones. (Photographs by S. A. Barrett)

thod of boiling the contents of the basket without burning the container over a direct fire was common in northern and central California, where pottery and stone cooking vessels were not used. The atole mush was eaten by dipping the fingers or a mussel shell scoop into the communal basket.

Less commonly, the Indians mixed acorn flour with a red clay to "sweeten" it and baked it as bread in earth ovens. These ovens had linings of stones and were pre-heated with a wood fire. The remaining coals were raked out, and the dough was placed on the heated stones. Coverings of leaves, coals, and finally of earth conserved the heat during the twenty-four hour baking period. Acorn bread prepared in the traditional manner is sweet and black, but assumes a formidable rock-like hardness if not eaten in a few days.

Studies of the nutritional value of acorns for cattle fodder during World War II revealed the oak as a rich source of starch and vegetable oils. The acorn was certainly adequate for human needs if prepared properly and supplemented occasionally with fish, meat, and fruits. As a further interesting sidelight on the use of ground plant materials in general, the accounts of early frontier physicians and modern archaeologists frequently mention the advanced wear of adult Indian's teeth —the result of chewing ground materials in which grit from the milling stones had been mixed.

The California buckeye *(Aesculus californica)*

was another food-producing tree of the coasts and valleys of the state. Buckeye nuts, like acorns, were poisonous before processing. Many aboriginal groups gathered these nuts in the fall, removed the outer husk, and cooked them whole. Later, the brown inner husk was removed, and the buckeye meat was ground into meal. The flour was leached for about ten days in a shallow pebble-lined basin on a stream bank or in tightly-woven basketry containers which had been lowered into pools of running water. Sticks were placed beside the pool for each day of processing to mark the passage of time. Finally, the meal was cooked into gruel and immediately eaten.

The seeds of the islay or holly-leafed cherry *(Prunus elicifolia)* were prepared similarly as a base for soup.

The toyon *(Heteromeles arbutifolia)* produced abundant red berries in California's chaparral belt. The berries were collected in baskets and roasted over coals or were tossed in a parching basket with heated stones or coals. The nuts of the California laurel *(Umbellularia californica)* were collected and roasted when needed. Jojoba or goatnut *(Simmondsia chinensis)* was the source of rich oily nuts in the desert mountains. These nuts could be eaten immediately or made into a drink.

Several swamp plants were utilized by the Indians. The cattail *(Typha* spp.) provided edible

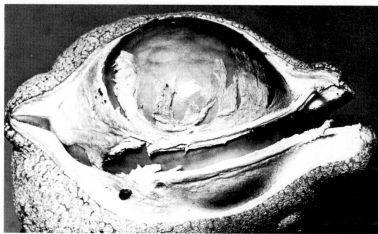

roots and young shoots. The soft material from the heads of these plants was used as disposable diapers. The Arrowhead or Tule potato *(Sagittaria latifolia)* is a tuberous pond plant of northern California. Indian women waded into the water in late summer, pushing baskets before them, and loosened the tubers with their toes. The entire plant would float to the surface and could be placed in the basket. After roasting, the tubers were skinned and eaten immediately or were mashed into flour.

The Indians of California made extensive use of various liliaceous bulbs. Some species of mariposa lily *(Calochortus* spp.) were unearthed with pointed digging sticks and eaten raw, but most were roasted in stone-lined earth ovens until soft and brown. The early miners of Gold Rush days adopted these bulbs as a survival food. The camas *(Camassia quamash)*, the staple plant food of the Pacific Northwest, was prepared in a similar way until reduced to a sweet mass that could be eaten at once or dried in cake form and stored. The Indians tried to collect the camas while it was producing its characteristic blue flowers. After the flowering season, it was often confused with the white-flowering death camas *(Zygadenus venenosus)*, a fatal plant to eat. Other notable bulb plants used as food included the wild onion *(Allium* spp.) and the indian onion *(Brodiaea* spp.).

Seeds of a great variety of smaller plants were economically important to the California Indian. Chia *(Salvia columbariae)* is one of the most famous examples. This sage grew in large quantities and produced small grayish seeds. The plant was bent over a large flat basket and was beaten from above by a basketry seed-beater to dislodge the seeds. These seeds were ground into a meal, rich in a sticky mucilagenous substance that expanded in hot water. Cakes and biscuits could be made from the flour and had a tasty nut-like flavor. The high nutritional value and digestibility of Chia was supposed to sustain an Indian for a full day on a forced march. It was also reputed to have neutralized the alkalinity of water from desert oases. *Salvia carduacaca* produces larger seeds which were used in the same way.

Top, the California buckeye, and, below it, a nut with its outer husk removed. This food source was poisonous before processing. (Charles Webber photos from CAS Picture Collection.) In the two lower photos the buckeyes are being husked and then the mashed meats are being poured into a leaching pot. (Photos by S. A. Barrett)

The tansy - mustard *(Descurainia pinnata)* and peppergrass *(Lepidium fremontii)* produced seeds which were beaten into baskets, roasted on parching trays, and ground into meal along with other seeds to make pinole flour. The lacepod *(Thysanocarpus curvipes)* was used similarly.

A wide variety of plants provided the Indian with green vegetables. Wild cabbage *(Caulanthus crassicaulis)* and the new leaves of the prince's plume *(Stanleya* spp.) were boiled. Miner's lettuce *(Montia perfoliata)* was eaten raw or cooked. This plant of the shade forest was adopted by the

The seeds of lacepod, right, were ground into flour, and miner's lettuce, far right, was eaten either raw or cooked. (CAS Picture Collection.) Below, a field of salvia. Its seeds were a source of flour used to make a sort of bread. (Photograph by Harry H. Haworth)

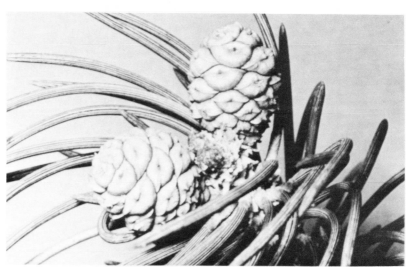

Manzanita berries, top left, were gathered for food. (Photo by Robert L. Hoover.) Top right, crushing manzanita berries. Left, gathering tarweed seeds. (Photos by S. A. Barrett.) Above, piñon pine nuts, another important food source. (Charles Webber photo from CAS Picture Collection)

"sourdoughs" of the Gold Rush era and was even used as an emergency food in England during World War II. It has a strong mustardy flavor.

The Indians of the California deserts had less of a variety of plant resources, but they intensively utilized some of those available plants. In the region east of the Sierra Nevada, the Indians practiced vertical transhumance—the seasonal exploitation of food resources at differing elevations. Small mobile bands collected wild grass seeds in the valleys of the Great Basin during the spring and then traveled up the mountain ranges in the fall to harvest the seeds of the piñon pine *(Pinus monophylla)*. This tree presently grows between 3,500 and 9,000 feet elevation along the eastern Sierra slopes and sporadically in the parallel ranges of the Great Basin.

Paiute bands erected temporary brush shelters near piñon groves in the late fall. Men with long forked sticks dislodged the cones, and the women collected them in large burden baskets. The cones were piled in heaps and burned to dry the pitch and cause the cone scales to open and release their seeds. The Indians struck each of the inverted cones at the base and knocked out as many seeds as possible. Each nut shell was cracked with stone grinding implements before winnowing the shells from the seeds in shallow baskets. The nuts could be eaten dried or were roasted and stored for later use.

In the lower Mojave and Colorado Deserts, the mesquite *(Prosopis juliflora)* and the screwbean *(Prosopis pubescens)* were the most important food plants. The ripe beans were collected, sun-dried, and stored in openwork baskets. The entire pod was ground into meal without removing the seeds. The Indians added water and allowed the resulting concoction to ferment for several hours to improve the taste. The fresh pod and drink were both eaten without cooking. The pods were often pulverized in slender pestles of mesquite wood.

Several desert plants of the agave and cactus families were important sources of food to the Indians. The mescal or century plant *(Agave* spp.) sends up a large flowering stalk from the center of its rosette of leaves in the spring. The Indians pried out the flowering heads with sticks and baked them overnight in covered pit ovens, sandwiched between agave leaves. The baked heads were sweet and juicy. Many were eaten on the spot, but others were formed into cakes, dried, and stored for the winter. The cakes were sometimes used as the base for a sweet drink after being boiled in water. The flowering buds of the agave could also be roasted and dried for winter use. Agave seeds were ground into flour for use as a gruel.

Of the cacti, the beavertail *(Opuntia basilaris)* and prickly pear *(Opuntia occidentalis)* were most important sources of aboriginal food. The fruits were knocked down with sticks and

collected in large baskets. After tediously brushing off the fine short spines, the fruits were cooked in pits for about twelve hours. These fruits which were eaten raw were first carefully peeled. This author can verify the delicious flavor of fresh cactus fruits, though it varies with the species. Someties the fruits were dried and the seeds ground into meal. The Paiutes ate the flower buds and young joints of the beavertail cactus.

The increased interest in ecology and survival arts has focused attention on the aboriginal food plants of the world. California, with its unique wealth and abundance of native plant life, is a particularly rewarding area of study. Though tastes vary widely, the knowledge of Indian uses of foods plants is a satisfying excursion into our gastrononmic past. ✤

Among the desert plants used for food were the beavertail cactus, above, and the agave, left. (Charles Webber photo from CAS Picture Collection)

DESERT SAN NICOLAS

The large sandspit at the southeast end of San Nicolas, where Captain Nidever and Charles Brown landed in 1853.

The wind blows away the sand covering San Nicolas' ancient cemetery, and now and then a robust Nicoleño skull is revealed. (Courtesy Clement W. Meighan; see his "The Nicoleño," *Pacific Discovery,* January-February 1954)

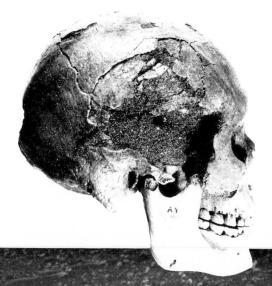

ROBERT M. NORRIS

SIXTY MILES south of Port Hueneme lies San Nicolas, a barren, flat-topped island of about twenty square miles. Of all the southern California islands, San Nicolas is the most distant from shore. Politically, it is a part of Ventura County, although the county authorities there, like most other southern Californians, are seldom concerned with it.

An unknown visitor to the island shortly before the turn of the century was much impressed with the wind-swept desolation he saw there; the island seemed to him to be blowing into the sea. This traveler referred to San Nicolas as the "Passing Island," an appropriate name in many respects. The past century has seen the disappearance of the last of the Channel Island Indians—the famous Lost Woman of San Nicolas—and even the dogs that lived with the Indians. Now, there are only one or two survivors of the thousands of sheep that were grazed on the island after 1860. As if this weren't enough, the persistent winds and occasional rains are carrying the island itself into the sea, particle by particle.

Although the island was named by Sebastián Viscaíno in 1602, the first white man to see it was probably Ferrelo, Cabrillo's pilot, who left Santa Cruz Island one February day in 1543 in a small launch to search for other islands reported off the inner group. Doubtless, many travelers during the 17th and 18th centuries passed close by San Nicolas, but few of these took the trouble to land and fewer still bothered to comment on it in their journals. The lack of even a fair anchorage and the forbidding, barren appearance of the island probably caused many of these early travelers to seek other more favored landfalls. By the early part of the 19th century, when many trading ships were operating illegally in Californian waters, San Nicolas had more frequent visitors because of the relative safety afforded by its isolation. Many of these traders and hunters found it advisable to elude the Spanish authorities by spending some of their time at the outer islands. One of these men, a Captain Whettemore, who was in the sea otter trade, visited San Nicolas in 1811. He landed his otter hunters, a group of thirty well-armed Aleutian Indians from Sitka. The Captain had business in Baja California which did not require his crew of otter hunters and he therefore sailed without them, returning a few months later. During his absence the Aleuts got into

cisco in the *Peor es Nada* and was lost at sea. During the following years, the islanders, who were eventually taken to Mission San Gabriel, all died, and the last survivor of their race, still on the island, was probably forgotten by nearly everyone but the padres at Mission Santa Barbara. They remained hopeful that one day the Lone Woman might be found because they continued to receive occasional reports from visitors to the island who claimed to have seen a woman's footprints on the beach sands. Finally, in 1853, Padre Gonzales of the Mission persuaded Captain Nidever of Santa Barbara to go in search of the last surviving Nicoleño.

Captain Nidever failed to find the woman on either his first or his second visits. However, he did find unmistakable evidence that she was still living. Thus encouraged, he made the third trip accompanied by Mr. Charles Brown and a number of Barbareño Indians. Brown landed on the southeastern end of the island—on the large sand spit. Here he arranged his Indians in line, a hundred yards or so apart, but within speaking distance, and had them move slowly forward, painstakingly combing every inch of the island. Late in the morning they came upon a hut

Eighteen years alone on California's desert island, an Indian woman outdid Robinson Crusoe

a dispute with the islanders, probably about the women, and systematically butchered all the poorly armed island men and boys, or so the story goes.

Word of the massacre eventually reached the Mission padres at Santa Barbara who arranged with Captain Sparks of that city to set out with his little schooner, the *Peor es Nada* ("Better than Nothing"), to bring back the remaining women. Captain Sparks sailed in 1835, twenty-four years after the Aleuts had done their terrible work. When the *Peor es Nada* reached San Nicolas, seven or eight women were taken aboard—some accounts say as many as twenty. One of the women either hung back when the rest went aboard, or later jumped over the side and swam ashore, supposedly protesting that she had forgotten her child; it is not clear what actually happened. In any event, she alone remained on the island, for faced with a developing storm Captain Sparks feared to wait in San Nicolas' dangerous anchorage and set sail, intending to return for the Indian woman later on. The islanders were landed at Santa Barbara and later taken to San Pedro. A short time after his return to Santa Barbara, Captain Sparks sailed for San Fran-

Limpet shells (*Megathura*), with the centers broken out and the edges ground down, became favorite Nicoleño ornaments. Fishhooks and beads were also of shell. Other objects—whale figures, whistles, pipes, miniature canoes— were carved out of steatite (soapstone). (Courtesy Clement W. Meighan)

Indian shell-mound filled with quantities of land snails, abalones, and sea urchins. (Author)

made of whale ribs and brush, near which they found a basket of feathers. Brown ordered the Indians to scatter the feathers and temporarily abandoned the search. Later the same day, upon revisiting the hut, they found that the feathers had been replaced in the basket, but still no woman was in sight.

The next day when the search was renewed, Brown caught sight of a figure struggling up the hill toward the hut and bearing a heavy load. By the time Brown and the Indians reached the hut, the Indian woman was sitting skinning a sea lion, guarded by her dog who growled menacingly as Brown and the Indians approached. She rose as Brown drew close, and bowed toward him. When the Indians reached the hut, and saw her, they all knelt. Upon seeing people of her own race, she came toward them and offered them food. She indicated by signs—none of the Indians could understand her language—that she would have come to them, even if they had not first found her. Brown and his party spent the following month on the island and gradually learned from the lone woman how she had lived alone eighteen years by catching fish, abalones, and sea urchins which were plentiful along the island shore. She showed them how she occasionally crept up on a sleeping sea lion and killed it with a heavy rock.

On the way back to Santa Barbara, the weather was bad and the sea rough and she was much frightened. She begged the sailors to placate the wind or sea gods, or so they interpreted her signs. She recognized all the islands and had names for them. Upon landing at Santa Barbara, she was terrified at her first sight of horses and cattle and doubtless much impressed with the city itself. In all likelihood she was born on San Nicolas and had never been away before.

After her arrival on the mainland, she was cared for by Captain Nidever and quickly adapted herself to the strange ways of the people in whose midst she found herself. She became a favorite in the community and spent much of her time visiting the various Mexican families and dancing for them. The padres at Mission Santa Barbara christened her Juana Maria, to which the townspeople added Peor es Nada in memory of the little schooner that had brought her relatives to the mainland years earlier. Although the padres at the Mission had Indians from all over southern California brought to Santa Barbara, none could speak her language. Only one very old woman was even able to understand any of her words. Juana Maria Peor es Nada was therefore forced to make all her desires known by means of sign language.

After only six weeks in Santa Barbara, she sickened and died, most probably because of the great change in diet. She was about 45 years old at the time. It is reasonably certain, however, that her last days in Santa Barbara were happy ones because Captain Nidever did his best to see that she was comfortable and not in need. With her passing went the last member of a once numerous and prosperous people.

For some years after the departure of the Lone Woman, San Nicolas had no inhabitants save the foxes, mice, lizards and the more or less itinerant birds. Sometime after 1860, sheep were brought to the island and grazed by a succession of solitary herders, many of whom were Basques. As is so often the case, the efficient sheep ate the short island grass faster than it could grow, and large tracts of the island formerly protected by grass and chaparral

Abalone exposed on the rocks along the
northwest coast during low tide—this was
an important part of the Nicoleño diet.

were laid bare to the savage attack of wind and rain.
About 1940, when the military removed the last of
the herders and most of the sheep, many deep gullies
and barren tracts of sand dunes had spread over areas
formerly covered by short, thick island grass. Thousands of bleached, empty snail shells cover the drift-
ing sand where vegetation once flourished. In recent
years, with no sheep to interfere, the grass is gradually creeping back over the bare spots and loose sand.

Surprisingly enough, even San Nicolas did not
escape the wild enthusiasm associated with the land
boom of the 1880's in southern California. In 1886,
an unusually optimistic real estate promoter divided
the entire island into lots. It is not known whether
any of these were sold, but if they were, we have no
record of any owners coming to claim their share of
California's desert island.

Today, San Nicolas is a Naval reservation and is
closed to the public. The Indians and their dogs are
gone; the sheep herders and their sheep are gone—
only the descendants of the foxes, lizards and mice are
there to form a living link with the past. ❧

The author's
brother,
Kenneth Norris,
standing beside
a fretwork
carved over
the years in
sandstone by
sand-laden
winds.
(Author)

⩗ Some areas
are covered
with shells of
land snails
stranded by
the receding
tide of grass.
(Author)

THE HAUNTED CANYON

Joel Hedgpeth

THE CANYON OF DEER CREEK winds its way across the lava plateau of Tehama County, California, south of Lassen Peak, as a sheer walled trough, about thirty miles long. The stream that threads the bottom of this canyon starts as a brook among the sedges and grasses of a meadow in a parklike area between the aspens and lodgepole pines of the mountain country. The canyon itself begins as a shallow valley in the heavy forest at the lower end of the meadow. Soon there is an abrupt drop over which the stream is catapulted in a spectacular waterfall, and the valley becomes narrow and rocky. As the stream gradient increases, the walls of the canyon become higher. In the middle part of the canyon the walls are gaunt battlements nearly a thousand feet high.

Here and there a break in the canyon wall permits the entrance of a side stream. The tributary canyon is often flanked by pillars and pinnacles

Graham's cabin on Deer Creek, Tehama Co., Calif.

of brown and gray lava, encrusted with palette-like daubs of yellow, green, orange, and lavender lichens. The stream in the depths of the canyon tumbles over rubble and around huge boulders or slips through sluice-like channels of solid rock. In summer the water is low and warm, in winter it is a fury of cold white energy capable of throwing huge trees high up on benches or jamming them between rocks where they remain for decades. Smaller drift, summer and winter, finds its way southwestward with the stream to the Sacramento River.

There are a few level patches in this almost inaccessible canyon, and on nearly every one there is an abandoned cabin, slowly falling apart. They look as if they had always been there, these forlorn ruins, and as if no one had ever lived in them. There is usually a table on trembling legs, or a bench built against the wall, and often there is a worn-out stove. Now and then a hunter or a fisherman spends a night in one of them, and some are used by the cattlemen, but always when a stranger comes upon them he finds no sign of life except the scurrying of a pack rat beneath the floor or the buzz of hornets around a nest under the roof. How the lumber, even the few boards and two-by-fours, was carried down the long rocky breaks in the sheer canyon wall, is something of a mystery—probably on mule or horseback, but that must have been a tedious business for both man and beast.

Graham's cabin, perhaps the oldest on the creek, was built sixty or seventy years ago, of square-hewn logs cut from a nearby pine grove. Old Man Graham seems to have made a sort of living trapping, and raised most of his food on a few roughly level acres on both sides of the stream near his cabin. The most accessible of the cabins is just inside the mouth of the canyon on a little flat of three or four acres. It is a little frame shanty, perhaps twelve feet square, and its walls are papered with newspapers bearing the date of January 1, 1911. The headlines tell the story of the death of Art Hoxie in an airplane crash. There are reports of interviews with other aviators of the day — Moissant and Johnson — who remembers them now? The stock market was light on the last day of 1910: less than 100,000 shares changed hands. The latest book of Gibson Girl drawings had just been issued for the holiday trade. One wonders what the man who pasted these newspapers on the wall was thinking as he did so, and when he left the cabin. He had thought well enough of his place to plant a few roses, which still grow and bloom there after thirty-five years.

The inevitable gold diggings, universal in the California mountains, are marked by the indestructible piles of gravel on the benches around Polk Springs, deep in the canyon. But this is not gold country, this lava-bound region, and no one ever made his salt here. At Polk Springs there is also an abandoned hard rock mine, financed by stock sold in England. Perhaps the shares can still be found in English garrets or lumber rooms, hidden away in old trunks.

The sheer lava walls of the canyon are pocked with shallow caves like solidified bubbles, some of them high on the faces of the cliffs, where only hawks and owls have ever been, and others near the ground, with smoke-blackened walls that indicate they were once the dwelling places of men.

Alders, laurels, and willows grow along the stream. On the benches there are oaks and stunted pines. Here and there near the canyon rim is a grove of larger pines. At the lower end of the canyon, in the foothills outside the forest belt, the vegetation is chiefly willows and scrub laurel. At the edge of the lava plateau, where the level acres of the Central Valley are spread along the Sacramento River, the canyon comes to an abrupt end. The stream, freed of its narrow rock channel, meanders down to the river in a shallow gravel wash, bordered by large cottonwood trees and thickets of willows.

What white man first saw this canyon, we do not know. Perhaps it was John Bidwell, who named the streams in this country (without much originality), and suggested Deer Creek to Peter Lassen as a likely spot to settle. Lassen blazed his own trail across the mountains—it was a very bad route—from the headwaters of the Humboldt in Nevada, to bring settlers to his new city on the bank of Deer Creek. The last part of his trail followed the lava ridge north of the canyon down to the valley and his ranch, which was a couple of miles from the river. Lassen's settlement, ambitiously named Benton City, is remembered only by specialists in local history. The Lassen ranch even-

tually fell into the hands of Leland Stanford, who made a show place of it, with solid red brick barns and warehouses. During the prohibition era the wine grapes which were the particular pride and main resource of the ranch were pulled up; today the big barns are empty and the little town of Vina dozes beside its large, unused railroad station. At the highway, as it crosses Deer Creek, there is a stone monument beside a boulder-lined hole. This, an old cellar, is all that is certainly left of Benton City.

Long after the days of Peter Lassen and Benton City the original inhabitants of Deer Creek canyon lived in its untraveled recesses, and the manner of their going has made it haunted ground. Their last village, which they called Wowunupomotetna, the Hiding Place of the Bear, was only fifteen miles from the railroad. From the rimrock they could see the strange smoking beast on its way along the river. Yet for thirty years no white man knew of this village, and few believed that the once-feared Indians of the canyon still lived.

At the beginning of their end, the Yahi, as they called themselves, were much like any other northern Californian Indians. They were a hunting and food gathering people, whose acknowledged territory was the slice of lava crusted foothill country along the watersheds of Mill and Deer Creeks. The Yahi were the southernmost branch of a larger people, the Yana. All were foothill Indians, and the settlers called them Mill Creeks, without distinguishing the separate groups. The Yahi were, however, different from their neighbors and relatives in one important respect. They were used to fighting for their own, and the rocky canyons of their country with innumerable hiding places gave them a secure refuge from which to carry on their fight. But like their neighbors, they had no tribal organization, and they were without a strong leader.

How and when the Yahi first found themselves in difficulties with the settlers has not been recorded. Old Peter Lassen never had any trouble with them during his years on Deer Creek or while leading wagon trains through their country. But the Gold Rush brought a new variety of the human species to California, the rough character who regarded the Indian as a sort of vermin, in the same class as the wildcats and the rattlesnakes. There is a record that in 1851 one of these individuals, encountering an Indian whose looks displeased him, hung the redskin from a tree as a

Looking upstream from the mouth of Deer Creek Canyon. (Photograph by O. R. Smith)

lesson in deportment for the rest of his kind. Although this Indian was almost certainly not of their tribe, as the incident took place some distance south of Deer Creek, the news of it doubtless reached the Yahi.

The fundamental difficulty, of course, was the destruction of the game animals which were the Indian's meat supply. It was no rare thing for white hunters to kill several bears in a single day and leave the carcasses to rot after taking only the hides and tongues. What they did to the smaller animals which were even more important to the Indian economy has not been considered worthy of record. Cattle stealing by the Indians was an inevitable result of these inroads on their food supply, although it is certain that the Indians did not understand the white man's peculiar sense of property. Nor did the settlers trouble themselves about the fine points of Indian territories or different kinds of Indians. On their punitive expeditions into the hills they often killed the first band of Indians they met. If the chase was futile, they would go out of their way on the return trip to ambush some entirely innocent Indians.

The story of the fifteen years between that first hanging and the massacre of the Yahi is a tangled and bloody tale. There were long and futile chases through the mazes of the Deer Creek country, murders and abductions of whites by the Indians in reprisal, and counter-reprisals by the whites. The most determined expeditions were led by settlers from neighboring regions who had no immediate grievance, rather than by those nearest to the Yahi country.

During one hot September a troop of cavalry blundered over the hills without seeing an Indian. A Mrs. Dirsch was murdered, and the northern Yana were reduced to a remnant over the protests of their white employers, and the pockets of the dead were picked for their wages. The Lewis children were kidnapped. The boy was killed, and the girl, thankful, escaped by following Deer Creek downstream. These stories are still told in the country, often with bloody and obscene elaborations.

One version, told to me by one of the county's

noted spinners· of tall tales, is evidently a blend of several incidents:

I can tell you all about the damned Indians. They came down to the valley and stole some children. They killed the little boys and left them on a rock pile near here, and they went on with the girl. Somehow she got away when they left her behind with an old squaw. She remembered that her father told her to go downstream and she'd always get some place, so she came right down Deer Creek. She got down and she told folks about it, and a fellow—he's a dead shot—his name was Thomas, got up a posse and came right up to the meadows after them. They caught up with the Indians—he could see their camp smoke—and they surrounded them. Nobody shoot till I give the word, he said, and they killed every one of those Indians.

The murders which led to the disastrous end of the Yahi occurred on Concow Creek, far south of their range, but the Indians' reputation was against them. Mrs. Workman, her hired hand, and Miss Rosanna Smith, who had just arrived from England, were killed by Indians. Unprintable details have gathered around this killing, together with a confused story of several hundred gold sovereigns, which no one has ever found. To avenge these murders seventeen white men, most of them neighbors of the victims, set out to finish the Mill Creeks. Whether they trailed the Indians across the half dozen canyons between the site of the crime and the Yahi country, or assumed the direction of the trail, cannot be determined at this late date. At any rate, a trail was picked up just south of Deer Creek, and was followed across Deer Creek and into the smaller canyon of Mill Creek. On the eve of August 15, 1865, near a place now known as Black Rock, the avengers approached the Yahi camp.

Early in the morning the Indians were surrounded. Half the party worked down from the upstream side while the others blocked off escape downstream. When the alarm was given in the camp, a swift, brief massacre followed. The Indians, trapped in their narrow canyon, were poorly armed and unable to inflict any casualties on their attackers. When it was over, the creek was clogged with bodies and the sand bars between the rocks were sticky with fresh blood. After all the men had been killed, there was an argument. Should they let the women go, or kill them also? This was settled by turning them over to the neighbors from

Concow Creek, who "dealt with them as they saw fit." A few years later a visitor to the place counted nearly forty-five skeletons.

There was one known survivor of this massacre, a boy with six-toed feet. The boy had caught the eye of one of the guides, who had an "odd taste about such things." A squaw was saved to take care of him, but it was a long climb out of the canyon and she had been wounded in the foot. When she refused to carry the child farther, she was shot. Five years later Hi Good was killed by his six-toed Indian boy in an argument over money.

The massacre of 1865 was the end of the Yahi as a hostile nation, but not of all the people. Some, perhaps, escaped from that disaster, others were somewhere else at the time. A few years after the massacre some Indians came to an outlying ranch, which happened to be Hi Good's place, to give themselves up and be taken to the reservation at Round Valley in Mendocino County. While the Indians waited around for some person of authority to arrive, one of the ranch hands amused himself by casting a rope over a tree limb. His idea was to hang a steelyard and weigh himself, but the Indians had had enough of the white man's ways—for them a rope over a tree limb had but one meaning. Without trying to recover the bows which they had brought with them in token of their surrender, they ran away. It was to be nearly forty years before one of these Indians, then the last survivor of his race, was to talk to a white man again.

There was one more massacre, in April, 1871. A band of about thirty Indians was trailed to a cave after a steer had been wounded by an arrow. All of these Indians were shot by the cowboys. One of them shot the children with his .38 calibre revolver because his .56 Sharps "tore them up so bad."

The surviving handful of the Yahi kept out of sight. Occasionally they would rob a cabin, and rarely someone caught a fleeting glimpse of an Indian disappearing into the thickets or rock piles. Only the recluses who lived in the lonely cabins along the stream and the cattlemen who worked in the country believed that there were still wild Indians living in the canyon. Old Man Graham, in his rough cabin of square-hewn logs, had more than his share of trouble with them, and set out poisoned flour for their benefit. The stories brought down to civilization by these hermits were laughed off by the townfolk as old timers' yarns.

But it was impossible to dismiss the incidents of 1908 as fiction. A surveying party, brushing out a line for a proposed water power development (which has never materialized), blundered into the middle of an Indian village hidden in a dense thicket of laurel trees.

The night before, two of their party had returned from a stroll, soaking wet, with a story of having been threatened by a naked Indian with a huge spear. They had escaped by swimming across the stream. Their fellow surveyors had thought it a fine, realistic story, and complimented

it seem that the band itself was reunited after this dispersal. Ishi, the brandisher of the spear, did not care to talk about this part of his life and his exact relationship to these people was never established. For the next few months the village was visited by all sorts of curious people, among them anthropologists from the University of California, whose professional interest brought them back to the scene several times. The Indians had abandoned the site altogether. It has since been burned out by a brush fire, and no trace of it remains.

In August, 1911, nearly three years after the

Ishi with salmon spear, May 1914. (From Univ. Calif. Publ. Amer. Arch. and Ethn., Vol. 13, No. 2, 1918, courtesy of the University of California Press)

them on getting wet to substantiate it. Now here, in broad daylight, they had found the Indians. Two of them ran off into the rock pile at the base of the cliffs. One remained, a paralyzed old woman, who begged for water in almost forgotten Spanish.

The village itself was a cluster of three or four small huts of boughs, so well concealed that they were invisible from the cliff overlooking the laurel thicket in which they had been built. When the surveyors returned later in the day, the old woman was gone. They took away the effects the Indians had left behind in their flight as souvenirs, not realizing that the Indians needed them in order to survive.

No one ever saw these Indians again, nor does

discovery of this hidden village, a half starved Indian appeared in the yard of a slaughterhouse near Oroville, thirty-two miles south of Deer Creek. His hair was burned short in token of mourning and his only clothing was a cast off undershirt. He cowered in a corner while the dogs barked at him, and he was sick with fear. The sheriff was summoned, and the Indian was taken off to the county jail.

At a loss to know what to do with him, the sheriff placed him in the insane cell. The Indian knew no English, or any other language but his own, and he became a nine days wonder in the press. The University's anthropologists, hoping that this was one of the survivors of the Yahi village, sent Professor T. T. Waterman to try out

Ishi demonstrating his bow and arrow. (From Univ. Calif. Publ. Amer. Arch. and Ethn., Vol. 13, No. 2, 1918, courtesy of the University of California Press)

a vocabulary on him. It was not the same dialect, but one word was familiar to the Indian: *su wini*—yellow pine. In this manner, Ishi, the last stone age man in the United States, came down from the hills.

Chaperoned by Dr. Waterman and an old survivor of the northern Yana tribe summoned to act as interpreter, Ishi left for San Francisco. First he wanted to hide from the train, which he believed to be some sort of evil demon. Once in San Francisco, he soon adjusted himself to civilization. The high walls of the tall buildings did not awe him in the least; after all, they were hardly as imposing as the cliffs of his homeland. But he never ceased to be amazed at the number of people in the city.

Street cars delighted him. He watched them for hours, marveling at their size, the noise of the gong, and the snorting of the air brakes. Automobiles impressed him less. Soon he learned to accept the works and doings of white men with apparent calm. When an airplane was pointed out to him, he was only mildly curious. It seemed quite natural to him that a white man should be up there. A water faucet was much more interesting and practical to Ishi.

He was a find for the anthropologists. All of his life had been lived by the primitive skills and crafts which had long since been forgotten by other California Indians. The language he spoke was virtually unspoiled. He was an excellent craftsman, especially at making bows and arrowheads. Dr. Saxton Pope, an ardent archery enthusiast, became his friend and personal physician, and learned much about the Indian ways of hunting with the bow and arrow from Ishi. His dialect proved too much for the interpreter, who condescendingly regarded him as a savage, but authorities on Indian languages came great distances to listen to him and record his stories.

The Board of Regents of the University of California formally appointed Ishi a museum helper, and he was given a room in the anthropology museum, which then adjoined the Medical School on Parnassus Heights in San Francisco. Here he made a wonderful collection of arrowheads, most of them from bottle glass. Bromo-Seltzer bottles were his favorite material—he liked the blue color. Although he never learned much English, he managed to do his own shopping by the expedient of pointing out the desired item in the store. He preferred the comforts of the museum, the chairs, a bed, the shelter, and the water that could be turned on and off, to the primitive life he had formerly known, and at no time did he want to return to his old way of life. Even the idea of a camping trip along Deer Creek did not appeal to him, but once reassured that he was not going to be left behind in the mountains, he agreed to go along.

When Ishi first came to civilization he was in perfect health, a typical specimen of the stocky California Indian type. He had never worn shoes or clothes, and he soon recovered from the hardships of his years of wandering after the break-up of the last village. He let his hair grow, became fat, and was contented with his lot. But he did not have the white man's immunity to the diseases of civilization, and soon contracted tuberculosis. He died a few months after the onset of the disease.

After the tradition of his people Ishi was cremated with his bow, a quiver of arrows, and some food. His remains, placed in an urn, were deposited in a San Francisco cemetery. The inscription reads: "Ishi, the last of the Yahi Indians. Died March 25, 1916."

Unfortunately little has been written about the character and personality of this man Ishi. Primitive or wild men brought to civilization are common enough, and some people have been quick to point morals from the episodes, usually in favor of the simple life. The noble savage stoically accepting the complications of civilization, yet wasting away for the carefree life of his native heath is the familiar pattern for these incidents. During the days of Rousseau and Chateaubriand there was a deluge of this sort of thing, and some of it got tangled with the political thinking which underlies our own philosophy of government. Since the development of modern anthropology, however, this has gone out of fashion. It appears that the simple life is far from simple, but is complicated by customs as artificial as our own. Nevertheless, the character of Ishi indicates once again how much of our civilization makes no essential contribution to our spiritual well being.

AUTHOR'S NOTE. The principal sources for the life of Ishi and the history of his tribe are the papers of T. T. Waterman and Saxton Pope, in *University of California Publications in American Archaeology and Ethnology*, Vol. 13, Nos. 2 and 3, 1918. There are some pamphlets by "old timers" of the region, of indifferent historical value, and hard to obtain, the best of which is "Fighting the Mill Creeks," by R. A. Anderson, Chico, California, 1909. Recently there has been published a series of studies, "The Conflict between the California Indian and White Civilization," by S. F. Cook (*Ibero-Americana*, Nos. 21-24, University of California Press, 1943), which cover the entire problem. No. III of this series, "The American Invasion, 1848-1870," deals especially with the reduction of the Indian population since the Gold Rush.

To understand Ishi, we must remember that not only was he the last of his people, he was also the survivor of a submerged culture in the midst of a complex one beyond his comprehension. All his life, until his final years, he had lived in the fear and belief that the white man would destroy him on sight. His people before him had trusted no neighboring tribe. Ishi, who loosed arrows at white men after being frightened away thirty-eight years before by another white man hanging a rope over a stout limb, had every right to expect that he had not long to live when caught in that slaughterhouse yard in Oroville. But times had changed. It was no longer the style to shoot or hang Indians simply for being Indians. Instead, he was given a warm room in a museum and befriended by men interested in the manners and customs of his people, and by a doctor who wanted only lessons in using the bow and arrow.

Perhaps it was simply because he was a stranger among people whose ways he did not understand that he seemed to be a gentleman, yet he did by instinct the right things according to the standards of the civilization in which he found himself. As Dr. Waterman wrote, "he convinced me that there is such a thing as gentlemanliness which lies outside of all training, and is an expression of inward spirit. He never learned to shake hands but he had an innate regard for the other fellow's existence, and an inborn considerateness, that surpassed in fineness most . . . civilized breeding."

Whatever the reason, this Indian impressed all who knew him as something more than the last survivor of a tribe whose bloody history was alive only in the memories of the older settlers. Not the stern and noble savage, for he had spent too much of his life in hiding to outface people with the glittering stare of popular tradition, but a gentle, kindly man who did his best to adjust himself to his new circumstances. He was lonely and unhappy at times, as anyone would be when reminded of the tragedy of his people, but he was usually serene and sure of himself.

It may have been the innate resources of a life spent among hills, trees, and elemental things that gave Ishi his spiritual strength and enabled him to adjust himself to such a different life from the one he had known for more than fifty years. A sympathetic visitor to the canyon in which he lived would like to think so. Even one who knows nothing of the story of Ishi would not be surprised to meet a ghost from the past around the next turning of the trail between the rough-hewn lava walls with their bright crusts of lichen and their smoke-darkened caves.

BIGTIME AT *CHAW'SE*

Elizabeth Leite
Photographs by the author

THE home team—two men and two women—sit in a line facing their opponents at perhaps two yards' distance. They rhythmically drum against the log at their feet, beating time to their song with decoratively carved sticks. In unison they sing, the younger man taking the lead, his mother and the middle-aged couple singing more softly. Born of these golden, oak-covered foothills, the ancestral Miwok lands, the young native Californian and his quietly composed mother play the hand game one more time. During the weekend festivities they have been part of a team four times, and they will win four out of the five games, extraordinary good luck. This round the men hide the "bones," carved and painted cylinders perhaps four inches long and one inch in circumference; two are white and two are white with a black stripe around the middle. The ends gleam brightly in their dark hands.

The opposing team—composed of the Miwok tribal leader, three grade-school children, a young mustached man, and two women—watch the players intently. They joke among themselves and direct teasing comments toward the players, whose volume boldly increases as the men ready themselves in anticipation of the guessing. The players sing their power song to a crescendo, clearly and brightly, the vowel-rich syllables threading in and out of the steady drumming. They actively perform theatrics as they pass the bones from hand to hand, deceptively masking their movements beneath lapsize fringed game blankets. Like Coyote the Trickster, with power and deception they will fool their opponents.

The leader, a good natured man in his fifties, points a marker stick left, upriver. The younger man and his taciturn Paiute partner slowly and ceremoniously open their hands. The black and white bones lie positioned downriver, to their left, the leader's right. The bad guess costs the oppo-

Above, a few of the more than 1000 mortar-holes at Grinding Rock
State Park, where generations of Indians ground acorns into meal.

33

Right, Miwok youths in traditional costume performing a demonstration dance at Yosemite (courtesy of Yosemite Natural History Association). Below, members of one of the teams with lap game blankets hiding the bones during the hand game.

nents two marking sticks. Luck is holding; one more round and the game will be over. Their song swells with expectancy and good humor. The drumming heightens in volume. Suspense builds as they begin perhaps the final round.

The drumming can be heard throughout the meadow, even on the surrounding hillsides, reverberating the Indian way, as the day winds down to end BigTime, a yearly event at Indian Grinding Rock State Historic Park (*Chaw'se*). The official, state-sanctioned event commemorates and celebrates the acorn harvest and the California indigenous people who once ground their staple food here, under the flickering shade of hundred-foot, wide-canopied valley oaks (*Quercus lobata*), in granite outcroppings where grinding holes number over one thousand and petroglyphs attest to duration of heritage.

No less than one hundred years ago, the regular thud of pestle hitting mortar rock resounded in a constant rhythm, just as today the hand-game drumming fills the meadow like a beating heart. At these mortars women pounded the nutritious acorn into meal for gruel and bread, and powdered herb and seed for food, medicine, and flavoring.

Perhaps thirty adults, both white and native Californian, and half that many children sit scattered now beneath the bark-covered sunshade, the *ramada*, talking softly among themselves. A few women rock babies. Some drink coffee while they watch. Most pay little apparent attention despite the fact they, like the players, have staked bets on a winning team. Yet they obviously lend support by their physical presence, their joking commentary. The pot, matched evenly dollar for dollar on each team, lies between the adversaries, dollar bills forming a tidy pile. Those who wager will either lose all or double their investments.

Many of these people are direct descendants of the Sierra Miwok, a people who lived within a narrow strip of the Sierra Nevada foothills along the watersheds of three parallel east-west rushing rivers. The waters acted to separate the people into distinct groupings, whose customs and technology varied slightly. But overall, the Miwok formed a cohesive culture stretching along the western Sierran slope for about two hundred miles, from south of Yosemite National Park north into the Maidu country around Auburn, along the modern road to the casinos at Lake Tahoe.

This hand game lies deep in the cultural heritage of all California native peoples. Passed from generation to generation, the knowledge of moves, of songs and subtleties, contributes to the rich cultural remainders of a dispossessed but not defeated culture. So, too, the dances performed for spectators and kin earlier in this day and the day before by the hosting Miwok dancers and the visiting troupes reaffirm what it means to be native Californian in the 1980's.

The present game, the second of the afternoon, lasts longer than many—over two hours. Each team began with five markers, which neither has either lost or gained. The players are tired. Some played late into the previous night. A few men met to talk "man's talk" in the Roundhouse even as the darkness faded into dawn. The singing, however, brings renewed strength and the cheerful banter between players entertains all assembled. I tap my foot to the drumming, closely watching the young man on whom we have cast approval. The tribal leader feigns ignorance. He denies he knows the rules. His nephew, the weekend winner, jokes about old people, about women and children. Teasing and derogatory remarks attack tribal affiliation, individual power, prestige. Humor runs rampant. Occasionally the bones are passed to a child who changes a winning streak to failure, for children are rich in the power of deception. And then the older players are teased still more. This loving, off-hand jocularity underlines a deep respect for the elders, for continuity and the old ways, for the passing of culture to a new generation, for pride in what is left. The friendly rivalry, the hint of personal power, of good luck and even talent, increase individual prestige.

Winning or losing does not seem important here. This is the hand game. Music and theatre, magic and power occur in the course of the game. The bet simply enhances the festivity, provides the observer reason to pay attention. But win or lose, no one goes away unhappy. The good feeling generated will last till the next coming together. And

Cedar bark dwellings constructed in traditional manner as part of a village recreation. Poles of young incense cedar lashed with wild grape and honeysuckle vines provide a framework for mature cedar bark strips, making a warm and dry shelter.

for the entire nation.

Inside the ceremonial Roundhouse, constructed in one old and correct way, with door facing east, smoke hole in the center, bark-shingled roof supported by handhewn oak columns and walls of layered stone, the air feels cool and even a little moist despite the blazing sun. A frog croaks between drum beats, punctuating the rhythm. Somewhere among us, he escapes the burning afternoon heat. A shaft of light pours through the smoke hole, cutting a circle of light on the earthen floor.

Some dances are sacred. The participants know this. Most Indians know this. Many spectators do not. They take pictures. The male dancers curve the round of a circular path, bent forward at the waist, stepping with intricacy on bared feet, bowing the head side to side, arms and shoulders rocking to the regular beat, abalone shell beads jingling brightly. During certain songs the men and boys blow bone whistles which alternate with or emphasize the foot drum, a wood-covered hole-in-the-ground opposite the door, by the setting sun. With each lowering of the log pounder, the entire Roundhouse floor becomes a musical instrument. The dancers complete their cycle, as they began, with backs facing the fire and the observers, who sit sprinkled throughout the remaining seven-eighths of the sacred space on the ground or on a wooden bench which edges the entire circumference. Perspiration glints on bare backs. Smoke burns the eyes and tickles the nose. A few coughs and sneezes break the rhythm of the chantlike songs, the resonating earth. A baby cries.

The women also dance, generally flanking the

stories of this year's games will continue through the coming seasons.

Near the pole-supported bark-roofed sunshade, Chaw'se hosts several other historical reconstructions. Cedar bark sleeping structures, shaped like the proverbial teepees of the plains Indians, suggest a technologically simpler time. Beneath the widely branching oaks, their circular floor space remains empty of the skins and baskets, stone and bone implements, and other items of day-to-day necessity. Beyond them, crouching low to the ground, partially subterranean in the ancient manner, the Roundhouse shows its profile against the sky. Park workers, tribal council members, and some non-Indian volunteers were instrumental in making Chaw'se what it is today—a model of native American historic parks

men with a line. Each dancer moves slightly backward and side-to-side while remaining in one spot. They rock their bodies to the rhythmic pounding in a roll which moves the shoulders and the body, first to the right and up, then to the left and up. Miwok women hold strings of clinking beads in front of them which shake in time to their movements. Visiting women bend their arms at the elbows, palms open, arms tight against their sides. Behind the drum a line of singers chants the prayer-song, a polysyllabic litany. Each cycle completes with an emphatic "HO!" of applause.

Among the tribes represented here, style delineates tribal differences. But these are mainly ornamental flourishes. The overall pattern remains constant. The beat, the harmonious ritual sequence of the dances, the relationship of men to women—all demonstrate a cultural continuity which at one time spread throughout California.

Children dance; children play the game, these the carriers of culture from old to young. The dance captain proudly explains, "I learned this dance from an old woman now gone a long time. I taught her dance to the girls." And six teenage Miwok girls perform the basket dance, gracefully shuffling forward from a squared position in their buckskin dresses, into the center of the dance space and beyond, passing each other, slowly and gracefully, an ancient basket held at the shoulder. They perform the ribbon dance, fragile ropes of shining ribbon draped over their outstretched arms. Others show the Pomo coyote dance, men and boys stepping with alternatively slow and rapid steps, pausing for moments in the beat as though to catch a breath. Even a two-year-old boy dances, clad in red flicker feather head band, eagle

feather skirt, white leggings, and red loincloth. Dust swirls rise as the dancers complete their cycles.

Many dances will not be performed. So sacred, so potent, they will be hidden from spectators like myself who cannot experience the depths of their power and mystery. Later a Pomo woman explains to my husband and me: "We come to share our way in this place. We know it is right. This is powerful medicine for our old and sickly. The grinding rocks held food. They held healing herbs. This is powerful medicine for our old and sickly left at home."

She glows with energy and exuberance after she dances in her multicolored dance dress which, like an Egyptian tunic, pulls over the head and covers her from head to foot. Equally exuberant, she gathers manzanita berries later that day as treats for her grandchildren, so passing forward ethnic food preferences along with more spiritual matters. Native berries plopping into an empty cereal carton demonstrate the blending of old and new, traditional with contemporary.

Dust eddies gather and fall as the cars bounce into the meadow, through dry yellow grass beneath enormous deep green oaks. Young boys collect parking fees and provide directions. They wear international orange vests, looking official and apparently enjoying the importance of their duties. During the weekend several hundred cars will come and go, while only a few remain throughout, parked along the edges under the trees. These vehicles carried some visitors over two hundred miles, the Pomo and Wintun from interior California, the Paiute from over the crest of the Sierra into Nevada, and even a Karok family

Left, Miwok youths in traditional dance costumes (from "Indians of the Yosemite" by Galen Clark, C.A.S. picture collection). Below, early photograph of Chowchilla Indian in war dance costume.

from far to the north among the redwood forests and rushing waters of the Klamath River, almost at the Oregon border. Long ago these tribes would have spoken mutually unintelligible, non-related languages. These visitors all speak English and consider themselves kin. They pitch tents or sleep in campers. Perhaps the children sleep under the stars as the evenings are mild, and filled with a waning but yet rounded moon and the light of the Milky Way. People come and go from the Round-house, from the *ramada* and the cultural center, enjoying this coming together, this remembrance of the way. They play the hand game, dance their dances, re-establish friendships.

Children are everywhere. Dark-eyed babies in strollers, hand-held toddlers, schoolchildren, adolescents, young adults. They come with their parents to share community and spirit. A few dance, rigorously trained from infancy. A few play the hand game with the adults. Mainly, they amuse themselves as children will, in the ball field playing "Indian football," a game similar to soccer, or among themselves by their campers and tents, drinking sodas and eating hotdogs, eating frybread and jam. This is BigTime, a modern gathering of the tribe, like Fourth of July and harvest rolled into one, a weekend party with cousins, friends, and a few interesting strangers.

Spectators like myself attend BigTime to view the dances, to enjoy the deep pit barbeque lunch (a tribal council fundraiser), to see a few Native Americans. Many come with cameras and money to purchase authentic craft objects. Much food will be eaten; much coffee and soda pop drunk. Cameras click as the men hoist succulent beef and venison from its hidden subterranean oven, wrapped in aluminum foil and encased in water-soaked burlap to prevent burning. This meat, prepared in the old way with a few modern

technological variations, remains underground from Friday evening to Saturday noon, secretly steaming beneath a sheetmetal cover and piled earth, resting on a bed of fine oak coals. Indians and spectators alike eat from plates heaped high with crisp salad, spicy beans, fragrant tender meat. The strangers may return next year, having enjoyed the feeling of the event, the beauty of the place, the all-pervasive ritualistic easygoing nature of the day, the shared meal.

Park interpretive workers who are also Miwok tribal council members stage BigTime, presenting aspects of their culture to the public in the hope of increasing multicultural awareness. President Reagan, while still governor of California, declared the weekend of the fourth Friday in September, Native American Days. And thus each year the big party repeats itself, with food, dance, and song. It has layers of meaning attached to its occurrence—the official interpretation, community entertainment, and the deeper Indian meaning.

For beyond reaffirming the value of old cultural practices, beyond recognizing the positive nature of cultural differences, beyond simply having a good time, BigTime at Chaw'se serves another valuable social function. It is a true "gathering of the tribe," but the tribal concept has been extended to include all Native Californians who may choose to come. At home, perhaps on a reservation, a *rancheria*, in a small town, most share close ties of relationship—cousin, aunt, uncle, sister, brother. The young must seek suitable sweethearts elsewhere. BigTime provides the opportunity to form new intertribal and inter-familial marriage connections. Families bond new ties for the future among eligible youth. Few teenage observers are present at the late Saturday evening game. Like adolescents everywhere the young slip off by themselves to play and court, to

Early photos of California Indians. Below, a woman with carrying basket. Right, woman weaving a basket (Galen Clark, C.A.S. picture collection).

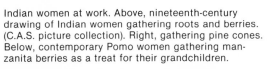

Indian women at work. Above, nineteenth-century drawing of Indian women gathering roots and berries. (C.A.S. picture collection). Right, gathering pine cones. Below, contemporary Pomo women gathering manzanita berries as a treat for their grandchildren.

Left, central Sierra Miwok family, 1913.
Below, left to right: Miwok man (photos
courtesy of Museum of Anthropology,
University of California, Berkeley); hand game
at Yosemite reconstructed Indian village
(Yosemite Natural History Association);
Indian mother and baby (Galen Clark, C.A.S.
picture collection); and contemporary
Indian father and child.

find a new boyfriend or girlfriend. This setting encourages intertribal marriages, and so strengthens the Native Californian culture.

The owners of a red pickup truck plastered with bumper strips accentuate this point. "I'm proud to be Indian!" "I'm a Miwok Indian!" "Official Indian Truck!" They are young marrieds with several little children.

Most of all BigTime provides the opportunity to experience cultural pride. The visiting team, composed entirely of elderly men, sings as one voice in the language yet spoken today along the banks of a huge lake which is home to the Pomo. Beside blue waters rich with fish and lined with acorn-laden oaks, ancestors sang the same songs these players use today, the women carrying a higher tremolo accompaniment in times past. An entire extended family plays the game, dances and sings, celebrates the Pomo way with those assembled, awakening old friendships and creating a few new ones. They like to remember these old ways. The teams, Miwok versus Pomo, sing their songs and beat their rhythms. In the end, who will be more powerful? But even this pride is subject to taunts and teases, lighthearted humor, personal jests and poking fun.

The last hand game of the weekend ends. The young Miwok and his mother, the Paiute and his wife, are the winners. The players continue another round, pretending not to notice that the winners have all the marker sticks. This playfulness dissipates the tension and intensity of the two-hour competition. The losers trickle away gradually, while the winners gather round to collect their due. Like myself, all thank the team, the young Miwok in particular. A relaxation seeps over the remaining company, like a gentle fog blowing in off the Pacific one hundred fifty miles west. We pick up our things to leave, nod goodbye to the winning team, for whom I would like to think we brought good luck, and cross the game field to the meadow and our car. Almost empty now, the meadow begins to appear as it did in centuries past. The oaks, giants of their kind, still shade huge circles on the dry grass even in the late afternoon heat. Darkness hovers along the meadow edge where incense cedars and an occasional pine screen the light before it reaches the hard-baked earth. Golds and greens, iron rich reds, and grey-white of the grinding rocks color the landscape in its autumn hues. A few people remain, park workers and friends cleaning up, and a few families preparing their campers for departure.

BigTime completed, smell of crushed grass, of pine pitch, a leaf drifts earthward. Listen to the echo of the drumming, of the pounding of stone in bedrock mortar, children laughing in this meadow. Remember the old way, Miwok way. ✤

AN ISLAND CALLED CALIFORNIA

To the European explorers, California and the west coast of North America represented, in many ways, the most distant and difficult land to reach, with an unexplored continent on one side of it and the planet's largest ocean on the other. Yet the richness of resources and living conditions offered by the Mediterranean climate of California, and the lush rainforests to the north, were a powerful inducement to discovery. One of the most persistent of explorers' legends was that California was not part of the mainland, but was an island. And, considering the mountain, desert, and ocean barriers surrounding it, ecologically speaking it was.

Long before the Gold Rush had changed San Francisco from a quiet village to a hectic city, the San Francisco Bay area was an object of study by explorers, geologists, and naturalists, in part because the bay was a superb anchorage and the surrounding land therefore potentially of great value. However, the Spanish occupance of the region did not, for a long time, produce much in the way of scientific study, as the Spanish were largely interested in converting the Indians. Hence, the most productive expedition prior to the Gold Rush was that of the British captain, Frederic William Beechey. In 1826, between two summertime voyages in search of the western end of the Northwest Passage, Beechey spent the winter in San Francisco, dispatching various teams of crew members to study the geography, botany, and wildlife of the Bay area. The story of his visit to San Francisco is presented in "The Beechey Expedition Visits San Francisco" (1969), by A. Lincoln, Professor of History at the University of San Francisco.

After the Gold Rush, when San Francisco had become a major city, interest in cultural and scientific matters developed rapidly. The California Academy of Sciences was founded, and soon developed a program of scientific research and public exhibits. The land on which the Academy's offices and museum was constructed, on Market Street, was donated by a prosperous piano maker, horticulturist, and real estate investor, James Lick. Lick's interest in the scientific and cultural aspects of the city was great, and a number of institutions were wholly or partially funded from his estate. But the beneficence for which he is still best known was the observatory. He had a lifelong in-terest in astronomy and the possibility of space exploration, and in the later years of his life worked enthusiastically to establish what was to be the finest observatory of its time. In "James Lick's Observatory" (1978), Owen Gingerich, Professor of Astronomy and History at Harvard University, narrates the events leading to the establishment of the Lick Observatory. (His research was greatly assisted by Mary Shane, Curator of the Lick Observatory Archives, and the article is based on his James Lick Centennial Lecture, presented at the University of California in Santa Cruz on October 11, 1976.)

One of the oddest episodes in the history of the exploration of California was the notion that California is an island—this despite the 16th-century explorations that proved the Gulf of California to be closed at its northern end. Yet for almost 200 years, in part perhaps because of the legends that grew up about the voyages of Sir Francis Drake, all European maps showed California as an island. And the geographic truth was finally established not by a scientist or explorer, but by a Jesuit priest, Father Kino, whose extensive horseback exploration of the region around the north end of the Gulf, and into what is now southern California, confirmed the connection between California and the rest of the continent. In "The Passage By Land to California" (1966), the story of his discoveries is presented, along with his map, by Ronald L. Ives, who for several decades was a widely published writer in many magazines on the history and geography of the Southwest.

One of the earliest explorations of the west coast of North America was that of Sir Francis Drake—who is believed by some historians to have been the first European to look upon San Francisco Bay. The controversy over Drake's landing place has been chronicled in many *Pacific Discovery* articles. Presented here, in "Portus Novae Albionis—Rediscovered?" (1954), is an early article by one of the staunchest defenders of Drake as discoverer of San Francisco Bay, California businessman and historian Robert H. Power. In a letter discussing the inclusion of this article in the anthology Mr. Power states: ". . . the evidence in my opinion is now definite that the conclusion reached in the article is correct."

THE BEECHEY EXPEDITION VISITS
SAN FRANCISCO

A. Lincoln

ON November 6, 1826 H.M.S. *Blossom,* commanded by Frederick William Beechey, sailed into the Golden Gate to begin a visit that was more productive scientifically than that of any previous expedition to Northern California.

Captain Beechey, though only 30 years old, had already served 20 years in the British Navy and had been on a number of scientific explorations. When only 17 he fought in several dramatic naval engagements which resulted in the capture of two French frigates. During the War of 1812 he served in the campaign against New Orleans and was in one of the boats which swept across the Mississippi River with troops, seamen, and marines in an unsuccessful attempt to create a diversion in favor of the British attack on the American lines under General Andrew Jackson.

With the return of peace Beechey served on three exciting scientific expeditions. In 1818 he took part in Commander John Franklin's polar expedition. In 1819 he was placed in charge of

surveying, charting, and drawing curious objects and scenes for Commander William Edward Perry's attempt to sail the Northwest Passage by way of Lancaster Sound, Barrow Strait, and Melville Sound. They wintered in the Arctic. Next summer they were blocked by massive ice floes when about halfway through the passage. In 1821 Frederick William Beechey was dispatched with his brother Henry on an overland expedition to survey an extensive area of the North African coast, and to explore its classic region of the old Greek Pentapolis and report on the antiquities of Cyrenaica.

In January 1825 Beechey, soon to be made captain, was placed in command of the H.M.S. *Blossom,* a 427 ton sloop. At Woolwich the vessel was double-hulled and fitted out to make its way against ice barriers and to engage in extensive exploration. Because of the necessity to save space and weight to adjust for the stores and the required scientific equipment taken aboard, the *Blossom's*

The *Blossom* off the Hawaiian Islands. Painting by William Smyth, one of the artists of the expedition. (From Alan Moore's *Sailing Ships of War,* London: Halton and Truscott Smith, Ltd., 1926.)

The Entrance to San Francisco Bay.

The Fort in one with Yerba Buena Isl.ᵈ lands over the Bar in 4 1/2.ᵐˢ No ship should cross it further North on account of the rolling swell.

The *Blossom* entering San Francisco Bay. This drawing appeared on one of the expedition's maps published by the British Hydrographic office in 1833, and is reproduced from *The Maps of San Francisco Bay,* published by the Book Club of California, San Francisco, 1950.

The Presidio of San Francisco. Painting by Richard Beechey. (Courtesy of Warren Howell.)

complement of officers and men was reduced to 102 and its armament to 16 guns.

In May 1825 the expedition sailed from Spithead, England, with instructions to sail eastward as far as possible along the north coast of Alaska during the summer of 1826 and again in 1827. It was hoped that the *Blossom* would meet and aid the Captain John Franklin Expedition which was attempting to come through the Northwest Passage from the opposite direction. When the Beechey Expedition was not in the Arctic area it was to visit and survey those parts of the Pacific that were relatively unexplored. It was also to collect rare and curious specimens which would add to scientific knowledge in the various branches of natural history.

Although Captain Beechey twice failed to meet Captain Franklin, he sailed much farther along the northern Alaskan coast than had any previous navigator. Many new geographical fea-

tures were discovered, including Point Barrow, which Beechey named for the famous promoter of Arctic exploration. Here the expedition was forced to turn back by an impenetrable ice barrier when only 146 miles from where the Franklin Expedition had been forced to stop. After each voyage into the Arctic the *Blossom* sailed down the Pacific coast to Northern California to explore this little known area, to secure supplies for the ship, and to restore the health of the crew.

Sailing through the Golden Gate, November 6, 1826, Captain Beechey was impressed with "the magnificence of the harbor." It seemed sufficiently extensive to contain all the British navy. Its convenient coves offered many anchorages. The countryside was diversified with hill and dale, partly wooded, and partly pasture lands of the richest kind, abounding in herds of cattle. The Captain predicted that since it "possesses almost all the requisites for a great naval establishment" and is

Drawn by R. Beechey Midⁿ   *H.M.S. Blossom.*
PRESIDIO OF SAN FRANCISCO   *Novʳ 1826*
New California

"so advantageously situated with regard to North America and China, and the Pacific in general, that it will, no doubt, at some future time, be of great importance."

Admiralty mate James Wolfe, able diarist and chartmaker, excitedly wrote that they had found a "Canaan which if not exactly flowing with milk and honey offered something more substantial." A few days later he wrote that the consumption of fresh vegetables, fruit, and meat, and the opportunity for hunting and horseback riding helped materially in restoring the health and enthusiasm of the *Blossom's* crew.

Captain Beechey, like other explorers before him, was amazed by the contrast between the material advantages of the country and the lack of enterprise in its owners. The fort on the bluff near the Presidio was in such dilapidated condition that it seemed ready to topple over the precipice and into the bay. Anchoring at Yerba Buena cove, the English were amazed to learn that the presidio and the mission were the only buildings for many miles.

Several of the explorers hired horses from some Californians who came down to the anchorage to meet them, and then set out on a tour of inspection. The journal of Richard Beechey, the Captain's 18-year-old brother, describes their first visit to the presidio.

The roads were good, winding over steep hills, but through very few trees and those only in the low ground near the small lakes. The cattle were abundant . . . and were on the whole in very good condition. Half an hour's easy riding brought us in sight of the Presidio or "Safeguard." It is a square enclosure . . . formerly completely surrounded by a mud wall, which is now more than half destroyed. We rode up to the grand entrance as we supposed from a soldier who carried something like a musket, and were proceeding through when we were immediately stopped in a formal manner and given to understand that there was no thoroughfare, but that we might pass over the broken down parts of the wall into the enclosure which seemed to us altogether incomprehensible.

All the houses including the Commandante's were in miserable condition. Young Beechey noted that the interior of the Commandante's home was "very little better than the outside with no furniture except 2 sofas and a writing table with several plates and pictures by way of ornament."

Captain Beechey in his *Narrative* wrote that one enclosure was "little better than a heap of

The Mission of San Francisco. Painting by Richard Beechey. (Courtesy of Warren Howell.)

MISSION OF SAN FRANCISCO

rubbish and bones on which jackals, dogs and vultures were constantly preying." Except for a tottering flagstaff, three rusty cannons, and the half-uniformed sentinel parading the gateway, they would not have believed it was a seat of authority. The Captain later predicted that there would be a transfer of ownership unless a change should occur in the policy of the Mexican government.

Finding little of interest at the presidio, the English concluded their inspection tour. They remounted and pressed on toward the mission, over a road made impassable by the profusion of bushes and overhanging branches. Richard Beechey felt that the mission had a better appearance than the presidio. It was built in the style of a village. Its homes were better constructed and some were whitewashed in front. The church was not impressive from the outside, but the interior far surpassed what they expected from the impoverishment of the area. Padre Tomás Estenega served them a very hospitable repast of tea, bread, apples, and California brandy.

During both of their visits to California the officers and seamen of the *Blossom* were impressed continually with the hospitality and kindliness of the mission padres. However, Captain Beechey was very critical, perhaps overly critical, of the mission system. He also felt that the padres, who were by far the most intelligent men in the area, had been "so long excluded from the civilized world that their ideas and their politics, like the maps pinned on the walls, bore the date of 1772."

Captain Beechey's two-volume *Narrative of a Voyage to the Pacific and Beering's* [sic] *Strait* is of great value to the historian because of the long and vivid description of life in Northern California shortly after it became part of the Mexican Republic. The famous California historian, Hubert Howe Bancroft, has acclaimed Beechey's observations as "more evently accurate and satisfactory than those of any preceding navigator."

Captain Beechey planned to make a coastal survey from Monterey to Cape San Lucas after the visit to San Francisco Bay. He hoped that on the return from the Arctic the following fall they could complete the hydrography to the north left unfinished by Captain George Vancouver. However, the expedition failed to secure, in either San Francisco or Monterey, the medicines and ship's stores essential to meet the hardships of another long and hazardous voyage into the Arctic ice. The Captain was afraid the Mexican naval base at San Blas would not have these much-needed supplies either and the *Blossom* would have to sail as far

south as Lima at a great sacrifice of time. It was felt that it was necessary to sail across the Pacific to Macao or Canton, China, for the supplies. Hence the plans for a California-Oregon coastal survey were dropped.

From November 6 to December 28, 1826 and from November 18 to December 5, 1827 the Beechey Expedition completed the first thorough and scientific survey of San Francisco Bay and its borderlands. Hundreds of soundings were recorded. Before 1826 only the·most elementary maps of the areas had been drawn and they were almost totally devoid of soundings and navigational instructions. The Captain was pleased to find that the California authorities, who restricted the activities of Captain George Vancouver and other earlier visitors, were now very cooperative and offered their services in whatever way they might be required. Three of the *Blossom's* officers, who were dispatched overland to Monterey to make arrangements to secure supplies unavailable in San Francisco, were given as an escort a dragoon with a very fancy blue and red uniform and two vaqueros (cowboys) to drive nine horses to be used when those they mounted became fatigued. The diary of this round trip furnished Beechey with much information in regard to California. Commandante Ignacio Martinez granted officers permission to make a comprehensive survey and even entry to the forts to take necessary sightings and measurements. The only requirement stipulated was that when this was completed, a copy of the chart should be left with Mexican authorities.

On the day after the arrival the *Blossom's* sails were unbent, lower yards and topmasts struck, and the crew commenced stripping the ship in order to completely refit the riggings. A rope walk was set up on shore. Astronomical instruments were landed, and an observatory erected upon a hill nearby. A large barge, fitted out as a schooner with two complete suits of sails, was hoisted out and rigged. Clinker-built of mahogany, decked and coppered, it was as large as the space on the *Blossom* would allow. During the long voyage the men felt better knowing that the 38-foot barge could provide refuge for nearly all hands. The barge had been constructed and equipped purposely at Woolwich dockyard to take soundings and for surveying among islands and along rugged coastlines.

By the end of the second visit to California, the charting was completed from the north coast of San Pablo Bay and Carquinez Strait to the southern tip of San Francisco Bay at the mouth of the Guadaloupe River. A number of trips by various officers to the San Jose mission and the overland expedition to Monterey helped sketch in the primitive roads and other features.

The expedition was responsible for the naming of two of the Bay's best known islands. Observing that long lines of pelicans were continually nesting on a rocky island adjacent to the Golden Gate, Captain Beechey felt sure that this island, the odor of which was decidedly offensive, was the one an earlier Spanish navigator had called Alcatraz or Pelican Island. It was so designated on all of the maps made by the expedition. Actually in 1775, Captain Juan Ayala, whose ship the *San Carlos* was the first recorded vessel to enter the Golden Gate, gave the name "Isla de los Alcatraces" to a larger island a few miles to the south. Beechey called this one Yerba Buena because of the wild mint *(Micromeria chamissonis)* which grew plentifully there. For almost 100 years its correct name was uncertain. Goat Island, Bird Island, and Wood Island were some of the names it was given. In 1931, however, a popular campaign restored the name that Beechey had given it.

Another significant mistake was made in mapping the Bay area. It was, however, later corrected. On the maps three rivers—the Jesus Marie, the Sacramento, and the San Joaquin—were shown flowing into the waterway east of Carquinez Straits. This was one of the few times second-hand information was incorporated into their scientific reporting. The Jesus Marie was probably an alternative mouth of the Sacramento River.

In a special section of his *Narrative of a Voyage to the Pacific,* Beechey included six pages of detailed information for future navigators entering and leaving San Francisco Bay. He discussed geographical features to be used to obtain bearings, the safest channels, and the best methods for taking advantage of the prevailing winds and tides. He also warned of reefs, sand bars, and other hazards to be avoided.

Halfway between Alcatraz and Yerba Buena Islands a very treacherous obstruction to navigation was discovered. It was a rock about 190 feet long and 100 feet wide and only five feet below water at low tide. For the next forty-four years it was known as Blossom Rock. In April, 1870, San Francisco papers announced that Colonel A. W. von Schmidt, a well known construction engineer, who had been granted a $75,000 contract, was ready, as *The Chronicle* phrased it, to "extract this ugly tooth from the mouth of that fair daughter of Neptune—San Francisco Bay." The Colonel was prepared to explode 4,300 lbs. of dynamite in

the huge bake-oven-shaped cavity he had drilled into the side of Blossom Rock far below the surface. On Friday afternoon, April 23, 1870, every man, woman, and child in San Francisco, said *The Chronicle,* turned out to watch. A *Daily Alta California* reporter, who with hundreds of others observed from a ship, noted that on North Point, the wharves and the sandy hills, human beings presented an almost unbroken front. Telegraph Hill, he wrote, looked like "a swarm of flies on a sugar loaf." The *Daily Alta California's* description of the complete destruction of the worst obstacle to safe navigation in the Bay was especially dramatic.

> The scene was one of the most brilliant and imposing ever witnessed in the city, and one that will be long remembered. . . . The sight was terrifically grand. A large circular volume of water about 400 feet in diameter shot into the air to the height of about 100 feet, while in the centre and amalgamated with the water could be seen black volumes of smoke and a sheet of stones, the latter ascending far above the water and presenting on the whole the appearance of a vast volcanic eruption. . . . The heavy volume of water returned to its kindred element, and after a lapse of some seconds the stones and timbers came showering down with terrible fury. The water around the rock for a distance of nearly one thousand feet, changed its natural greenish hue for a yellow-muddy dirty color. . . . Every steamer and tug-boat blew their whistles and dipped their colors. Bells were rung and guns were fired. . . . Blossom Rock [was] a thing of the past.

A copy of the map drawn by the Beechey Expedition was left with Commandante Ignacio Martinez before the *Blossom* sailed out of the Golden Gate in January, 1828. Governor Jose Maria de Echeandía ordered it sent to him in

Water color of San Carlos Mission, near Monterey, by William Smyth. (Courtesy of Peabody Museum, Harvard University.)

San Diego, but it cannot be found in either the California or Mexican archives. However, two copies are in the Contra Costa County Hall of Records at Martinez. In September, 1862 a deed was recorded to the Rancho San Pablo and the boundaries were established by the Beechey map. The original grant, confirmed by Governor Echeandía in December, 1827, was bounded on the north by the Rancho Don Luis Peralta and on the south by Canada de Pinole. It is interesting to note that the Contra Costa County seat was named for Commandante Ignacio Martinez and is on the site of his Rancho Pinole.

More recently the Beechey map has been used in law cases to establish real estate holdings. In one the successors in interest of a Spanish grant claimed Belvedere to be a peninsula of the mainland, and therefore within the boundaries of a Spanish grant which embraced the whole Tiburon area. The other party, Kershaw, claimed that Belvedere was an island. A certified copy of the English explorer's map was obtained and used as evidence, and decided the case against Kershaw. Later in the Mare Island Cases (U.S. vs. tSewart and U.S. vs. O'Donnell) the Beechey map was used to show that an area northwest of Mare Island was not a part of the federal naval base.

During the twenty-five years following the publication in 1833 by the Hydrographical Office of the British Admiralty, the Beechey charts were printed with only minor revisions and additions in France, Russia, Germany, and the United States.

In 1841, Eugene Duflot de Mofras, an attaché of the French Legation in Mexico, made a semi-official tour along the Pacific coast. In 1844 the French government published his four-volume *Explorations du Territorie de l'Oregon, des California et de la Mera Vermeille* and a large folio *Atlas*. Duflot de Mofras' map of the San Francisco Bay, as he acknowledged, used a Beechey chart, translating its text into French and the soundings and elevations into meters. The only important change was an inaccurate extension to include the Sonoma area, and north to the Russian River including the Russian settlements which de Mofras visited. In 1852, M. D. Tebenkov's impressive *Atlas of the Northwest Coast of America,* published by the Russian government, included a map entitled "Harbor of San Francisco in New California, from the English Capt. F. W. Beechey." The titles, text, and measurements of the Beechey chart were translated into Russian. Two years later Henry Lange's *Atlas von Nord America,* printed in Mainz, Germany, used de Mofras' modification of the Beechey map. The first comprehensive map of Northern California by Americans was drawn in 1841. It was a poor one by the United States Exploring Expedition under the leadership of Commander Charles Wilkes. It was included in an *Atlas* which was a part of the Expedition's multi-volume report and was not published by the United States government until 1858. The entrance of the port as well as the San Francisco and San Pablo Bays were based on the Beechey maps with additional sound-

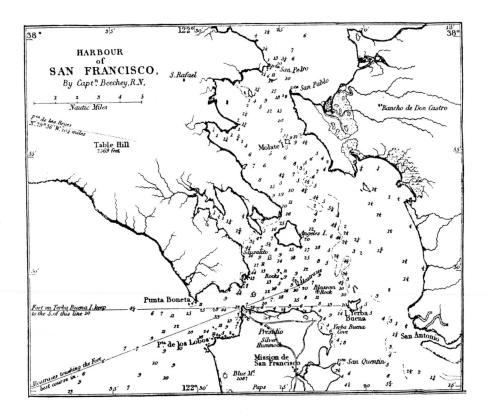

Right, Captain Beechey's map of the San Francisco Bay area. This was the first accurate map of the region, and the best one until after the Gold Rush. *Left,* detail, showing depth soundings in the bay.

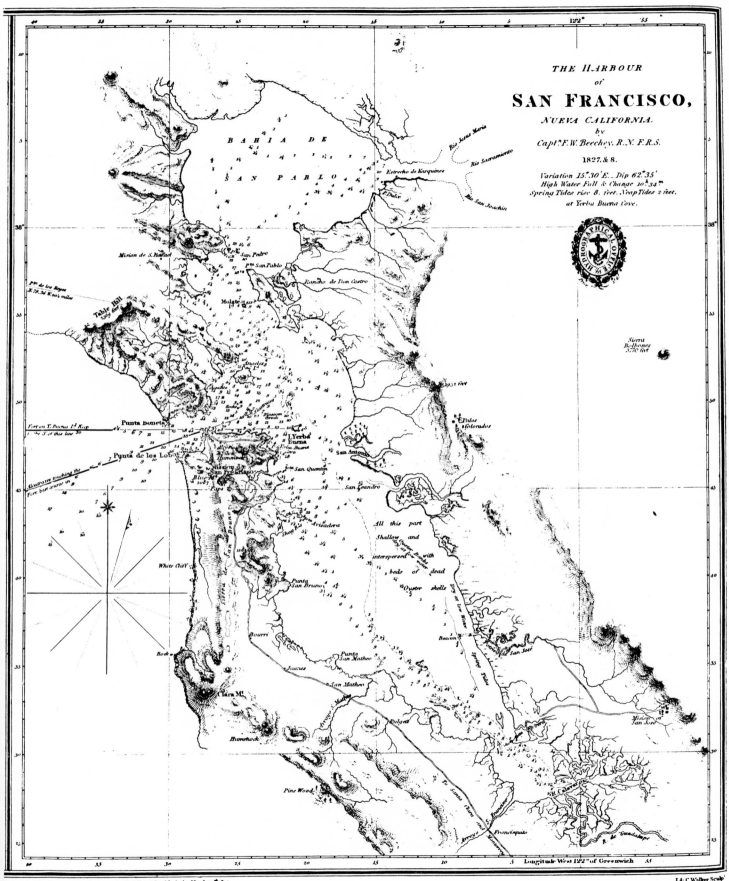

THE HARBOUR
of
SAN FRANCISCO,
NUEVA CALIFORNIA.
by
Capt. F.W. Beechey, R.N. F.R.S.
1827. & 8.

Variation 15.°30'E. _ Dip 62.°35'
High Water Full & Change 10.ʰ34.ᵐ
Spring Tides rise 8. feet. Neap Tides 2 feet.
at Yerba Buena Cove.

BAHIA DE
SAN PABLO

Rio Iesus Maria
Rio Sacramento
Estrecho de Karquines
P. Dute
Rio San Joachin

Mision de S. Rafael
P.ᵗᵃ San Pedro
P.ᵗᵃ San Pablo
Rancho de Don Castro
Molate Isl.ᵈ

P.ᵗ de los Reyes
N.79.30 W.20's miles
Table Hill
504 feet

Sierra
Bolbones
3,710 feet

Angeles
Isl.ᵈ

1052 feet

Angelo

C. Palos
Colorados

Fort on Y. Buena 1.ˢᵗ Kap
the S. of this line 30
Punta Boneta
Alcatraces touching the
Fort bent course in 9
Punta de los Lobos
I. Yerba
Buena
Yerba
Buena
San Antonio
Mision de
San Francisco
Blue
1081
San Quentin
Paps
San Leandro

White Cliff
San Bruno
Shoal
Avisadera
Punta
San Bruno

All this part
Shallow and
interspersed with
beds of dead
Oyster shells

Beacon
Old San José
Dry at low Water

Bourri
Rock
Juares
Punta
San Matheo
San Matheo
Spring Tides

Tara M.ᵗ
Rulou
Mision of
San José

Horseshock
Arroyo S. Matheo

Pine Wood
To Sierra Tiers out
Arroyo
Principuito
R. de Guadalupe
S. Calaveras

ing to Act of Parliament at the Hydrographical Office of the Admiralty March 10.ᵗʰ 1833.

J. & C. Walker Sculp.ᵗ

49

ings and some minor modifications of the shore-lines.

The best maps of the gateway to the mines during the California gold rush were also dependent on Beechey's survey. Commodore Cadwalader Ringgold, who had been in California with the Wilkes expedition, was again in San Francisco in 1849. Ringgold was asked by some San Francisco citizens to prepare a series of accurate charts for immediate use. In 1850 the first of five editions of his *A Series of Charts and Sailing Directions* was published. In his text Ringgold acknowledged that his charts of the harbor entrance and the bay itself were based primarily on Beechey's well-executed surveys. The Commodore also heralded as "truly accurate" Beechey's six pages of advice to future navigators for entering and leaving San Francisco harbor. They were incorporated into Ringgold's ten

pages of "Sailing Directions." The American Commodore paid a special tribute to Beechey's writing ability when he prefaced his five-page excerpt from the English captain's description of the harbor, by saying "the pen of the illustrious navigator, Beechey, will convey to the majority of my readers a more adequate idea of the harbor's beauty and adaption to the purposes of a great agricultural and commercial community than any remarks I could make."

During the early American period, the Beechey charts with their minor modifications and extensions remained the best available charts to navigators entering the Golden Gate. California had been a state for several years before the Beechey maps began to be superseded by those issued by the United States Coast and Geodetic Survey.

This geological map of the bay region first appeared in *The Zoology of Captain Beechey's Voyage* by Alexander Collie, London: H. G. Bohn, 1839.

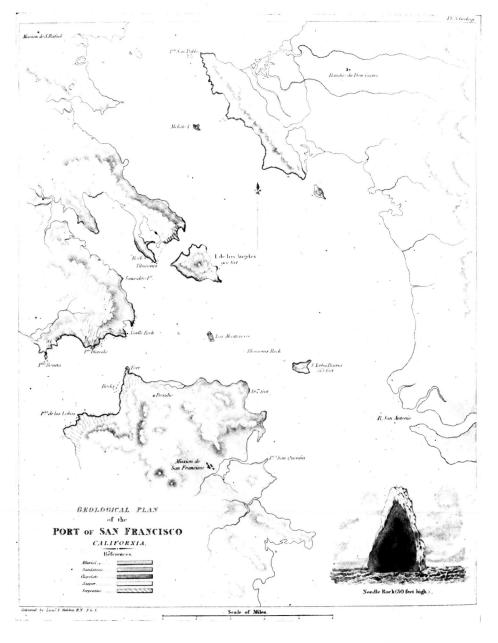

JAMES LICK'S OBSERVATORY

Owen Gingerich

Photographs courtesy of Lick Observatory

TO SUCH astronomical philanthropists as Yerkes, Hooker, Carnegie, and Rockefeller, American science owes a great debt. And yet I cannot imagine celebrating their anniversaries in quite the same way that we can commemorate James Lick, who applied his San Francisco real-estate fortune to many scientific and educational enterprises. For with Lick, the building of a great telescope seems to have been his own idea, and although it was fostered and encouraged by others, he set the specifications and determined the site in his own idiosyncratic way. That Lick Observatory remains one of the great astronomical institutions of the world owes much not only to Lick's fortune, but to the inspiration that he instilled in the non-astronomers who actually built the observatory. Lick Observatory was the first mountaintop observatory, and played a key role in bringing American observational astronomy into worldwide ascendancy.

The story of James Lick's life is remarkable by any standard. He was born in Pennsylvania in 1796, when George Washington was serving his last year as President. In 1819 the young Lick began his years of wandering, temporarily settling in Baltimore as an apprentice piano maker. Migrat-

ing to South America, he established himself as a master piano maker, first in Buenos Aires, then in Valparaiso, and finally in Lima.

After nearly a decade in Peru, Lick became increasingly eager to try his luck in California. James K. Polk had been elected President on an expansionist platform, promising to extend the Union from the Atlantic to the Pacific, and Lick felt sure that California would become part of the United States. On January 7, 1848, Lick sailed through the Golden Gate. He had brought along his workbench and tools, but never again would he hang out his shingle as a piano builder, for the 51-year-old Lick had quickly decided to gamble his future on San Francisco real estate. Within twenty years, when a local newspaper made a survey of the wealthiest men in town, Lick ranked first with $750,000.

How Lick became interested in building the world's largest telescope is a bit of a mystery. In 1860 a young Portuguese-American, George Madeira, was lecturing on astronomy and geology throughout California. Lick attended one of his lectures in San Jose and afterward invited the young man to visit his ranch for several days. Together they observed the heavens through

James Lick, above, who amassed a fortune in San Francisco real estate,
gave it away almost entirely to educational and cultural institutions, of which
one of the best known is Lick Observatory, atop Mount Hamilton in California.

acter. It required months of careful approaches and the proper presentation of facts to change his views of location. He next had a notion of locating it on the mountains overlooking his millsite near Santa Clara, and thought it would be a Mecca, but only in the sense of a show.

Gradually I guided his judgment to place it on a great elevation in the Sierra Nevadas . . . At the same time, by my presentation of facts and figures of the cost and maintenance of other obseravtories, he named the sum of $1,200,000 in one of his wills, as the sum to be set aside for founding the James Lick Observatory, and for its support.

In making him acquainted with the size and performance of the telescopes of the larger observatories, I naturally mentioned the great reflector of Lord Rosse. That seemed to fire his ambition and at the next interview he insisted on a refractor of six feet in diameter. It required long and patient explanations to get him down to forty inches, which was the diameter we finally adopted.

In addition to his own interventions on behalf of the observatory, Davidson urged Joseph Henry to encourage the strong-minded millionaire. In the correspondence, which is preserved in the Smithsonian Archives, the Smithsonian secretary wrote:

While there are thousands of enterprising men in our country who have talents for accumulating wealth there are but a few like yourself who have the wisdom and enlightened sympathy to apply it as you have done. There is in most men an instinct of immortality which induces the desire to live favorably in the memory of their fellow men after they have departed this life, and surely no one could choose a more befitting means of erecting a monument to himself more enduring or more worthy of admiration than that which you have chosen.

Henry went on to say:

It should be recollected, however, that, besides a suitable building, funds are required to sustain, properly, an establishment like that of the Academy. A curator will be necessary and the means for publishing the proceedings. Furthermore, an establishment of the kind ought to have the means of consecrating to science any one who may be found in the country possessed of the peculiar character of mind in a marked degree for original investigation.

By the following year Henry was even more specific; he not only urged Lick to appoint the best

Madeira's telescope and at one point the young man is said to have exclaimed, "Why, if I had your wealth, Mr. Lick, I would construct the largest telescope possible." Probably these words planted the seeds for Lick's greatest monument.

On the other hand, Joseph Henry, then secretary of the Smithsonian Institution, liked to think that *he* had persuaded Lick to build a great observatory when he met the Californian in the Lick House in 1871. Two years later, when Prof. George Davidson, President of the California Academy of Sciences, called upon Lick to thank him for the valuable lot he had just deeded to the Academy, Lick told Davidson of his intention to bequeath a large sum of money for a telescope "larger and more powerful than any existing." Naturally Davidson was most interested in such a significant scientific venture, and the Academy president offered his encouragement and advice. Davidson described the ensuing encounters as follows:

James Lick originally intended to erect the Observatory at Fourth and Market Streets. His ideas of what he wanted and what he should do were of the very vaguest char-

available astrophysicist, but even singled out the English astronomer Norman Lockyer, the self-trained spectroscopist and founder of the journal *Nature*. Lockyer was a dynamic individual who is personally credited with far more scientific contributions than Edward Holden, the man who in fact became the first director of Lick Observatory. There is no disputing the tremendous scientific contribution made indirectly by Holden in bringing together a truly remarkable staff in the first decade of the Lick Observatory's operation. It is probably idle to speculate whether Lockyer could have done as well in staffing the mountain. Both Holden and Lockyer seemed always immersed in controversy, and one might imagine that the newspapers would have found as much to criticize in Lockyer as they were to find for the much-harassed Holden.

Meanwhile, back in San Francisco, the aging Lick was quite irked to discover that he could not will his money directly to the state for the construction of an observatory. He was obliged to place his fortune in the hands of a trust commissioned to carry out his wishes. The Deed of Trust specified the construction, on the borders of Lake Tahoe, of

> a powerful telescope, superior to and more powerful than any telescope ever yet made, with all the machinery appertaining thereto and appropriately connected therewith, or that is necessary and convenient to the most powerful telescope now in use, or suited to one more powerful than any yet constructed, and also a suitable observatory connected therewith. Provided, however, if the site above designated shall not, after investigation, be deemed suitable by said Trustees, or a majority of them shall select a site on which to erect such telescope, but the same must be located within the State of California.

Toward the end of 1874 Lick became more and more impatient about the slow progress the trust had made in the few months of its existence. In principle Lick had signed away his entire fortune, and when he resolved to revoke his trust deed and write a new one, it was judged legally impossible. Lick simply hired an astute lawyer to break the trust, expecting years of litigation. Without going into court directly, the attorney took the matter to the public press and managed to form a "public opinion" so that the first five trustees willingly resigned.

As chairman of his second board of trustees, Lick named Captain Richard F. Floyd, a dashing

Captain Richard F. Floyd, who abandoned retirement plans to build the observatory.

southerner who had acquired distinction in San Francisco business and social circles. For two or three years he had commanded steamers on the west coast; hence the title "Captain." His wife was the heiress to a fortune, so he retired at an early age to his estate on Clear Lake about 100 miles north of San Francisco. In front of his pretentious dwelling was moored a 72-foot steamer as well as a yacht and several smaller boats. When Captain Floyd planned this home, he might well have anticipated a life of luxurious ease in idyllic surroundings. But the course of his life was abruptly altered when he was introduced to James Lick in 1875. Upon their first meeting Lick had taken an immediate liking to Floyd, and with uncanny acumen he exclaimed that this was the very man he wanted to build his observatory. In retrospect one must wonder if such a successful observatory would have been established without Captain Floyd's dedicated leadership. F. J. Neubauer, in his articles on the history of Lick Observatory in the old *Popular Astronomy,* wrote that "From all that can be gathered from the records, it is not an exaggeration to state that the Lick

Observatory, as it finally came into being, was the brain child of Captain Floyd."

The second trust brought about several important changes. First, Lick reserved the right during his lifetime to hire or fire the trustees. Second, the contemplated observatory was deeded to the Regents of the University of California rather than the state. Finally, Lick was persuaded to relocate the Observatory from Lake Tahoe to Mount Hamilton, a move that pleased him since the mountain was located in his favorite Santa Clara County. D. D. Murphy, mayor of San Jose and a member of the second trust, influenced the County Supervisors to build the necessary road to the top of the mountain. He also took the necessary steps to obtain the land, which was done through an act of Congress.

Although happy over the selection of Mount Hamilton as the site for his observatory, Lick was still distressed at the slow pace of his trustees. On a Sunday morning in August, 1876, Lick astonished his friend Charles Plum by announcing his intention to discharge the trustees except for Captain Floyd. Lick ordered Plum to return at 3 p.m. with a new slate, but as Plum departed, he realized that such a misson could not be legally transacted on a Sunday. The next morning, however, the new board of trustees was appointed. When the change in trustees became known, rumors flew that the old man was insane. Lick feared that his will might be attacked by his Pennsylvania heirs and his trust broken. He ordered his trustees to assemble a jury of the most eminent doctors to examine him and to issue a written report on his mental condition. All nine agreed that he was in sound mind and "perfectly conscious that one who leaves so much money, if found vulnerable, would be plutarchic carrion for litigious vultures." But for Lick himself the end was very near.

Almost exactly 100 years ago, early in the morning of October 1, 1876, James Lick died quietly in his room at Lick House. Flags throughout the city flew at half mast. For three days the body of James Lick lay in state in Pioneer Hall while thousands of San Franciscans passed the elegantly draped casket. On the afternoon of October 3 the funeral procession, attended by a full quota of dignitaries, moved slowly to Masonic Hall for the elaborate services. The casket was then placed in a vault at the Masonic cemetery; ten years later it was moved to its final resting place under the great telescope of Mt. Hamilton.

A certain amount of litigation hung over Lick's estate, and several years elapsed before all the claims were cleared and the properties could be sold. This proved quite fortunate, because in 1876 the country was in the throes of a depression, and the sale of the real estate at that time would not have supported all of Lick's charities.

The problems facing the third board of trustees included the fact that at the time of Lick's death they had not been formally elected, and Lick's properties were threatened by the necessity of raising $40,000 for taxes. The secretary to the trustees, Henry E. Mathews, took it upon himself to collect the sum. The secretaryship was a highly responsible position that required initiative and an endless amount of tact. Captain Floyd had chosen Mathews to fill this important position, and he performed with unusual efficiency and harmony. Mathews was a professional photographer for a time before entering the services of the trust, and many of the early photographs of Lick Observatory were taken by him.

The third member of the trio that brought about Lick Observatory was Thomas E. Fraser, the superintendent of construction. A native of Nova Scotia, he had become the trusted manager of the Lick properties in Santa Clara County a few years before Lick's death. It was Fraser who introduced Captain Floyd to Lick. He was a self-educated construction engineer, and the highest paid employee of the trust. When the observatory was all but completed he resigned, dying just a few years later at the early age of forty-one. His friend, Captain Floyd, died almost exactly a year earlier, at the age of only forty-seven years.

Mary Shane, in her unpublished history of Lick Observatory, has written:

> in eight years from the beginning of active work, the finest observatory of its time was built, equipped and in operation. This was primarily the achievement of three remarkable men; Floyd, Mathews, and Fraser. None of these men had astronomical training, but they were completely dedicated to making the Lick Observatory the finest institution of its kind. They achieved this through ingenuity, perseverence and such arduous work that the endeavor essentially cost Floyd and Fraser their lives.

Although the Mount Hamilton site had been selected and secured, progress in obtaining the "largest possible telescope" was considerably slower. Lick himself had inquired about the cost of such an instrument from the obvious expert, Alvan Clark, who had built the 26-inch refractor for the Naval Observatory. Clark's estimate of

Above, Lick Observatory shortly after its completion. Left, Thomas E. Fraser, superintendent of construction of the observatory. Far left, the interment of James Lick, on January 8, 1887, in a vault beneath the 36-inch refracting telescope.

$200,000 outraged Lick, who believed the Cambridge telescope maker was taking advantage of him. Only after James Lick's death could the trustees proceed with a contract for the 36-inch lenses to be figured by Alvan Clark and Sons. The glass disks were ordered from Feil and Company of Paris. The flint glass arrived safely at the Clark's

factory in 1882, but the crown glass cracked during packing. The Feil brothers had immense difficulty producing another disk, succeeding only after nineteen failures and at a cost that drove the firm into bankruptcy. Finally in October, 1885 the crown glass was delivered to the Clarks, and the finished objective arrived safely on Mt. Hamilton on December 29, 1886. Almost a year later the last carload of tubing arrived from Cleveland, accompanied by Ambrose Swasey who personally supervised the mounting of the great telescope.

Although the taming of the mountain and the building of the physical plant had been carried out by truly dedicated non-astronomers, the astronomers, too, were pioneers facing rugged and extreme conditions. The early history of Lick Observatory is to some extent the history of 25 years in the life of Edward Singleton Holden. Holden was a man of enormous energies. For example, in his first five weeks as director of the observatory he wrote no less than 504 letters in his own hand. Holden was first recommended for the job when he was still a junior staff member at the U.S. Naval Observatory. There he had become an assistant on the new 26-inch refractor, then the largest in the world. Holden worked under Simon Newcomb, who was at that time America's leading astronomer, and a year later Newcomb recommended Holden to the first Lick trust as a possible director for the planned observatory. Since Holden was not yet 28 years old and had had only a year of practical experience in observatory work, this tells a great deal about Newcomb's high esteem for Holden.

In 1876 the Navy sent Holden to England to examine scientific instruments, and in London Holden first met Captain Floyd. From this time on there must have been some tacit agreement that Holden would eventually take over the observatory directorship. As the observatory headed for completion, the Regents of the University of California appointed Holden President of the University, and he served rather uneventfully for a year and a half. Holden became Director of Lick Observatory on June 1, 1888, and perhaps the best testimonial to his leadership as director is the list of senior staff that he had assembled by this time: S. W. Burnham, J. M. Schaeberle, J. E. Keeler, and E. E. Barnard. The fact that ultimately Holden was unable to hold this staff together at Lick Observatory tells more about the lonely conditions on an isolated mountain, especially difficult for families, rather than any failure in Holden's personality.

Some of these difficulties are graphically recounted by Holden in his retiring Presidential Address of the Astronomical Society of the Pacific, an institution that Holden was largely instrumental in founding:

> Every necessary of life at Mt. Hamilton must be provided by individuals, except water. That is furnished by the Observatory. To distribute this, we have a system of four reservoirs, with several miles of pipes. . . . All the motive power used in revolving the great dome, or in raising its floor, depends on the water-supply, and the slightest accident to the wind-mill, to a reservoir, or to the pipes stops the work of the great telescope. After every snow-storm a whole day's work, and sometimes more, is necessary to get the re-

volving parts of the dome into satisfactory working order. . . . The reservoir capacity is not sufficient to store enough water to carry us through the dry season. Hence, every year it has been necessary to use for domestic purposes some of the rain-water collected during the winter and stored for use as power. All this water has passed many times through the hydraulic rams, and is therefore covered with a heavy film of oil, and is really unfit for use, and produces more or less illness when it is used. But it must be used. There is no other. There is absolutely no present remedy. It will be necessary to provide a greater storage or a greater supply. Either of these things can readily be done; but either will require an expense which there is no present way of meeting.

Holden was a prolific writer and first-class publicist, always willing to supply readable articles to news magazines. He wrote on topics as diverse as "The Picture Writings of Central America," "Our Country's Flag," and biographies of William Bond and William Herschel. Perhaps he wrote too much, because for some reason the popular press took a dislike to him, and his lengthy rejoinders seldom helped his local reputation. Simon Newcomb, in his autobiography, addressed the question of Holden's administration. He wrote:

> To me its most singular feature was the constantly growing unpopularity of the director. I call it singular because, if we confine ourselves to the record, it would be difficult to assign any obvious reason for it. . . . Nothing happens spontaneously, and the singular phenomenon of one who had done all this becoming a much hated man must have an adequate cause. I have several times, from pure curiosity, inquired about the matter of well-informed men. On one occasion an instance of maladroitness was cited in reply.

> 'True," said I, 'it was not exactly the thing to do, but after all, that is an exceedingly small matter."

> "Yes," was the answer, "that was a small thing, but put a thousand small things like that together, and you have a big thing."

Finally, at the end of 1897, Holden felt obliged to resign. However, I do not wish to end on this negative note, but rather with a brief survey of the scientific results achieved in that first decade. This can be done in part by looking at the early publications of the Lick Observatory, and in part by reviewing the interests of each staff member.

S. W. Burnham, the oldest man on the original staff, had led a remarkable double life. During the day he had served as a court stenographer in the United States Circuit Court in Chicago, but during the night he had acquired an international reputation as a double-star astronomer. His Chicago observatory had been a backyard affair, but it boasted a particularly fine 6-inch Clarke lens. From 1866 until he came to Lick Observatory he also had access to the 18½-inch Dearborn refractor, with which he made some of his famous observations. It was Burnham who was invited in 1879 to bring his 6-inch telescope to Mt. Hamilton in order to conduct a site test. Burnham used the opportunity to detect some new double star systems, and he had concluded that, "So far as one may judge from the time during which these observations were made, there can be no doubt that Mt. Hamilton offers advantages superior to those found at any point where a permanent observatory has been established." At Lick, Burnham pursued his double-star obseravtions, which fill volume 2 of the Lick Observatory *Publications*.

Below, the library of Lick Observatory. Below left, tourists visiting the observatory.

Early projects of the 36-inch refractor, largest in the world at the time of its completion, included a photographic atlas of the moon, and a study of the apparent radial velocities of nearby stars, leading to the conclusion that the solar system is moving toward Vega at 12 miles per second.

Burnham was very popular with the public, and his resignation in 1892 brought considerable unjust blame on Holden. It was simply a matter that Burnham could not see any sense in maintaining two establishments, one on the mountain and the other in San Jose where his children attended school, and he could return to the Circuit Court in Chicago at a much higher salary than he received at Lick Observatory.

F. J. Neubauer reports that John Schaeberle was a "born bachelor, that kind who attends the YMCA gymnasium regularly, taking care of his health in a common sense way." He had graduated from the University of Michigan, had made several successful telescope mirrors, and had discovered several comets. Holden placed him in charge of the meridian circle at Lick Observatory, but he is probably most famous for the 40-foot camera lens of his own design used to obtain large-scale photographs of solar eclipses. Since Holden already had

Arrival of the 36" O.g.
at Lick Observatory,
2:30 PM. Dec. 27, 1886.
— Beautiful Day.

WORLD'S LARGEST TELESCOPE DEDICATED AT LICK

SAN JOSE DAILY MERCURY.

a large permanently-sited observatory, he risked the criticism of other professional astronomers by investing so much in solar eclipse expeditions to distant parts of the world. However, the eclipse team achieved an impressive record of results. Schaeberle and Burnham first used the long camera in December 1889 at Cayenne in South America. It was used again in Chile in 1893 and in Japan in 1896.

At 31, Edward Emerson Barnard was the youngest member of the original staff at Lick Observatory. He was an expert professional photographer in his home town of Nashville, Tennessee, but at the same time he had become a dedicated amateur astronomer. In 1877 Barnard met the great Simon Newcomb, with whom he discussed his ideas about photography as applied to astronomical observations. Newcomb encouraged the young man, and by 1881 Barnard announced his first discovery of a comet. At Lick Observatory he specialized in stellar photography, and Volume 11 of the Lick Observatory *Publications* contains over 100 plates of star fields and comets taken by him. His most acclaimed observation at Lick was the discovery on September 9, 1892 of the fifth and innermost satellite of Jupiter. Back in Chicago, Burnham proudly displayed a telegram from his young friend, and he extravagantly proclaimed to the press that "the discovery of this satellite is the greatest astronomical achievement of the century." Barnard stayed with Lick Observatory until 1895 when George Ellery Hale persuaded him to accept a professorship at the new Yerkes Observatory.

It is no exaggeration to say that James Keeler was the best trained scientist on the original staff. After receiving a BA from John Hopkins, he became an assistant at Allegheny Observatory. He went abroad for a year, studying physics in Heidelburg and Berlin, returning to Allegheny Observatory until his appointment as assistant to the Lick Trust two years before Lick Observatory formally opened. With the 36-inch telescope and a grating spectroscope, he measured the wavelengths of the bright lines in nebular spectra. His accuracy was sufficient to show that—like stars—gaseous nebulae have measurable motions toward or away from the earth. In 1891 Keeler left Lick to become Director of the Allegheny Observatory in Pittsburgh. During that time he designed a spectrograph with which he confirmed that the rings of Saturn are meteoritic in nature, and he became co-founder with George Ellery Hale of the *Astrophysical Journal*. In 1898 he was recalled to Lick Observatory to succeed Edward Holden as director.

Holden, throughout his administration, was remarkably successful in securing special funds and gifts for various projects. In 1895 he had convinced an English amateur, Edward Crossley, to donate his three-foot mirror, together with its mounting and dome, to Lick Observatory. Subsequently he persuaded the Wells Fargo Express Company and the Southern Pacific Railroad to donate the freight charges to bring the telescope from Britain to Mt. Hamilton, so that Lick Observatory would have the largest reflector in America.

The mounting for the Crossley telescope was very clumsy and designed for a much higher latitude in England. It was not until Keeler took an active interest in the Crossley that successful photographs were made with it. His pictures revealed how greatly spiral nebulae outnumbered all the other hazy objects detectable in the sky, and his success with a reflecting telescope paved the way for the successful design and application of the larger reflectors that were soon to dwarf the 36-inch Crossley. In 1900 Keeler was quite unexpectedly cut down with a heart attack, bringing his directorship and his astronomical career to a premature end at age 43. His marvelous photographs of the nebulae were posthumously published in Volume 8 of the Lick Observatory *Publications*.

To end this account of Lick Observatory in the nineteenth century, let me quote a poem penned on an early page of the Lick Observatory logbook by the superintendent of construction, Thomas Fraser:

Here pride and arrogance will sink to mites
Glassed with a billion suns and stellar lights;
Sordid villainy will all its courage loose;
And wealth learn how its treasures it may use.
How use them for a noble lasting end
As here is done by California's friend.
No words are meet to praise the illustrious Lick
Through ages long his high panegyric,
The Sun and all yon glittering Stars will write
With penciled rays of there unfading light
And commets coursing through the Milky Way.
Sound his high praise till Earths remotest day.

Right, E. S. Holden, first director of the Lick Observatory. Below left, the 12-inch refractor, used for early studies of double stars. At right, the Crossley 36-inch reflecting telescope in its original mount. Studies of spiral nebulae made with the Crossley paved the way for the development of much larger reflectors. Far right, the Andromeda Galaxy as photographed with the Crossley. One of the few galaxies other than our own visible to the unaided eye, it is a member of the Local Cluster, and is similar to our own Milky Way.

THE PASSAGE BY LAND
TO CALIFORNIA
Ronald L. Ives

ONLY about three centuries ago, most well-informed geographers were certain that California was "the largest island in the world," separated from the mainland of North America by the Strait of Anian, a body of water that began at the mouth of the Gulf of California, and extended northward for a great distance, eventually joining with either the Pacific Ocean or the Northwest Passage.

This strange and persistent misconception was widely held despite the competent and accurate explorations of Francisco de Ulloa (1539) and Hernando de Alarcon (1540), both of whom sailed the length of the Gulf, and found it to be a closed sea. Immediately thereafter, Melchior Diaz, one of Coronado's most competent captains, journeyed from central Sonora, Mexico, and reached an inland point about a day's journey south of Calexico, California. His graphic description of the mud volcanoes at Cerro Prieto, Baja California del Norte, a unique location, assures us that he was there.

Many historians believe the legend of the insularity of California grew out of an erroneous report that Sir Francis Drake had sailed through the Strait of Anian, and "completely around" the island of California during his voyages in that area about 1579. For this report, says a later chronicler, "this malevolent heretic is well punished in this life and also in the next — paying forever for his evil deeds there in Inferno." Unfortunately for the pious chronicler, Drake never made any such claim, and his logs, kept by his

chaplain, Francis Fletcher, are straightforward seamen's reports, many parts of which can be verified beyond any reasonable doubt.

Recent investigations show that the actual perpetrator of this gross geographical error was one Fray Antonio de la Ascension, who accompanied and described the work of the Vizcaino expedition of 1602-1603.

About 1705, European geographers suddenly did an about-face, and most maps after that date show California as a part of the North American mainland, with shore configurations and place names much like those on modern maps. Reason for this change is not stated in most histories of geography. It was not until the second decade of this century that the source of the more accurate cartographical data was surely identified, although folklore, legends, and secondary accounts indicated the existence of a file, somewhere, of a large number of maps and documents by a Father Kino, who apparently had explored extensively in the Arizona-Sonora borderlands.

While delving in the Archivo General y Publico, in Mexico City, during the academic year 1907-1908, Herbert E. Bolton, a young historian from the University of Texas (he later went to Stanford, and then to Berkeley), found 433 small folio pages in the Seccion de Misiones. Study of these showed that here, at last, was the legendary Kino journal, best known as the "Favores Celestiales."

In 1705, Father Michele Angelo Tamburini, Father General of the Jesuit Order, in acknowl-

Above, "And the other ocean lies that way — —". An early artist's conception of how the missionary-explorers gathered information. Woodcut from Miguel Venega's *Noticia de la California* (1739).

Photographs by the author

edging some of Father Kino's documents, hoped "that they may all be approved in Mexico, in order that they may be published." This publication finally took place in Cleveland, Ohio in 1919!

Outstanding among Bolton's discoveries was Kino's map of 1701, the famous "Passo por Tierra a la California," which showed clearly and accurately the continuity of the lands from Sonora to Baja California. So dependable is this map that it was not completely supplanted for more than 200 years, and a modern traveller, using this map and the accompanying journals, can find almost every place listed on it, usually at the first attempt.

Unlike many of our important scientific advances, which grew out of a "flash of insight," gathering of the data for this map was the work of 20 years of intensely hard labor, involving literally thousands of miles of horseback travel, scores of latitude measurements with an astrolabe, and the exploration and pacification of parts of Baja California, Sonora, Arizona, and Alta California (our present state). Although Father Kino is best known as one of the truly great missionaries of the later seventeenth and early eighteenth centuries, sometimes being called "the Apostle to the Pimas," the record shows most clearly that he was also an outstanding explorer and cartographer.

Born in Segno, in the Val di Non, near Trent, Italy, on August 10, 1645, Father Kino arrived in Mexico City in the spring of 1681, at the age of 36, after a tempestuous journey, interrupted by pirate scares and shipwrecks, from Genoa, Italy, via Cadiz. The last leg of the journey took only 98 days!

While awaiting orders in Mexico City, he found time to study all available maps of the lands of New Spain, and also to write up and publish his observations of the Comet of 1680.

At the time of Kino's arrival in Mexico City, another attempt was being made to colonize California, then regarded as an "earthly paradise on the right hand of the Indes." Designated leader of this expedition was Admiral Don Isidro Atondo y Antillan, a competent and experienced soldier. To his staff, with the rank of Royal Cosmographer, was assigned Father Kino, who also had missionary and ecclesiastical duties.

The first colony, near La Paz, was a prompt and dismal failure. At a new site, San Bruno (Lat. 26°13′ N.; Long. 111°24′ W.; Alt. 25′, MSL.), a mission and fort were built, and small gardens were planted. Many trips were made westward

Below, Father Kino's famous *Passo por Tierra a la California*, drawn in 1701 from exploration notes augmented by instrumental measurements of latitude. This version is a tracing by the author of Kino's map.

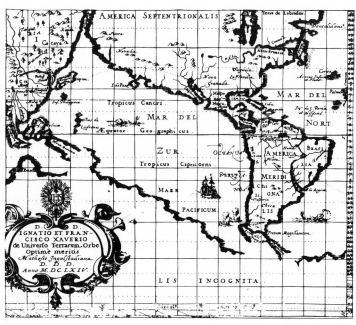

Above, a detail of Adam Aigenler's world map of 1664. This map, one of the few of that time which showed California as a part of the North American mainland, and Father Aigenler's field manual were extensively used by Father Kino during his explorations.
(Print courtesy of Library of Congress)

63

across the Sierra de la Giganta, to learn more about this land. Despite miles of arduous travel, nothing even faintly resembling the "earthly paradise" was found. A later missionary in about the same area (Father Johann Jacob Baegert, S.J.) emphatically stated that "California is the worst place on earth."

Diaries of this expedition tell not only of shortages of everything from food to horseshoes, but also detail the problems of gathering information from the Indians, the searches for trails and water holes, the attempts to grow crops in a land where water was both bad and scarce, and the long hungry waits for delayed supply ships.

While here, Father Kino made the first good map of the southern part of the peninsula; and made and mapped the first crossing of the "New Province of San Andres," from the Gulf of California to the Pacific. This journey, from San Bruno to the Boca de San Gregorio, via the canyons of Comondu and the Cadegomo, was as difficult as Balboa's crossing of the Isthmus of Panama. Along the same route, only a few years later, the missions of San Juan Londo (1699), San Jose de Comondu (1709), and La Purisima de Cadegomo (1712) were founded. At the latter site today is the historic and hospitable town of La Purisima.

Among the notes and observations made during this attempt at colonization was one which later proved most important. While exploring the beaches on the Pacific coast of the peninsula, Father Kino found many large and beautiful blue shells, full of mother-of-pearl; and also noted that

Right, map showing the route of the Kino-Atondo Expedition across Baja California in 1684-85. So clear are the descriptions in the original documents that the route of the expedition can be followed today, and most of the camps identified within a few feet.

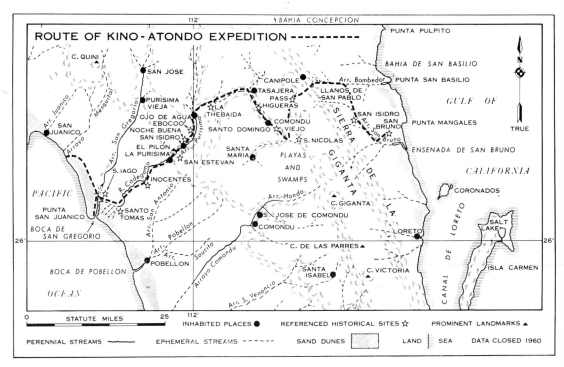

these shells were not present on the beaches of the Gulf of California.

After nearly four years of efforts, the would-be colonists were not only worn out and suffering from scurvy, but also convinced that San Bruno was not the place for a colony. Soon a relief ship took the many sick to the mainland of Mexico, while Father Kino and Admiral Atondo planned a search for a better colony site.

While Admiral Atondo went off on a pearl fishing expedition, with native divers who had been "kept in jail — in order that they might not flee," Father Kino, on the ship of Captain Don Blaz de Guzman, sailed north in the Gulf of California, seeking a better colony site.

Sailing northward from the mouth of the Rio Yaqui in mid-June, they discovered a new bay, which they named San Juan Bautista. This, the drowned mouth of the Rio de Sonora, is now known as Kino Bay. While there, they explored the estuary, now called the Laguna de la Cruz, and made the first recorded contact with the Seri Indians, who still inhabit Tiburon Island and the adjacent shores of Sonora.

Rejoining the Admiral, whose pearl fishing efforts were producing much sweat and little wealth, they returned to Matanchel (near the present San Blas) for supplies. On orders from the Viceroy, they put to sea again immediately, to intercept the incoming Manila Galleon, and to warn that overloaded vessel of a lurking pirate band. Crossing the Gulf in record time, they intercepted the Santa Rosa, and convoyed it safely to Acapulco, where the small fleet arrived on December 20, 1685. Kino's account of the voyage agrees quite closely with that of William Dampier, chronicler for the pirates.

Ordered to Mexico City by the Viceroy, Father Kino soon obtained a new field assignment to the then-unknown lands of the Seris, Guaymas and Pimas, in the frontier province of Nueva Vizcaya (northern Sonora and southern Arizona). With him he carried a Royal Edict, directing that no convert in that province should be forced to labor in the mines or on the ranches for a period of 20 years after his conversion, and that those who volunteered for such work should be paid a fair wage. For violations "grave penalties shall be imposed."

Father Kino rode northward to his new assignment on the ancient Camino Real, following in part the course of Alvar Nuñez Cabeza de Vaca and Francisco Vasquez de Coronado. Arriving in Oposura (now Moctezuma) at the end of February, 1687, he reported to the Father Visitor, Rev. Manuel Gonzalez, S.J.; was briefed on the local situation; and soon travelled up the valley of the San Miguel River to the Pima settlement of Cosari, where he immediately founded his first mission, Nuestra Señora de los Dolores, a short day's ride east of the modern town of Magdalena, Sonora.

Mission Dolores, Father Kino's home base for the rest of his strenuous and productive life, was far more than just an ecclesiastical outpost. Soon the mission grew into a largely self-sufficient frontier community, consisting of a church, which functioned as a fort in time of danger; quarters

The fertile Magdalena Valley supplied much of "the bounty of Sonora" which supported Kino's missions, and gave a surplus for export to the new missions to the north and west.

Right, two views of Mission San Ignacio. This structure built on the site of Kino's original mission still serves as the parish church of San Ignacio, Sonora.

Above, typical arboreal desert country in southern Arizona. Peaks on the horizon are Mt. Diaz named for Melchior Diaz, an early explorer in this nearly waterless region. (Photo by Ted Barnett) Kino's explorations through Arizona led to his founding Missions Tumacacori, *right*, 18 miles north of present Nogales, and San Xavier del Bac, *far right*, near Tucson.

for the fathers and their military guards; a storehouse; and many corrals. Surrounding the mission were cultivated fields, worked by the converts; and farther away the range lands, supporting large and growing herds of horses and cattle. Each mission was started with aid from the older establishments; and each, in its turn, furnished supplies for the establishment of other missions "mas alla."

Almost before the adobes of Mission Dolores had dried, other sites were picked in the immediate vicinity — San Ignacio, Imuris, and Remedios. Some of these missions, like Dolores, are now in ruins, due to failure of the water supply. Many others, however, enlarged and rebuilt in subsequent years, are the centers of modern communities. Typical is Mission San Ignacio de Caborica, now the parish church of the modern Sonoran community of San Ignacio.

As Mission Dolores became self-supporting, Father Kino began his major explorations in Pimeria Alta. Alone, or with only one or two white companions, he rode down the valley of the Rio de la Concepcion, establishing missions on the way, and eventually reaching the barren shores of the Gulf of California, where he hoped to find a good seaport, from which the bountiful crops of Sonora could be sent to aid the missions of California.

Northward explorations, into lands "whither up to this time time no father had entered," led to the founding of missions Cocospora, Guevavi, Tumacacori, and San Xavier del Bac; and to the discovery of the famous Casa Grande Ruins. Tumacacori, twice rebuilt after Kino's time, was destroyed by Apache raiders in 1821, but the ruin, restored by the National Park Service, is now a National Monument, with a historical museum and growing research center.

Mission San Xavier del Bac, on the outskirts of modern Tucson, was founded by Father Kino in 1700, and during his lifetime was the supply point for his extensive northerly and northwesterly explorations. Three quarters of a century later, San Xavier was the home base of Fray Francisco Hermenegildo Garces, O.F.M., who, working with the Indian, Sebastian Tarabal ("El Peregrino"), guided Juan Bautista de Anza across the deserts and mountains to Mission San Gabriel. Two years later, in 1776, De Anza led a band of settlers from Mexico over this trail, and up the coastal Camino Real to found the colony of Yerba Buena, now the City of San Francisco.

Soon, with missions strategically located over the relatively well-watered lands of Pimeria Alta, Father Kino searched farther afield, journeying to and down the valley of the Gila River, eventually reaching the Colorado, across which he saw lands that he believed to be those of California. While returning from one of these journeys, he saw that his Indian companions had some beautiful blue shells, exactly like those he had seen on the Pacific coast of Baja California (but not on the Gulf coast), some years before. From this observation he concluded, most correctly, that the Indians had a trade route from the Pacific coast to central and southern Arizona. Surely, he reasoned, if the Indians could bring shells from California to Pimeria, the Spanish could send supplies from Pimeria to California.

During more than 40 journeys of exploration, Father Kino crisscrossed the deserts of northern Sonora and southern Arizona, breaking trails that are still known, and sometimes used, even today. Much of this travel was through the arboreal deserts of what is now the extensive Papago Reservation, in southern Arizona. Often alone, but occasionally with one or more white companions, Father Kino rode all day, at "pony express" speeds, then spent much of the night in conferences, discussions with the Indians, and ministering to the aged, the sick, and the dying in the isolated camps of "The Desert People."

As the explorations extended, Father Kino mapped a workable trail from Caborca to Yuma. This, later to be known as the Camino del Diablo (Devil's Highway), and to be marked by "two graves to the mile" is one of the most difficult desert trails in North America. Parts of it are now Mexican Route 2, the paved road which connects Caborca with San Luis, via Sonoyta.

Eventually, convinced that he had found a land passage to California, he notified his close friend and immediate superior, Father Visitor Manuel Gonzalez, and soon the two fathers were riding westward toward the Colorado, to verify the discovery.

Using the shortest trail, through Sonoyta, they rode over the Camino del Diablo to the country of the Yumas, and then descended the eastern bank of the Colorado to its mouth, measuring the latitude carefully at several places. Near the head of the Gulf, Indians gave him more of the beautiful shells "from the opposite coast."

Although Father Gonzalez was ill, they shortly crossed the Colorado on a raft, and travelled southwestward down the shore. On the morning of March 11, 1702, the two fathers watched the sun rise over the Gulf of California, "proof most evident that we are now in California." After making further pertinent and correct observations, they returned to the Colorado and recrossed it uneventfully.

After an unsuccessful attempt to cross the Great Sand Dunes, which were and are a serious barrier to travel on the Sonoran shore of the Gulf, the trail to Yuma was retravelled, and then the Camino del Diablo. At Sonoyta, Father Gonzalez could no longer ride, and he became worse instead of better during a rest of three days. From Sonoyta to Mission San Pedro y San Pablo de Tubutama, considerably over 120 miles by trail, Father Gonzalez was carried in a litter "with great care, and with much charity and love" by stalwart Papago volunteers. "All possible remedies" were tried, but Father Gonzalez died only a few days after his arrival in Tubutama.

Now, although the land passage to California had been discovered and mapped by Father Kino, and had been seen by an official witness, that witness was dead, and another official verification was needed. This took quite a bit of doing, as the regular mission activities had to be carried on as usual; funds were short, also as usual; and time was running out for Father Kino, who was in his 57th year, and who, some years before, had been described as "an old and twisted prop."

With the active support of General Don Jacinto de Fuensaldaña, commandant of the presidio of Fronteras, the long-planned expedition got under way in 1706. Detailed as military escort, "to be eyewitnesses and inform themselves of everything for the purpose of reporting juridically in Mexico" were Alferez Juan Matheo Ramirez and Commander Juan Antonio Duran. Ramirez was designated official chronicler, and a separate report was prepared by Fray Manuel de la Oyuela y Velarte, a Franciscan guest.

Travelling by way of Tubutama and Coborca, the party soon reached Sonoyta, where a day and a half were spent in missionary activity. Next camp was the watering place of El Carrizal. From this friendly place, they went southwestward, toward the Sierra de Santa Clara, which Father Kino had visited twice before. This jumble of peaks and craters, now known as Pinacate, reminded Father Juan Maria Salvatierra of "the state of the world in the general conflagration." On an earlier visit, he and Father Kino had identified the main peaks as an extinct volcano.

Riding in one day from El Carrizal to the

Above, Father Kino and his companions crossed hundreds of miles of bare Sonoran plains in search of a good harbor on the Gulf of California from which supplies could be sent from Sonora to California. Typical is this view looking eastward from Flat Hill near Bahia la Cholla. *Below left,* the Rio de Sonoyta and the lavas at Pinacate were stops on Kino's route through this territory, which is shown on the map, *bottom right.*

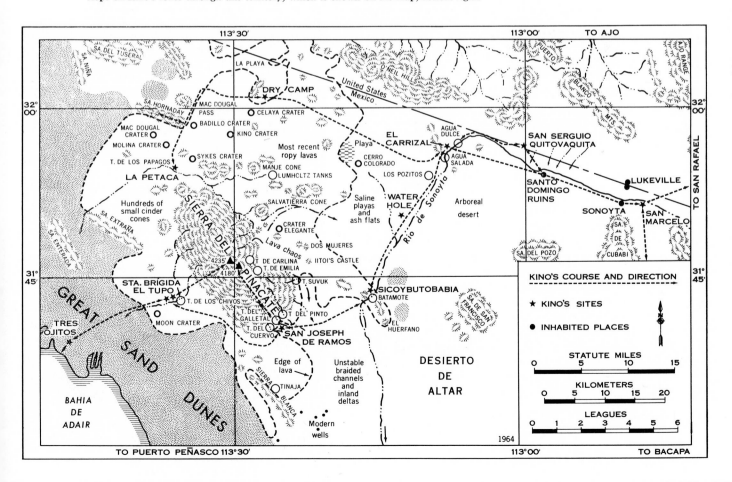

sub-summit, where they left the unsaddled mules, the party climbed the nearest peak (Carnegie Peak, 4180 ft.), made detailed observations, and spent the night. The next morning, November 6, 1706, while the observations were being repeated, Fray Manuel, "at the cost of very great toil," ascended the more northerly and higher peak (Pinacate Peak, 4235 ft.), and again saw clearly "with even more detail" the continuity of the lands of Sonora with those of California. All witnesses being thoroughly convinced, the party descended to the subsummit, saddled the mules, and rode four leagues down the lava slopes to a water hole. There, a Mass of Thanksgiving was celebrated, breakfast was eaten, and all set out northeastward for El Carrizal, which was reached that night. Travel for the two days (November 5 and November 6, 1706) was approximately 90 miles, and included a 3500-foot ascent over lava flows.

By a direct route, and wasting no time, the party returned to Mission Dolores, where Ramirez prepared the official report of the exploration, which all signed. Here, also, Fray Manuel prepared his independent and agreeing report. The joint report, now an official document, or *juracion*, was to be forwarded to General Fuensaldaña, who had promised to send it to Mexico City by special messenger, and from there, perhaps. "even to the King." Just as the report was ready to be sent off, they learned to their "great sorrow that our Lord had just taken the General to Himself." The report, nevertheless, found its way to Mexico City, and its content was soon spread through the civilized world.

The 1706 journey to Pinacate was the last of Father Kino's geographically important *entradas*, but he remained productively active for some years thereafter. On March 14, 1711, Father Kino rode westward from Mission Dolores to Magadalena, where he planned to dedicate a new chapel in honor of St. Francis Xavier, "The Apostle to the Indes" a land where Father Kino had once hoped to serve. "When he was singing the Mass of Dedication" he was suddenly stricken, and was taken to the Spartan quarters of the resident father, Agustin de Campos. There, "a little after midnight, Father Eusebio Kino died with great peace and edification." He was buried in the chapel which he had helped to dedicate, but the site of the chapel, and of his grave, is still being sought by historical archaeologists.

The voluminous Kino records were "lost in the files" for almost two centuries. With the finding and publication of his diary by Herbert E.

The goal of Kino's expedition, the barren shore of the Gulf of California, seen from the summit of Punta Peñasco, Sonora.

Bolton, in 1919, public interest was aroused in Father Kino and his works. In the ensuing years, the Jesuit explorer was the subject of a dozen books, and more than 100 historical papers, and the subject is by no means worked out even today.

Monuments in honor of Father Kino have been erected in a number of southwestern communities, such as Magdalena, Nogales, and Tucson. On the 250th anniversary of his death, March 15, 1961, a Solemn Pontifical Mass was celebrated in his honor in Cathedral San Agustin, in Tucson, approximately on the site of Father Kino's San Agustin mission, in the country of the Sobaipuris, who lived where Tucson now is.

After years of labor and planning, the citizens of Arizona, with the consent and approval of the President of the United States, have placed in the National Hall of Statuary, in the Capitol Rotunda, in Washington, an heroic bronze statue of Father Kino, the work of Madame Suzanne Silvercruys. This statue will commemorate, for all of us, the great work of the Italian Jesuit who wanted to go to the Orient, but instead unravelled the geographic mysteries of the lands that have become Sonora, Arizona, Baja California, and California.

In tribute to the memory of Father Kino the monument, *above*, was erected in Tucson, Arizona. The heroic bronze statue of Father Kino, *left*, by Mme. Suzanne Silvercruys was donated by the citizens of Arizona and is in the National Hall of Statuary, Washington, D.C. (Photo by Karsh, Ottawa)

Portus Novae Albionis REDISCOVERED?

By
ROBERT H. POWER

FRANCIS DRAKE sailed away from the California coast on July 23, 1579. The place of his landing and departure has since been lost to history. Though every means of historical research has been used and several points are claimed, no sufficient evidence has yet appeared to prove the case for any particular one. The port of Nova Albion has eluded all searchers.

The first tangible evidence of Drake's visit to our coast was accidentally discovered in 1936 by Berle W. Shinn. Near Greenbrae, Marin County, California, in latitude 37°56' he picked up the plate of brass upon which Drake had inscribed his claim to Nova Albion for Queen Elizabeth "and herr svccessors forever." The Plate of Brass has been authenticated by experts, but no one can say Indians or white men had not moved it from where Drake nailed it to a post 375 years ago. Authorities, in fact, have thought it so likely to have been moved they have attached little importance to the place where it finally turned up, although because of it there has been some recent speculation upon San Francisco Bay as the anchorage of the *Golden Hind*. Drakes Bay, however, is still the locality most favored, with Bodega Bay second choice.

Consider for a moment the odds against the possibility that anyone would pick up this piece of brass 20 to 40 miles away at another bay and then drop it on the shore of the bay — the logical one I believe — where it was found. Certainly the Greenbrae location of the find should be treated as a significant fact, which authorities agree would be of great value if only it can be coupled with other facts.

The other clues every searcher must work with in the quest for Nova Albion are a border map on the Hondius broadside map of the world entitled *Vera totius expeditionis nauticae* (1590?); published accounts of Drake's voyage, such as *The Famous Voyage of Sir Francis Drake into the South Sea* (1589) and *The World Encompassed by Sir Francis Drake* (1628); and remarks by John Drake and others.

There is almost complete agreement that the Port of Nova Albion is in either Sonoma or Marin County because accounts of the voyage clearly state that the anchorage was near the 38th parallel, which crosses Marin from Drakes Bay to a point north of San Rafael and on across the southern end of San Pablo Bay. Also, the Plate of Brass was found in this geographical area.

The Dutch cartographer Jodocus Hondius compiled his broadside map after the voyages of Drake and Cavendish around the world. The decoration and text on the map, however, are confined to Sir Francis Drake and his voyage. On the west coast of North America on the Hondius map at approximately 38° latitude is a large inlet which is the Port of Nova Albion, and as a part of the border decoration there are three inset detailed plans of ports that Drake visited, one of them a bay called "Portus Novae Albionis." The source of these plans may have been the log of the *Golden Hind*, a document long lost. Two of them have been identified and found to be quite accurate. But the plan in the upper left corner of the broadside, the "Portus Novae Albionis," has never been satisfactorily oriented in California.

My quest to rediscover the Port of Nova Albion was begun by tracing the Hondius plan and then laying it over the geographical features of the Marin shore on a modern map. The greatest difficulty was in the lack of scale on the Hondius plan. But regardless of scale, those features of the plan consisting of a peninsula and an island resembled only Tiburon Peninsula and its island-like neighbor, Belvedere. Therefore I drew the peninsula on the Hondius plan on the same scale as Tiburon Peninsula on the modern map, and then copied the rest of the plan on the same scale so that the entire area on both plan and map could be compared. When the Hondius plan was again laid over the features of modern Marin, it encompassed an area from southern San Pablo Bay to Angel Island, and from San Rafael to Richmond. This brought the entire Hondius plan into essential agreement with the modern map.

The island and peninsula correspond to Belvedere and Tiburon. The *Golden Hind* is drawn where San Quentin Point should be. The rest of the inside shore of the bay corresponds to the San Rafael shore, the near-straight line corresponds to the straits of San Pablo, and the far shore compares favorably with the Richmond coast line. And, equally important, we find the tracing overlaps the 38th parallel by one half minute, and one edge of the Hondius plan parallels and nearly corresponds to the 38° latitude line. If northern San Francisco Bay is "Portus Novae Albionis," then the cartographer oriented his map with the latitude and longitude of the globe.

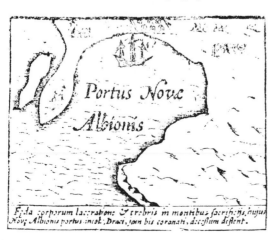

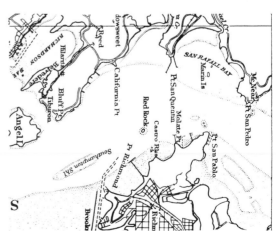

Belvedere   Mt. Tamalpais   Tiburon Peninsula   San Rafael   Richmond shore

Angel Island

(CAS photograph by George W. Bunton)

Why, then, did the cartographer ignore San Quentin Point, Angel Island, and San Pablo Bay? First, it is obvious the plan was drawn by sight from a single point. I asked a designer where he thought the draftsman stood when he sketched the plan. He quickly indicated a point off the end of the peninsula on the Hondius plan, basing his decision on the angles of the village stockade or fence shown on the plan and on the position of the Indian shown on the peninsula. A look at the present map strongly suggests that Angel Island is the very place where Drake's draftsman sat to draw the Port of Nova Albion 375 years ago.

As seen from Angel Island, the Port of Nova Albion has not changed in outline since 1579. Belvedere and Tiburon are both clear, but the details of the peninsula are not; therefore only a generalized coast was possible. San Quentin Point and the San Rafael coast blend into a gentle curve. The Straits of San Pablo allow only a restricted view of San Pablo Bay, which is far too distant to be drawn by sight from Angel Island. The Richmond coast is close at hand and in good perspective, making it significant that the same coast on the Hondius plan has more detail than any other portion, and in general agreement with the present outline of the Richmond coast. Also, it is reasonable to assume the artist might have omitted drawing the island from which he was making his sketch.

Consider now the odds that any other bay in Marin County has or ever did have a coast line similar to that of the Hondius plan; and consider also the odds in favor of a map that is almost geographically correct having borders parallel to true latitude and longitude lines. There is no other portion of the Marin or Sonoma coast that matches the Hondius plan so well. Moreover, Greenbrae, where the Plate of Brass was found, is within the area of the plan. These facts taken together strongly indicate that northern San Francisco Bay is indeed the Port of Nova Albion.

Before a conclusion can be drawn, however, the written accounts of Drake's voyage must be examined. The Famous Voyage gives a convincing indication that the Golden Hind was the first ship to sail through the Golden Gate, in these words: ". . . Till we came within 38 degrees towards the line. In which height

it pleased God to send vs into a faire and good Baye, with a good winde to enter same."

The combination "faire and good" emphasized with "it pleased God" can only be interpreted as meaning excellent. The words "into" and "enter" imply going through a restricted entrance, such as the Golden Gate, into a bay beyond. The need of wind indicates the entrance and bay were of some magnitude.

The World Encompassed, compiled from the notes of Drake's chaplain Fletcher, has passages that logically apply to San Francisco Bay. One of these states they rowed around for the first three days and then anchored the Golden Hind closer to shore. This again indicates a bay of larger size than Drakes or Bodega.

The same work also gives clues to terrain, flora, and fauna: "Besides how vnhandsome and deformed appeared the face of the earth itselfe! shewing trees without leaues, ground without greenes in those moneths of Iune and Iuly" (June 27 to August 2 by the modern calendar). "The in land we found to be farre different from the shoare, a goodly country, and fruitful soyle . . . large and fat Deere, which we sawe by the thousands, as we supposed, in a heard; besides a multitude of a strange kind of Conies."

San Quentin Point is rather barren and rocky, the grass is brown in July, and the buckeyes in Marin begin to lose their leaves in early July. The inland description is definitely inland Marin, and it is a typical description of the hilly area north of San Rafael where there is an abundance of oaks and acorns, and therefore ground squirrels ("Conies"), and open grass where elk by the thousands once grazed.

The Hondius plan also shows several trees which greatly resemble oaks and it is the only illustration of Drake's landing which was probably completely drawn in Nova Albion.

The Indians described in both The Famous Voyage and The World Encompassed have definitely been identified as Coast Miwok by Dr. Robert F. Heizer and by Dr. A. L. Kroeber of the University of California Department of Anthropology. These accounts of California Indians in 1579 are the rarest treasure in the narratives because they are the earliest descriptions of Indians on the California coast. The Coast

⋏ Angel Island was taken over by the Sixth Army on the day that the author and some Academy staff members landed there from the Academy's launch, and MP's kept the party from going farther eastward (to right in photo) where the view most nearly agrees with the Hondius plan. View across Raccoon Strait from Hospital Cove.

Credits—*Top:* Courtesy University of California Press. *Middle two:* Courtesy Clinton Duffy, former warden, San Quentin Prison. *Bottom:* CAS photo by G. W. Bunton.

Corte Madera Creek. There is an indication that the Plate of Brass was erected on a "Firme Post" at an Indian village and not at Drake's camp.

John Drake, cousin of Francis, who was aboard the *Golden Hind*, gave the following deposition to his Spanish captors five years after the voyage: "Francis Drake, on this journey, saw five or six islands of good land. He called one San Bartolome, one San Jaime, and another which seemed to be the largest and best, Nueva Albion. He remained here a month and a half."

Many authorities have ignored or discredited John Drake's statement about Nova Albion, but it has more significance than would at first appear. He could have remembered Nova Albion (Marin) as an island, providing he sailed on three sides of it. His complimentary tone suggests he thought well of Nova Albion, along with his cousin Francis who considered it worthy of naming after his homeland.

One descriptive item in *The Famous Voyage* that has always been used in arguing in favor of Drakes Bay as the place of anchorage, reads: "Our Generall called this Countrey, Noua Albion, and that for two causes: the one in respect of the white bankes and cliffes, which lie towards the sea."

The key to this passage is in the words "lie towards the sea." If the cliffs had been at the place of anchorage, the word *bay* or *harbor* would have been used, not the word "sea." The coast of Drake's Nova Albion was from San Francisco to Oregon, but it was probably named for the nearly white cliffs that face the ocean from Marin's outer shore.

The last paragraph about Nova Albion in *The World Encompassed* has always confused those who favored Drakes Bay because of the illogical time element involved. It relates how the *Golden Hind* sailed out of the harbor July 23 and landed on some islands July 24. The Farallones are 17 miles from Drakes Bay — too close to fit this time table, given the prevailing summer wind on these shores. They are, however, 37 miles from San Francisco, a reasonable day's sail.

"The 23 of July they [Indians] took a sorrowful farewell of us. . . . Not farre without this harborough did lye certaine Ilands (we called them the Ilands of Saint James) hauing on them plentiful and great store of Seales and birds, with one of which wee fell July 24. whereon we found such prouision as might serue our turn for a while. We departed againe the day next following, viz. July 25."

The location of the Plate of Brass, the geographical features of the Portus Novae Albionis, and the narratives combine to allow the following logical conclusion: Francis Drake on June 17, 1579, sailed the *Golden Hind* through the Golden Gate and anchored in northern San Francisco Bay. Three days later, he landed and set up a camp, probably on or near San Quentin Point.

Miwok inhabited the Marin peninsula and were concentrated mostly at Bodega and San Francisco bays.

The World Encompassed states that the place of landing and the camp site were three quarters of a mile from an Indian village. No archeological evidence of Indian villages has been found on the south side of San Quentin Point, but there was one not far away on

The profile of Tiburon Peninsula looking south from San Quentin (*bottom*) startlingly resembles the distant land across the cove in the old engraving (*top*) of the Indians crowning Drake — but where is the high hill to the left? The drawing (*upper middle*) of San Quentin Prison about 100 years ago shows one; the later photo (*lower middle*) has it partly excavated. Our present photo shows the new cell block where the hill *was*. A 100-year-old map in prison files calls the hill a burial ground of the aborigines, places an Indian village on the cove, and says whaling ships were beached there! It was drawn by a Spanish captain.

THIS GREEN AND GOLDEN LAND

The particular blend of summer-long sunshine and seasonal coastal rain known as Mediterranean climate is familiar to Californians. One of its distinctive features is a salubrious growing season that supports an ever-rich variety of flowers, shrubs, and trees, and also permits plants from many other parts of the world to thrive. In addition, California's climatic extremes of mountain and desert have stimulated the development of a variety of distinctive extremes in floral form. Some of the special trees of California have become major attractions for tourists from all over the world, and in seed or seedling form have been exported to many other places.

Although California has been known as the home of the biggest, the tallest, and the oldest of trees, the nature of the botanical situations that made these extremes of growth possible was not immediately apparent to explorers. The largest of the trees—the sequoias—have always attracted great attention, not only because of their extraordinary qualities as living beings, but also for their potential as a usable resource. Among the studies undertaken to learn their growth pattern was the one reported here, in "Youthful Years of the Big Trees" (1948), by Woodbridge Metcalf, who was Extension Forester at the University of California College of Agriculture.

Large areas of central and southern California are covered not by big trees, but by a low, dense, evergreen shrub vegetation known as chaparral. Although a goodly variety of plants and animals make up the chaparral habitat, it is the predominant shrub, chamise, that gives the habitat its well-known quality of being almost impenetrable. The function of fire in the maintenance of the chaparral habitat has long been a source of controversy, with some managers feeling that fire should be suppressed because of its potential for widespread damage, and others maintaining that periodic small fires are necessary for the chaparral to thrive. In "Chaparral" (1976), the ecology of chaparral and the function of fire in that ecology are discussed by David J. Parsons, Research Scientist at Sequoia and Kings Canyon National Parks.

Although the special qualities of many of California's trees were apparent on first look, the chief feature of the bristlecone pines remained hidden within its heart of wood for many decades. These twisted, scraggly-looking trees that grow high on the White Mountains of California and in several other states have turned out to be the oldest representatives of organic life on earth. The 7000-year sequence of tree rings they provide has become an important clue to the understanding of ancient climatic changes in the western regions of North America. In "The Ancient Bristlecone Pines" (1969), the story of research on these trees is presented by George Lindsay, Director Emeritus of the Academy, with photographs by Staff Photographer Lloyd Ullberg.

Not all the famous trees of California are noted for their extremes of growth habit. Oaks, in all their specific variety, grow throughout many parts of the country. But in California, the blend of scattered oak trees dotting a golden landscape of summer-dry grass has become known as a distinctive feature of the state's landscape, appreciated for its sky-revealing beauty and painted by many artists. And the oaks of California have an interesting botanical property. Although there are many subspecific varieties of oaks created by natural hybridizing, this takes place within each of the several subgenera rather than between them—a confirmation of the accuracy of the taxonomy. The research on oaks and their varieties is presented, in "Circus of *Quercus*" (1974), by writer-photographer David Cavagnaro, former Resident Biologist at Audubon Canyon Ranch and now widely known as a naturalist and teacher.

Because the climate of California permits plants from many parts of the world to grow well, it is not always necessary to travel far to study plants from other continents. A dozen botanical gardens, in all parts of the state, display worldwide plants in many groupings. Included are geographic, taxonomic, climatological, ecological, and horticultural arrangements—useful for both study and enjoyment. These botanical gardens, and the specialties they offer, are discussed, in "California's Botanical Gardens" (1966), by Elizabeth McClintock, currently Research Associate in the Department of Botany at the University of California.

WOODBRIDGE METCALF
Youthful Years of the **BIG TREE**

Much has been written about the veteran Big Trees of the Californian Sierra Nevada. Their massive size, great age, and stately grandeur have been extolled in poetry and prose, so that they are perhaps better known throughout the world than any other American tree. It is doubtless quite natural that much attention has been paid to these giants of the forest—virtually none to lesser individuals of the species, middle-aged and youthful Sequoias. Moreover, many people appear to believe that these great old trees are the last survivors of a vanishing race, that they are no longer able to reproduce their kind, and that when they die the world will know them no more. Happily these beliefs are not true; but, because so widely held, they must represent questions in men's minds. If there are young Sequoias today—giants of a distant future—what is their history, from seed to seedling, to sapling, to mature tree? How do they grow? Under what conditions? Are they strong or weak, many or few? What, in a word, are the chances for the species' survival, here in these few scattered groves on the west slope of the Sierra which together make *Sequoia gigantea's* last stand on earth?

Once the Big Tree's immediate future was secured, the giants saved from the ax by the creation of national parks and forests, answers to the questions of long-term survival were to be sought in knowledge gained through careful, detailed study of the entire life cycle of Sequoia, particularly of the critical early stages.

Modern scientific forestry supplied the techniques of study; the University of California, through the generosity of Horace Whitaker, furnished the "laboratory." Whitaker's Forest, 320 acres, 5500 to 6500 feet elevation, stands in the optimum region for *Sequoia gigantea*, on the slopes of Redwood Mountain in Tulare County. When he gave the tract to the University of California in 1910, Horace Whitaker specified in his deed of gift that it be used "for study and teaching of forestry and the enjoyment of the people."

Logging the area during the period from 1870 to 1876, mostly for sugar pine, opened up the timber stand, and evidently created ideal condi-

tions for forest reproduction. Though several old Sequoias were cut at that time, some two hundred veteran Big Trees remained, together with adequate seed trees of sugar pine, ponderosa (west-

ern yellow) pine, white fir, and incense cedar. Weather conditions between 1878 and about 1882 must have been exceedingly favorable, resulting in a dense seedling stand of all these species throughout the entire area. Five sample plots for study of growth and mortality were established in these young stands by the writer in the summer of 1915. All trees were tagged and measured at that time and have since been remeasured at

76

LEFT: *Three - year - old Sequoia seedling, showing the foliage typical of very young trees and new growth of older trees. This nursery-grown baby has produced a cone, of nearly normal size—although seed production usually begins when the Sequoia is 40 or 50 years old. (Photograph by W. C. Matthews)*

RIGHT: *A Sequoia veteran of Whitaker's Forest. Conical crown and rounded masses of dense foliage, average diameter of 10 to 12 feet, and average height of 225 to 250 feet, indicate that this and similar vigorous individuals have reached a mature middle age, 1000 to 1200 years. Young Big Trees in the background show the typical slender, feathery crowns of 60- to 70-year-old second growth. (Photograph by Woodbridge Marshall)*

West slope of Redwood Mountain from the clearing at Whitaker's Forest, 1926. The skyline shows the rounded crowns of old Sequoias. In the foreground, the tall, slender cones of 50-year second growth mingle with associated ponderosa and sugar pines, incense cedars, and white firs. (Photograph by the author)

about five year intervals. A sixth plot was marked off in 1940.

Periodically, Sequoia cones have been collected from which seed has been extracted and studied in the greenhouse and nursery at Berkeley by several members of the Forestry staff, including Professor F. S. Baker and Dr. N. T. Mirov. Sequoia seedlings have been grown in the nursery and many returned to the plantation at Whitaker's Forest, where under favorable conditions they are making extremely rapid and satisfactory growth. These studies, together with observations at other points, are the basis for what will be said here on the reproduction and growth of these remarkable trees.

The Sequoia's Seed

For such huge trees, Big Tree seeds are almost inconceivably small. The seed is like a tiny, golden brown wafer, or bit of sawdust, which will lie on the ground unnoticed by most people who pass through the woods. It takes from 80,000 to more than 100,000—about 90,000 at an average—of these tiny bits of life to make a pound.

The cones which produce the seeds need two growing seasons to mature. They are light green,

oval, about two inches long by one inch in diameter, and average between eight and twelve to the pound. Old trees bear them in great numbers in their crowns, but so far from the ground that one must use binoculars to observe them very closely. Trees apparently begin to produce cones when they are about fifty years old; even these young trees occasionally bear such quantities of cones that their slender tops are broken or deformed by the weight. Seed of excellent quality has been obtained from trees sixty to seventy years old as well as from veterans which have withstood the storms of two thousand winters.

An interesting and very significant fact is that a great many of the cones remain on the trees unopened for several years after the seeds mature. Some which have stayed on old trees long enough to become covered with lichen growth have yielded seeds which under test showed a germinative capacity of 42 per cent.

When they finally fall from the tree—some naturally, some blasted down by winter storms, some cut by squirrels for the food the seeds provide— the cones are firm in texture, bright green in color unless too old, and contain about 30 per cent moisture. The seeds are held between the heavy cone scales and surrounded by a purple, crystalline resin which when separated out may weigh half as much as the seed in any given sample. One hundred pounds of green cones will yield from three to three and a half pounds of clean seed. The biggest cones of bright green color give the best seed, its viability generally averaging around 50 per cent or up to 75 per cent in selected samples of the largest seed. The general run shows 35 to 50 per cent viability.

What Seedlings Need

Sequoia seeds respond promptly when propagated in greenhouse seed flats or outdoor seedbeds under usual nursery care. Seedlings grow rapidly when placed in cans or other containers and may be transferred to the field when one to two years old. They develop a large root system and are difficult to transplant successfully when more than a foot high. When set in the field they need good care and some irrigation during the first dry season unless placed where they have shade from the hot sun during critical afternoon hours. Otherwise very large losses occur.

Under natural conditions seedlings are rarely found in mature forest stands. Seeds falling on the litter and humus of the forest floor are evidently not able to establish themselves. Occasional seedlings will be found on exposed mineral soil along roads or trails, particularly where moisture conditions are good and overhead canopy not too dense. Even under these conditions, root competition from larger trees is generally so severe that seedlings are stunted or killed out entirely during the first year or two.

Thus it is evident that Sequoias, like white pines and other aristocrats of the forest, are quite fastidious about where they grow and require a special combination of favorable conditions to become established in large numbers. The beautiful young stands which did become established at Whitaker's Forest, Mountain Home State Forest, the Big Stump section, and similar restricted areas, were the result of a combination of favorable factors: (1) selective logging to open up the stand and expose areas of mineral soil; (2) adequate distribution of seed by squirrels or other natural means; (3) late rains in spring and early rains in fall during one or two years; (4) summer seasons free from extreme heat, dryness, and high winds; (5) successful fire protection for forty or fifty years.

The last is a most important requirement for the establishment of any young forest stand, though the use of fire to remove slash and other logging debris is a valuable aid in exposing mineral soil and providing suitable conditions for germination of seeds. Partial shade during hot afternoon hours and reasonable freedom from competition by roots of older trees are both of considerable importance. In general, Sequoias become established most easily along moist flats or on cool north and east slopes with sugar pine and white fir, leaving the drier sites to such drought-resistant species as ponderosa pine and incense cedar.

Struggle for Existence

Following the selective logging of the '70's in Whitaker's Forest, these factors combined to an unusually favorable degree. Germination of seed was good. Sequoia and other seedlings established themselves over a wide area, and as closely spaced as in a seedbed. This of course works two ways. Favorable conditions make for crowding, hence severe competition. During the first year or two the little trees are forced to fight for their very lives. Often one hundred or more seedlings will start to the square foot, and the fight for space to grow and the essential nutriments for life goes on continuously both below and above ground. In this struggle, which in many cases lasts for a hundred years or more, thousands will die and drop out where one succeeds. It is a great contest in which the victor in a local engagement must soon compete with other local champions in a gradually widening circle. Of all the starters, only an infinitesimal few win out to final victory. In the early months and years, moreover, outside influences such as rodents, grazing animals, frost, heat, drought, and floods all take their toll, to the advantage of trees which are most vigorous or fortunately situated. Thus, while greater vigor and rapidity of growth favor them, chance also aids the ultimate victors.

At the time the sample plots were established in 1915 the struggle had already been going on for about thirty-five years and showed no signs of letting up. Many dead trees had to be cut in order to give access to the plots for measurement of the living. Although their lower branches had been killed by shading, we soon found they were so numerous and so stiff and wire-like it was necessary to prune every trunk with a hand ax in order to tape-measure its diameter. At thirty to

When snow comes to Whitaker's Forest the slender young Sequoia crowns take on a new look as they bend gracefully under the white load. Occasionally some tops are broken by an overload of snow, but many quickly grow new leaders. This view across the plantation and swimming pool shows two veteran trees and their 65-year-old progeny. (Photograph by the author)

forty feet above the ground the crowns were so closely massed together that little sunlight came through, making it very difficult to identify tree tips for measuring total height. Three of the plots then showed a stand density of more than a thou-

sand trees per acre, a large proportion of them in the most crowded areas definitely weakened by the severe competition. A few vigorous individuals, however, had forged ahead in the race for height, showing signs of the dominance which many of them have maintained throughout the succeeding years.

In Plot One where 358 Sequoias and four white firs were at that time crowded into a quarter acre, the trees in the upper crown classes averaged only 35 feet in height. In plots where competition was mainly with associated species and not with other Sequoias, the better trees averaged 45 to 65 feet in height at thirty-five years; and in Plot Five where the soil was deepest and the Sequoias had more adequate room for development, the better trees averaged 87 feet in height at the same age.

Study of the figures taken during the last thirty-two years shows that the Sequoias not only grow exceptionally fast when conditions favor them, but are remarkably tenacious of life under competition. In Plot One only 109 trees were alive in 1947 of the 362 measured in 1915; however, though eight trees per year had given up the fight on this small area, a number of the suppressed Sequoias still clung to life though they have grown less than a half inch in diameter during the last quarter century and their crowns show only faint indications of green foliage. This refusal to give up the fight, though undoubtedly an attribute of champions, tends to prolong competition for many decades.

How Trees Appeared in 1947

The following brief summary of each of the plots will give an idea of the growth and condition of the trees after some seventy-two years of competition.

PLOT ONE. On this fairly dry quarter acre at about 6,200 feet elevation there remain 35 Sequoias in the upper two crown classes, the only trees of the original 358 measured in 1915 which still have a chance of survival. They now average 13.4 inches in diameter and 90 feet in height. The five dominant trees, perhaps the only ones which will be alive after another twenty years, now average 16.9 inches in diameter and 99 feet tall. There are still 75 Sequoias living on the plot which have lost out in the fight and are now clinging to life by a very slender thread. They average only 4.6 inches in diameter and 22 feet in height. Four white firs which have been somewhat isolated in a corner of the plot are still doing fairly well and average 9.9 inches in diameter and 45 feet tall. But they have little chance of survival.

PLOT TWO. This one-sixteenth acre plot contained only 13 Sequoias in 1915, and these were well distributed so that all had a fairly adequate chance for growth and development. They made rapid progress for the first decade, but more than half were badly broken by an ice storm in 1932. Road building took out one, and the falling of timber in 1947 broke several. The surviving four average 19.3 inches in diameter and 96 feet in height. One has a broken top but is recovering.

PLOT THREE. This quarter acre is on fertile bottom land along a fork of Eshom Creek at 5,400 feet elevation and when measured in 1915 was a good example of a mixed stand. Of the 251 trees then occupying the ground, 131 or 52 per cent were incense cedars. There were 64 Sequoias, 35 white firs, four ponderosa pines, four sugar pines, and 13 hardwoods—oak, alder, and willow. Now there are 29 Sequoias which average 26.2 inches in diameter and 112 feet tall, 12 cedars with average diameter of 8.3 inches and height of about 50 feet, and seven white firs averaging 17.4 inches in diameter and 120 feet in height. All other species have died out. A few white firs have held their position because favorably placed, but the Sequoias clearly dominate, unchallenged.

PLOT FOUR. Situated on moist bottom land west of Eshom Creek, this one-sixteenth acre plot in 1915 also contained a mixed stand, 76 conifers and one willow. There were 20 Sequoias, 16 of which still remain after thirty-two years. Nine are in the upper crown classes, averaging 19.1 inches in diameter and 97 feet tall. The cedars have fared badly in the contest, only 11 remaining of the original 26. These are all in the lower crown classes, averaging but 5.2 inches in diameter, their crowns hopelessly overtopped. The white firs have fared about the same, with but five out of nine remaining, their average diameter 5.4 inches and height about 35 feet. Only four ponderosa pines are left of an original 16, but that they have done a little better on this site than elsewhere is shown by their average diameter of 14.5 inches and height of 75 feet. All five sugar pines and the willow have died.

PLOT FIVE. This plot shows astonishingly rapid growth of the Sequoias which had sufficient room for development on deep soil at the north end of the clearing. In 1915 there were 27 trees on approximately a quarter acre—20 Sequoias, six incense cedars, and a fine sugar pine apparently somewhat older than the plot's other trees. Ten of the Sequoias held dominant positions in the stand in 1915, nine of them exceeding 90 feet in height. These dominant trees continued to push their slender, feathery tips upward nearly two feet a year; in 1947 nine of them averaged 158 feet in height and 42.5 inches in diameter. The

Fifty-year Sequoia second growth in Plot One. Densely massed trees have here fought for living space throughout their lives. More than half of those which started as seedlings have lost out in the ruthless competition, which still goes on. (Photograph by the author)

other 11 Sequoias were thinned out of the stand in the spring of that year to give the rest more growing room. Ring counts on the stumps of these trees put the age of the stand at some seventy-two years. The four remaining cedars have not had much competition from the Sequoias and average 24.9 inches in diameter and 72 feet in height. The sugar pine stands in the open at one corner of the plot, a tree of great symmetry and beauty. It increased in diameter from 40.2 to 56.6 inches and in height from 108 to 140 feet during the thirty-two years. It is probably about one hundred years old.

PLOT SIX. Established in 1940, this plot is about half an acre of bottom land along the fork of Eshom Creek north of the swimming pool. In the fall of 1938 some 40 trees in the lower crown classes were thinned out to give the better trees room to grow. This left 35 Sequoias and five cedars. When measured in 1940 the Sequoias averaged 21.5 inches in diameter and 113 feet in height, the largest diameter being 39.6 inches and the greatest height 143 feet. The five cedars were all suppressed by the Sequoias, showing an average diameter of only 10.2 inches and height of only 42 feet. Though the thinning was not heavy the trees have responded to the partial release from competition with an average diameter increase of 1.9 inches during the past seven years. Their average height is now estimated to be about 125 feet. It is evident that about one-third of the remaining trees can be removed during the next few years in order to stimulate growth of the others. The final stand on this half acre will probably include at one hundred years of age only ten trees. All the dense young stands are now being similarly thinned in order to relieve the excessive competition which otherwise would continue in them for many years. The dominant trees, Sequoias with an occasional well-placed white fir or pine, are generally in vigorous condition for future rapid growth.

The observations and measurements we have made in these plots bring out facts which may be briefly summarized:

(1) Sequoias grow more rapidly in height, diameter, and volume than any of their associates. The height growth of well located, dominant trees on good soil has averaged two feet per year for over seventy years.

(2) Sequoias will unquestionably dominate any stand in which they start on fairly even terms with any other tree species.

(3) The thickness and relative fire resistance of Sequoia bark after about forty years give them an added advantage over other trees.

(4) Sequoias in young, pure stands are so tenacious of life that periodic thinnings are desirable to relieve the better trees of excessive competition and maintain a satisfactory rate of growth.

(5) Young Sequoia trees have an ideal length and form for use as telephone poles, a fact which makes intermediate thinnings economically feasible.

With respect to forest economics, Whitaker's Forest furnishes an example of the future possibilities in a mixed timber stand dominated by Sequoia. During the past few years mature trees of white fir, sugar and ponderosa pines, and cedar have been selectively logged, throughout the forest's 320 acres, for the market. This sale of timber has removed approximately two million board feet of mature trees with very little damage to the young timber stands. This has made openings in the crown cover and exposed areas of mineral soil which should provide excellent seedbed conditions for new reproduction when favorable weather occurs. Some advanced growth of white fir is already on the ground and more will follow the next good seed crop. These young firs will be marketed as soon as they reach Christmas tree size and thus add moderately to the Forest's financial return. While the Sequoias will probably always make up the bulk of the trees in these stands, there are considerable numbers of sugar pine, ponderosa pine, fir, and cedar which will grow to merchantable size for posts, poles, and eventually for lumber. Thus it is estimated that under intensive thinning and forest management during the next quarter century the annual volume growth per acre will increase to at least 500 board feet, of which about two-thirds will be Sequoia. This will amount to an annual yield of 160,000 board feet of logs from the 320 acres besides poles and other products removed by continual thinning for relief of unproductive competition in the young stands.

Looking Ahead

The young stands at Whitaker's Forest have demonstrated the remarkably rapid growth rate of *Sequoia gigantea* during its youthful years. It is not a difficult tree to plant, and indications are that planting can greatly extend its natural range. Planted trees are making excellent growth at many points in California and as far north as Portland, Oregon. Extreme cold and dryness are its chief natural checks. Thus it is altogether likely that this noble tree may yield large quantities of lumber and other forest products from forest areas where it is now unknown, as well as from natural stands under modern, intensive forest management.

But above all, it is heartening to know that this greatest of trees will continue to spring by its own seed from its native Sierran slopes for untold generations, so only man does not destroy it in greed or carelessness. If man wills continued life to this small remnant of a once earth-circling forest of giants, only another and greater Ice Age, perhaps, can end its time on earth.

CHAPARRAL

David J. Parsons

THE traveler entering Sequoia National Park through the southern entrance passes through several miles of open oak woodland and steep brush-covered hillsides before arriving at the magnificent sequoia groves for which the park is so well known. To the casual observer, the steep, low-elevation, brush or chaparral covered hillsides seem to offer little of interest. Yet people who take the time to explore this area will find a fascinating assortment of plants and animals, many of which are unique to that vegetation type. They may eventually come to know and appreciate a community type which once covered much of California but today faces the multiple threats of progress and an ever-expanding economy.

The term "chaparral" is commonly used to refer to the low, dense, evergreen scrub vegetation which dominates much of the wildlands of central and southern California. The species that comprise it are characterized by deep roots and small, hard,

evergreen leaves covered with a waxy substance which reduces water loss during the long, hot, dry summer. Under California's typical Mediterranean climate, growth occurs during the cool, moist, winter and spring months and comes to a halt during the heat of the summer. At this time the plants lose much of their moisture and become highly susceptible to fire. The term chaparral comes from the word "chaparro" which was first used by the early Spanish explorers of the area and which itself is derived from a word for a similar-appearing vegetation type in the Mediterranean Basin. The term "chaps," referring to the leggings worn by horsemen in the early west to protect their legs while riding through dense brushfields, is credited with a similar origin.

The chaparral in California is a vegetation type which has remained too little appreciated. Despite having evolved over many thousands of years in close conjunction with periodic fire, it is

Top, dead remains of chamise and dense new growth of herbs several years after prescribed burning. (Photograph by Bill Jones.) Above, chamise stump-sprouting after a fire. (Photograph by David J. Parsons.) Below, buck brush, a common low-elevation chaparral shrub browsed by deer. Right, blue oak, a common tree of the chaparral zone. (National Park Service photo.)

now most commonly associated in the public mind with the threat of large destructive fires which must be avoided at all costs. What remains to be discovered for many is that the chaparral also comprises a unique, highly diversified, and pleasantly aromatic assortment of plants whose very existence is threatened throughout much of its range. An expanding suburbia, coupled with economic pressures to convert brushlands to grasslands in order to improve forage, reduce wildfire hazards, and increase runoff, has threatened the future of the community. Indeed, despite the fact that there are over 10 million acres of chaparral in California, what may be the last protected remnants of the California chaparral are found in the foothills of the southern Sierra Nevada in Sequoia National Park, and in Pinnacles National Monument.

Protected from many of the pressures of a technologically-based economy, the chaparral in these areas nevertheless faces another type of threat. For in the long run, over-protection from fire and the consequent buildup of hazardous fuels can be just as destructive as the various clearing activities. In the face of these conflicting forces, the National Park Service faces a major task in accomplishing its goal of preserving and maintaining the area in something resembling its natural state. The question now is whether even the chaparral that has been protected can be maintained as truly representative of the vegetation type as it was when European man first arrived on the scene.

In order to accomplish this task we need to know more about the natural successional patterns, including the historical role of fire and Indian burning, as well as the effects of recent management practices on chaparral vegetation. This knowledge must then be combined with the skill of trained resource managers to develop a sound program for the maintenance and preservation of this unique resource.

Within Sequoia National Park there are about 40,000 acres of chaparral. Ranging in elevation from about 1,000 to 5,000 feet, the chaparral is found predominantly on the steep slopes of the southwestern portion of the park. Much of this area is currently proposed for inclusion in the designated Wilderness Area of Sequoia and Kings Canyon National Parks.

The climate of this area has an annual precipitation of 25 to 35 inches, falling mostly as rain during the cool winter months. The summers are hot and dry with daytime temperatures frequently above 100° F. Under such a regime, growth occurs

Spanish bayonet against a backdrop of
mature north slope chaparral. (B. J.)

mainly during the short period in the spring when temperatures are not too high and ample water is available. This time of year is also characterized by a spectacular spring wildflower display. In the fall months there is more eye-catching color as the oaks *(Quercus* sp.), sycamore *(Platanus racemosa),* and other deciduous species that grow along stream courses and alluvial flats lose their leaves.

The predominant chaparral shrub of the area is chamise *(Adenostoma fasciculatum).* By far the most widely distributed of all chaparral species, the needle-leafed chamise dominates the steep, hot, dry, south and west facing slopes at lower elevations. It forms homogeneous fields of dense, nearly impenetrable brush, six to ten feet tall. On shallow, relatively unfertile soils, the cover of this single species may approach 100%. The herbaceous understory is sparse, being dominated by introduced annuals and occasional native bunch grasses. Occasional shrub associates include whiteleaf manzanita *(Arctostaphylos viscida)* and buckbrush *(Ceanothus cuneatus).* On dry rocky outcrops Spanish bayonet *(Yucca whipplei)* is locally conspicuous.

On the more mesic north and east facing slopes and at higher elevations, the chamise is replaced by a mixed, broadleafed chaparral. The mixed chaparral is characterized by a greater diversity, a more uneven cover, and heights which often reach up to 18 feet. It is characterized by such species as mountain mahogany *(Cercocarpus betuloides),* deer brush *(Ceanothus integerrimus)* and mariposa manzanita *(Arctostaphylos mariposa).* It is often associated with such tree species as the California buckeye *(Aesculus californica)* and interior like oak *(Quercus wislizenii).* At the higher elevations greenleaf manzanita *(Arctostaphylos patula),* snow brush *(Ceanothus cordulatus),* and chinquapin *(Castanopsis sempervirons)* characterize a lower-growing chaparral which is more adapted to cooler temperatures.

The low-elevation chaparral zones present an especially fine habitat for many species of wildlife. While the dense brushfields of the area do not in themselves constitute good habitat for most animal life, the region as a whole, with its associated annual grassland, oak woodland, and riparian habitats, supports quite a variety of birds and mammals. The California mule deer, the mountain lion, coyote, black bear, gray fox, and bobcat are among the larger species which frequent the area at some time during the year. Good habitat is also found for many birds, including the wren-tit, California woodpecker, scrub jay, brown towhee, California quail, red-tailed hawk, and along water courses the water ouzel. A variety of amphibians, reptiles, and insects are also present. In addition, this foothill region serves the important role of assuring valuable year-round habitat for such species as the mule deer, black bear, and mountain lion which winter in the lower elevations. This assures protection from hunters outside the park.

Other than for cursory sightseeing or occasional winter hiking, the recreation use of the low-elevation foothill zone is restricted almost entirely to swimming or fishing activities along one of the several forks of the Kaweah River. While the river activities specifically attract some people to the area, the zone tends to be looked upon by most visitors as no more than a buffer between the sequoia groves and wilderness high country, and the developed agricultural lands of the Central Valley. While this buffer role is a real one, it tends to draw attention from the fact that here is a fascinating and unique vegetation type whose existence is endangered.

The mosaic patterns created by the different chaparral subtypes as well as their relations to the associated annual grassland, oak woodland, and riparian vegetation are recognized as an intricate part of the natural biotic system. The understanding and maintenance of these vegatative mosaics and their associated wildlife patterns in their natural state are a major responsibility of the National Park Service. However even within the confines of a national park, natural conditions are not always easily maintained. For example, it is now recognized that fire has almost certainly been a part of the chaparral ecosystem for many thousands of years (perhaps hundreds of thousands).

The very nature of the community which we hope to preserve has evolved with and is dependent on a periodic fire cycle. However, as in most other wildland areas, a maximum effort in the last 60 to 70 years has been placed on the suppression of all fires in this zone. Now, if the chaparral is to be preserved in its natural state, ways must be found in which to reintroduce fire into its natural role. Furthermore, ways must be found in which to overcome any changes which may have resulted from the absence of fire during this time.

Prior to the coming of European man in the mid 1800's, the foothill areas were inhabited by the Western Mono (Monache) Indians. It has been estimated that at the time of the arrival of the first white man, Hale Tharp, in 1858, the population of the Western Monos in this area numbered about 2,000. There is evidence through early records and statements of living descendants of the tribes of the area that fire was used on a wide scale both to drive and hunt game as well as to improve wild food crops. Such practices were continued by the early European settlers for a number of years.

In addition to the cultural evidence for the historical frequency of fire in the area, the plants themselves show many signs of adaptation to periodic fire. Such specialized characteristics as the ability to sprout from the root crown, the production of seeds at an early age which can then lie dormant in the soil for long periods, the production of leaf chemicals which fall and accumulate in the soil and which inhibit germination and growth of seedlings or herbs until inactivated by fire, low moisture content during the drought period, and a structure which holds desiccated leaves and twigs laddered through the shrub, making for highly flammable conditions, are all specialized fire

Animals of the chaparral. Left, the red-tailed hawk can frequently be seen circling high above the foothills in search of squirrels or rabbits. Below, the mule deer, a common inhabitant of the chaparral zone, spends the winters at lower elevations and moves upward during the summer. (D. J. P.)

adaptations of this community. Furthermore, the lush and highly diverse herbaceous growth so characteristic of chaparral immediately following a fire is thought to be typical of a fire-type vegetation. With this remarkable recovery potential there is very little opportunity for species from adjacent communities to expand their range into the chaparral zone. Under a periodic fire cycle the successional pattern appears to be a successive regeneration of the same species.

On the other hand, when fire is excluded from a chamise-dominated chaparral stand for a long period, there is a decrease in growth activity and an increase in dead material. The stand becomes decadent and highly flammable. There is little or no reproduction. There is no indication of a succession of either new individuals or new species. It is obvious that in order to maintain its vitality chaparral needs periodic fires.

Based on such evidence, it seems apparent that the frequent fires which characterized the foothills before the coming of European man served to preserve a mosaic of different-aged stands of brush, prevented any significant buildup of fuels, and benefited wildlife by providing a continuous supply of tender young shoots for browse. The vegetation patterns had been selected for by a regime of periodic fire over a period of many thousands of years. This pattern of periodic fire was continued, and perhaps even intensified, for a short time following the coming of European man. During the late 1800's sheepherders commonly set fires in the fall in order to burn back the unpalatable

older vegetation and provide favorable conditions for the more palatable young vegetative shoots during the coming spring.

As the use of park land for grazing and other consumptive uses was curtailed during the 1890's, fire began to be looked upon as an evil which was to be avoided at all costs. A new era of suppression of all fires, whether man-caused or natural, had begun. There followed a buildup of fuels to unnaturally high levels. Where numerous small fires had once characterized the chaparral region and served to maintain a mosaic of different-aged stands, there soon began to develop a dense cover of old-aged and highly flammable material throughout. By the time the entire region had become covered with a vegetation about 30 to 35 years in age, there were no longer any natural breaks or recently burned areas to control the size of those fires which might get started. With this increasing and uniform flammability of the vegetation, the need for efficient fire suppression techniques became even more important. Those few fires which were not immediately suppressed threatened to become exceptionally large, such as the 5,000-acre Tunnel Rock fire in 1960.

Today, after a policy of total fire suppression has been in effect for over 70 years, a situation has developed such that almost the entire chaparral vegetation of the park is decadent and over-mature. This highly flammable situation poses a potential threat to life and property with every fire. The condition is highly unnatural, yet it is one which is difficult to do anything about. Even with

the current recognition of the need for fire to maintain natural conditions, things have gone beyond the point where we can allow fires to burn uncontrolled in the chaparral.

Unlike the higher elevation zones, where the rate of fuel accumulation has been much slower and naturally ignited fires are now allowed to run their course, in the chaparral all fires must be carefully controlled. In this zone each fire carries the threat that it might be the one which will sweep upslope out of control. Yet continuation of the present total fire suppression policy is not feasible. It would be against National Park Service policy to continue maintaining such unnatural conditions. In addition, the buildup of hazardous fuels has been so great that the efficiency of fire suppression techniques cannot keep pace. With the hot, summer-dry climate, it is impossible to keep fires from getting started. Thus it will only be a matter of time before the combination of an ignition source and a highly flammable fuel will result in a major wildfire. With such conditions there appears to be only one option left. That is to investigate the use of various manipulative techniques, including fire itself, to reduce the accumulated fuel hazard to a point where at least a semi-natural fire regime can again be instituted.

In an effort to tackle this problem, studies are currently under way to determine both the natural role of fire in the chaparral ecosystem and the feasibility of utilizing different manipulative means for accomplishing its reintroduction. Combining the findings of these investigations with those of other researchers on such topics as fire behavior, succession, fuel loading, and the use of such manipulative techniques as mechanical crushing and prescribed burning, an attempt will be made to produce a viable fuel management program for the low-elevation foothills of the park. Any such recommendations will necessarily call for a long term commitment on the part of the park managers to recognize the immediate need for a chaparral fuel management program. Contrary to the philosophy that all fire is bad, fire in the chaparral must be recognized as both natural and inevitable. The vegetation has evolved with fire and thus fire is necessary to maintain it in good health.

The formulation of a sound fuel management program which recognizes the essential role of fire in the ecosystem will be necessary in order to successfully respond to the challenge of preserving a remnant sample of chaparral vegetation for future generations. ❧

Top, deer brush and greenleaf manzanita, common in the mid-elevation zone, stump-sprouting after a fire. Center, deer brush in bloom. Left, chinquapin, a high-elevation shrub easily identified by its spiny fruit. (D. J. P.)

THE ANCIENT BRISTLECONE PINES

Photographs by Lloyd Ullberg
with text by George Lindsay

ARLY western explorers discovered these timberline trees, but nearly a century was to pass before the great significance of bristlecone pines would be recognized. They are the oldest living trees, and may well be the oldest living things on earth. One recently sacrificed specimen in Nevada was more than 4900 years old when it was felled.

John C. Fremont's exploring party found an unknown pine in Colorado in 1843, and in 1853 Captain Gunnison's botanist collected the same kind in the high Colorado mountains shortly before he and his men were killed by Ute Indians. At a meeting of the Academy of Sciences of St. Louis held March 17, 1862, its president, Dr.

George Engelmann, read a paper "On *Pinus aristata,* a new species of Pine discovered by Dr. C. C. Parry in the Alpine Regions of the Rocky Mountains." In his subsequent publication Engelmann said that the new trees which Parry found on Pikes Peak and high mountains of the Snowy Range were the same as those discovered by Gunnison, and he pointed out that some might exceed 1000 years in age and that their needles persisted for sixteen years—"a fact unheard of among pines, where leaves are said to endure generally for only three years."

We now know that bristlecone pines grow near timberline on high mountains of six of the

Above, Methuselah Walk leads through groves
of the oldest living things on earth.

southwestern United States. Most of the groves are on isolated, inaccessible desert peaks or ranges where perhaps they are relict remnants of a once more-continuous forest.

Many years ago Dr. A. E. Douglass of the University of Arizona started the research which ultimately led to the discovery, by others, of the remarkable longevity of bristlecone pines. We are all familiar with growth rings of trees. During the initial period of rapid growth large, thin-walled wood cells are produced, but later in the growing season when moisture, temperature, or other conditions become less favorable, the cells are small and the wood is denser. This variation forms the annual "tree rings" which allow us to count the years a tree grew. In a good year a wide growth ring is formed, while a narrow ring indicates poor growing conditions—in the Southwest this usually reflects a year of inadequate rainfall. Dr. Douglass, pursuing his interest in past climatic cycles, found that some trees growing in marginal areas had an annual tree ring variation of possible use in learning of past climates. Using primarily Rocky Mountain Douglas-firs, which are good for this purpose, he established a chronology extending back to 800 years before Columbus. By matching the ring-width pattern of logs in cliff dwellings with his chronology, he was able to establish the dates of those ruins.

Dr. Edmund Schulman continued the work in dendrochronology, the science which Douglass established, and searched for older living trees. He found a limber pine 1650 years old near Sun Valley, and this spurred on his search for even older kinds. In 1953 Schulman and Professor Fritz Went sampled bristlecone pines in the White Mountains of California, where the Forest Service had found a 940-year-old specimen, and Schulman's subsequent laboratory studies showed that these were indeed ancient trees.

Dr. Schulman then concentrated on bristlecone pines, sampling populations from Colorado to California. In 1956 and 1957 he conducted major surveys of the trees of the White Mountain Natural Area. The first one found to be more than 4000 years old he named Pine Alpha. Soon others in the 4000-plus age class were discovered, sixteen of them, nine of which are in an area Schulman called Methuselah Walk. One tree, which he named Methuselah, was more than 4600 years old. This exciting discovery culminated Dr. Schulman's life work. His report in *The National Geographic Magazine* of March 1958 was in press at the time of his death.

In 1953 the Forest Service had established a Natural Area in the White Mountains of east-central California for the protection of bristlecone pines, and in 1958 set aside 28,000 acres as a Botanical Area administered for "scientific study and public enjoyment." Academy photographer Lloyd Ullberg was one of the public who enjoyed the grove, and he showed me some of his excellent camera studies, including those in this article. Mr. and Mrs. Kenneth Bechtel learned of the bristlecone pines, and invited me to visit the White Mountains with them. Dr. C. W. Ferguson, Assistant Professor of Dendrochronology at the Laboratory of Tree-ring Research of the University of Arizona, who was an assistant to Dr. Schulman and is continuing dendrochronological research on the bristlecone pines and other species, volunteered to meet us in Bishop and visit the groves of ancient trees along with us.

As we drove south from Bishop Dr. Ferguson handed us a small piece of close-grained wood. We rubbed it and it smelled of pine. He told us it was a cross section of a tree fragment from the area we were to visit, that it contained a 400-year, high quality ring series, and that radiocarbon analysis indicated it was about 9000 years old.

We traveled south on Highway 395 to Big Pine, turned east on the Westgard Pass road, crossed the Owens River, and started the ascent of the White Mountains. Dr. Ferguson pointed out an area of big sagebrush *(Artemisia tridentata)*, where he had found 200-year-old plants. Higher up the mountains we came to forests of pinyon pine *(Pinus monophylla)* and Utah juniper *(Juniperus osteosperma)*, and at the summit of Westgard Pass we turned left onto a good paved road to the bristlecone pine area. Along it the Forest Service has developed an information center, where coralline fossils of Lower Cambrian age can be seen and collected, and a viewpoint with a magnificent vista of Owens Valley and the Sierra Nevada. Pinyon pines, the nuts of which are a most important food still used by Indians, gave way to grasslands at about the 8000 foot elevation, and at 9400 feet we saw scattered limber pines *(Pinus flexilis)*. At the Edmund Schulman Memorial Grove of the Ancient Bristlecone Pine Forest, the Forest Service had installed an audio-interpretive exhibit, picnic facilities, and trails leading to Pine Alpha and Methuselah Walk.

Bristlecone pines are not large trees. Those growing in protected areas are fairly straight, and although they are less than 50 feet tall, in some areas they were used for lumber in past times. All of them live in a harsh environment, just at timber-

Pine Alpha is 4300 years old, and it is the first tree known to have lived more than four millenia. It was discovered in 1956 by Edward Schulman, and is located in Schulman Grove. (This is an infrared photograph.)

Right, a young bristlecone pine tree, perhaps only two centuries old. Persistent needles which remain active for sixteen years give the branches a bottle-brush appearance.

Above, the honey-colored trunks are etched and eroded by wind-driven sand and ice crystals. *Right,* bristles on the scales of its small cones give the bristlecone pine its common name as well as its technical name, *Pinus aristata.*

line. The predominate soil is derived from dolomitic limestone, alkaline and not tolerated by most other trees. Annual precipitation in the bristlecone pine groves of the White Mountains is only about 12 inches. Perhaps the bristlecone pine's persistent needles, which astonished Engelmann more than a century ago, account for their ability to survive periods of even greater drouth. And they have grown slowly, often adding less than one inch to their radius in 100 years.

The oldest trees are in the most exposed locations. Pine Alpha, on a rock ridge, is 4300 years old, a twisted slab with only a narrow strip of bark on its protected side to connect its roots with its living branch. Its trunk has been eroded by wind-driven sand and ice crystals, and its dead limbs stand starkly against the sky. It was growing when pyramids were being built in Egypt, and it was a very old tree when Christ was born.

Dr. Ferguson suggested that we first drive on to see Patriarch Grove, at the north end of the bristlecone pine area. A graded dirt road, passable for most cars, branched off to the University of California's Crooked Creek high elevation research laboratory, where the effects of high altitude on plants, animals, and men are investigated. We drove onto the shoulder of Sheep Mountain, and from nearly 12,000 feet and above timberline we looked back down on the trees and then northward to White Mountain Peak, which is 14,242 feet high. It was cold, although summer, and we shivered as we admired the alpine plants flowering in great profusion.

The Patriarch is the largest known bristlecone pine tree, although it is only 1500 years old. The circumference of its multiple trunks is 37 feet. But much more interesting trees surround it. After our picnic lunch Dr. Ferguson conducted us on the most delightful "nature walk" of my experience. The forest was of remarkable trees, each one enticingly photogenic. Dr. Ferguson's quiet enthusiasm about his trees was contagious. Their honey colored, buff, or bleached trunks are polished and often satiny, and glow in the brilliant sun of the high altitude. The trees are gnarled and twisted into incredible shapes, and many look like standing driftwood. Needle-covered branches look like green bottle brushes. The cones are two or three inches long, and each scale has the bristly projection which gave the tree its name.

Dr. Ferguson pointed out young plants, only a foot or so tall, which were round bushes of many stems. These remain covered with snow much of the year. If one "leader" emerges through the snow

pack it may become a single-trunked tree, but in some cases, like the Patriarch, several basal branches grow and form trunks. A small sapling, however, may be more than half a century old.

We urged Dr. Ferguson to tell us about his work. In order to learn the growth ring sequence of living trees he extracts a core sample with a Swedish increment borer. The core, with a diameter smaller than a pencil, is surfaced and its growth rings are examined with a microscope. Data from these cores not only give the ages of individual trees, but also provide chronologic data. Each growth ring is assigned its actual calendar date, starting back from the outermost ring. The growth rings of about 1000 trees of the area have been analyzed, and their patterns of wide and narrow rings form the basis for cross referencing between specimens. This made possible the chronology and climate record of 4600 years, the age of the oldest known living tree in the White Mountains. But the wood of dead trees is resistant to decay, and cores from standing snags or fallen logs, whose growth-ring patterns overlapped those from living trees, allowed Ferguson to develop the chronology well past the 4600 years of Methuselah's life. He now has a continuous and dependable record to 5150 B.C., or 7118 years! The polished block which he showed us earlier in the day was radiocarbon dated at approximately 9000 years, and he has high hopes of finding overlapping samples of the intervening period so that a continuous record or chronology can be extended farther back in time. A few unimpressive pieces of loose wood may hold the key which will unlock the record.

Tree-ring dating requires skilled analysis and interpretation. Some trees grow in favorable sites where optimum growth is made each year; thus, their rings are fairly uniform in width from year to year. These are of little value for their climatic record, and the ring sequence from dead trees cannot be identified. On the other hand, trees which grow in harsher environments show greater variability in ring width from year to year and provide a more sensitive record. But as sensitivity increases, so does the probability that rings will be partially or totally absent about their circuit. Such a specimen is valuable, but difficult to analyze. In very bad years, growth may take place only in certain segments of the circumference of a tree, and if a core penetrates an area where there was no growth, no ring shows. With more than one core to examine, in the case of a critical ring, much more dependable information can be obtained.

There was abundant dead wood scattered

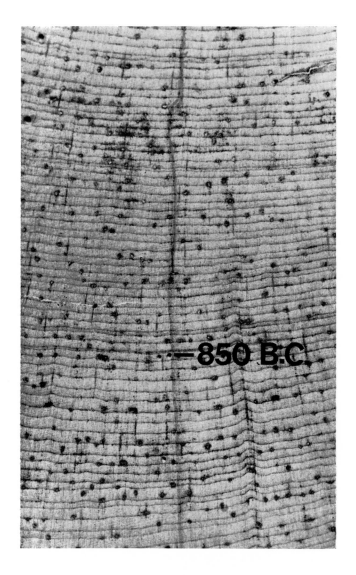

850 B.C.

good and poor years of the past—and in addition that this tree is so resistant to normal decomposition that a log on the ground may persist for thousands of years, and supply its own section of the ever-lengthening chronology.

What is to be learned from Dr. Ferguson's bristlecone pine chronology? We have mentioned climatology, and the record of climatic conditions it shows. Associated with this is biogeography, and the climatic changes which resulted in the retreat of the alpine flora, and other changes in the distribution of vegetation and related animals. Thus far the chronology has had limited application in archaeological dating, a primary use of dendrochronology in the Southwest, but a wood fragment from an archaeological site in the White Mountains has been dated in the early 1600's, and bits of charcoal provide dates throughout the A.D. period. And the rate of short-term geologic erosion has been determined for more than one area, by equating the amount of exposure of roots to the ages of the ancient trees.

A most interesting and valuable development is the relationship of dendrochronology and radiocarbon dating. Carbon-14 dating of wood of known age parallels the tree-ring chronology for the past 2000 years, but beyond that a discrepancy is shown, and radiocarbon tests indicate less than the actual age. Perhaps this is a reflection of magnitude of past solar activity and the number of sunspots, rate of carbon-14 generation, and terrestrial climate. The bristlecone pine chronology has confirmed aspects of carbon-14 dating of Egyptian artifacts, and tree-ring dated bristlecone pine wood was used to check the results of radiocarbon dating of oak used in Swiss lake dwellings. Carbon-14 tests of both the oak and the bristlecone pine control demonstrated that the dwellings were constructed nearly 6000 years ago, about 1000 years earlier than had been previously estimated.

The sun was pleasantly warm and the sky was cloudless as we sat on a log in that ancient forest and talked about the future. Are there dangers? While some ridges have only long-dead sentinels and no living trees, in most areas there is sufficient regeneration to keep the forest going. After all, it does not take many seedlings when the adults live more than 1000 years. Unfortunately, the danger to the bristlecone pine trees is from people. The beauty of this wild area has only recently become known, and the scientific significance and great age of the bristlecone pines has been recognized for only a decade. There is increasing public interest and appreciation of the wonderful trees,

A sanded cross-section of bristlecone pine wood which grew in the 800's B. C. The sequence of narrow and wide growth rings indicates climatic and moisture conditions of those ancient days. (Photograph from C. W. Ferguson, Laboratory of Tree-Ring Research.)

about, as well as many trees which had remained standing for a thousand years after death. Dr. Ferguson's 9000-year-old fragment was very likely dead and on the ground for most of that time. How does the bristlecone pine wood survive? First, it is dense and of a resinous nature which inhibits bacterial and fungal decay. The wood is also in "deep freeze" much of the year, which prevents deterioration, and in an arid environment when the temperature is above freezing. Very sparse undercover in the forest decreases the danger of burning, and I saw little evidence of borers or termites or other insects which damage most kinds of pine logs. There are no doubt other factors which give bristlecone pine wood resistance to destruction.

It is indeed fortunate that the oldest known living trees grow in stress areas near timberline and produce a sensitive growth-ring record of the

Left, bristlecone pines are resistant even in death. A gnarled skeleton can stand for many centuries, and a fragment of wood on the ground was found to be about 9000 years old. *Below left,* dendrochronologist C. W. Ferguson points out the bushy nature of a bristlecone pine seedling. (This photograph by George Lindsay.) *Below,* white dolomite slopes support a typical open-spaced forest of bristlecone pines. The trail at the bottom is Methuselah Walk, leading to Methuselah Grove.

and the unique and indefinable values of a visit to them. The Forest Service has developed roads and trails and facilities for the benefit of the public, which is good, but increased use of the area means increased dangers to it. In spite of requests and admonitions, many trees show sawcuts where people have removed pieces of sculptured wood as a memento or for profit. And the public cannot appreciate the potential research value of a piece of wood on the ground, so there is danger of its being taken for a souvenir or even to burn. It is important that the Forest Service have support for its efforts to adequately staff the Ancient Bristlecone Pine Forest not only during the few peak visitor months of summer, but throughout the year.

These and other stands of bristlecone pines are too valuable to be endangered or lost. They must be protected from wood collectors, and the groves themselves must not be used for sheep or cattle grazing, and any permits for such use must be purchased back. The very short grazing season means there is little profit either to the rancher or the Forest Service from such grazing rights, but even if there were, animal use of the bristlecone pine forest is incompatible with its best interests and must not be allowed. As the bristlecone pine area is developed for wider public use, future roads should avoid the groves, and future trails should avoid the trees. We are dealing with a truly unique national asset, the ultimate research and esthetic value of which cannot yet be forecast.

We were reluctant to leave this strange mountaintop environment of sky and rock and very old trees. Even as we drove down the grade we planned when we could return. The bristlecone pines do that to you.

Bristlecone pines grow in open forests at high elevations, in an environment hostile to most plants. There is little undergrowth. Shown here is the Patriarch Grove of old and young trees in the White Mountains of eastern California. (This photograph by George Lindsay.)

Majestic symbol of the California landscape, the twisted limbs of a valley oak stand bare against the winter sky.

CIRCUS OF QUERCUS

David Cavagnaro

Photographs by the author

DRIVE California in a big figure eight—north from San Francisco along the inner flanks of the coast range, east and then south along the foothills of the Sierra, across the Central Valley to Monterey County, south to San Diego, and then north again along the Tehachapis and the southern Sierra foothills—and you will hardly once be out of sight of an oak for more than a few miles at a time. In fact, travel anywhere except in the driest deserts and the highest mountains and you will find yourself always in the land of the oaks, for this is the nature of California.

Early and late settlers alike have been impressed by their dominance, for the indelible stamp of these grand trees has been left upon countless California place names. Oakdale, Oakview, Oakville, Big Oak Flat, Oak Knolls, and Paso Robles

are only a few of the spots on the map named in their honor. Had a botanist first discovered California, he might well have named the entire region Oakland. It would have been fitting, especially since few of the noble trees have survived the ravages of man in the city which did inherit the name.

The short history of our pioneering culture—and we are still largely a consuming, ravaging, pioneer breed—does not speak well of our treatment of the oaks. In the early days, oaks were cut from thousands of acres to heat growing towns and cities, most of which themselves were built in once-pastoral oak-grassland settings.

The valley oak, because rich bottom lands are its principal habitat, has suffered the most. The Central Valley was nearly cleared of these trees to make way for orchards and field crops, and the lush riparian woods, where valley oaks reached tremendous size in the river flood plains, were almost entirely removed to allow for the construction of the San Joaquin and Sacramento River levee systems. The magnificent trees which we take for granted as part of the landscape over hundreds of thousands of ranchland acres are actually for the most part doomed. A century of heavy grazing by cattle and sheep has most often prevented the establishment of seedlings. When the grand old giants have died one by one of old age, the rolling golden pastures of California will be bare.

The native peoples of California knew far more about oaks than we do, and they cared more, for the oaks provided them with acorns, one of their most important staple foods. Countless thousands of well-used mortars and pestles dug from the fields or found among the river rocks, and great slabs of Sierran granite pocked with grinding holes, attest to the immense human energy spent century after century preparing the annual acorn harvest. Even now, a few small bands make the autumn acorn pilgrimage, but even among the Indians it is a dying custom. Once in a while my wife and I bring in a harvest of the tasty nuts, leach them in hot water, and bake some sweet and delicious loaves of bread; but we come from another culture and live in another time. For us an empty acorn larder means nothing in terms of survival. We grind the crunchy meat in an electric blender, and somehow the feeling can never be the same.

There are at least two white men in California, however, for whom the oaks hold great meaning. Theirs has been a different quest, more intellectual than culinary, for they are University of California professors and taxonomists of the genus *Quercus*. For Dr. J. M. Tucker of Davis and Dr. C. H.

Muller of Santa Barbara, oaks have been a way of life. Their studies have taken them east to the Atlantic and south to Panama. Between them, they have probably examined every species of oak in the Western Hemisphere, and there are many. In 1942 Muller wrote an entire book on the oaks of Central America alone, and both botanists have published widely on their studies of North American and Mexican species.

Ten years ago I had the good fortune to be a student of Dr. Tucker. During four rather hectic autumn months my father and I travelled over 20,000 miles of the United States and Mexico gathering acorns and botanical specimens. By hand, one by one, we picked the little nuts until we had accumulated enough to fill the pickup truck three times over—sufficient acorns to feed a large Indian village for a year had gastronomy rather than botany been our mission.

It was a strange and beautiful occupation. We saw California when its hills were golden and the Appalachians when their forests were ablaze with autumn color. We felt the first frosts of Georgia and the last thunderstorms of Texas. We sampled pecan pie in every southern state, green coconut milk in Mazatlan, wild avocados in San Louis Potosi, and drove more bumpy, backwoods dead-end roads than I can remember. We were hauled to the courthouse in Shreveport, Louisiana, for running a red light while looking for street trees bearing acorns, and, on the flat, uninhabited, treeless Llano Estacado of the Texas Panhandle, home of the ground-creeping shinnery oak, an engineer stopped his quarter-mile-long freight train to ask us if we were collecting diamonds.

As a result of this trip, we, like so many other of Dr. Tucker's students, were thoroughly bitten

Oregon oak, right, in a winter ground fog. Left, its leaves, acorns, and a leaf gall produced by one of many species of oak gall wasps. Oregon oaks are extensively involved in hybridization, and produce fertile hybrids with both the blue and scrub oaks.

White oak species often hybridize where ranges overlap. Right, a cross between blue oak and Oregon oak in Sonoma County. Below, a blue oak in a pure stand in the inner Coast Range.

by the oak bug. But what about all those acorns? Dr. Tucker was engaged in a complex analysis of acorn proteins, another tack in his long pursuit of clues which might lead to an unravelling of the taxonomy and evolutionary history of the oaks. But why? Aren't oaks oaks, like maples are maples, one species listed after another as you see them in the plant books?

Well, yes and no. Let's take California as an example. Fourteen or fifteen species are listed in the various California floras. This would, on the face of it, seem simple enough. But many of these species are genetically highly variable. The leaves and acorns from population to population, even from tree to tree within a population, may vary tremendously in shape, size, and numerous other anatomical characteristics. Growth habits may vary also. Interior live oak, for instance, grows as a huge tree in the Sierra foothills and as a tough little bush in Coast Range chaparral; while Oregon oaks, which often rival the huge valley oaks in grandeur, grow as spreading, stunted, many-trunked clones at higher elevations. Besides their variability, many oak species hybridize, causing further confusion of their identification. No less than thirteen hybrid combinations have been reported from California. Studies of these problems have deepened our understanding of the evolution of the California flora and have helped clarify climatic fluctuations which have taken place in the recent geologic past.

Oaks extend far back in time. They belong,

together with beech, chestnut, and chinquapin, to the family *Fagaceae,* members of which appeared early in the fossil record of flowering plants. Our own tan oak, with its primitive, chestnut-like, herring-bone leaf veination, has come down nearly unchanged from a time when redwoods were dominant across North America. Separated from the true oaks in another genus, *Lithocarpus,* the tan oak is still associated with the redwood, isolated now in California as a retreating relict.

The genus *Quercus,* to which all other oaks are assigned, contains three subgenera in California. The white oak group contains *lobata,* the valley oak, *garryana,* Oregon oak, and *douglasii,* blue oak, all of which may reach tremendous stature and are widespread in the state. *Engelmannii,* or mesa oak, is a tree with blue-green leaves found near the southern California coast, while *sadleriana,* or deer oak, is a small shrub restricted to the Trinity and Siskiyou Mountains.

The remaining three white oaks are spiny-leafed evergreen shrubs found in hot, dry places. *Turbinella,* the desert scrub oak, grows on protected slopes and in desert washes in the southern part of the state. *Dumosa,* California scrub oak, and *durata,* the leather oak found on serpentine soils, are the primary oaks of the chaparral. In fact the word chaparral is derived from *chaparro,* Spanish for the evergreen oaks which are dominant in the Mediterranean version of this scrubby vegetation. From this word comes the term *chaparrajos,*

Common in both the Coast Range and the Sierra Nevada, the deciduous California black oak is perhaps at its most beautiful in Yosemite Valley, where the leaves of summer, left, are replaced by snow in winter, above.

103

Leaf forms of some hybrid oaks, parent species shown in black. Top row, the cross between interior live oak, at the left, and California black oak, on the right, is a sterile hybrid. The leaves shown are from individual trees found in various parts of California. The second row shows leaves of a hybrid swarm produced by Oregon oak, left, and scrub oak, right. The bottom diagram illustrates the random assortment of leaf as well as growth-form characteristics which is possible when tree and shrub species hybridize. Blue oak is on the left and desert scrub on the right, with two intermediate forms in the middle.

Canyon live oak, left, sometimes crosses with Palmer's oak, right, at the southern end of its range.

chaps for short, special pants worn by horsemen to protect their legs from the unbending and unforgiving chaparro.

A second subgenus contains just four closely related evergreen species. *Chrysolepis,* called canyon, maul, or gold cup oak, is widespread. It is probably the most variable in habit and habitat of all our oaks. Its dwarfed relative, *vaccinifolia,* the huckleberry oak, grows as a low shrub in the high montane Sierra Nevada, the Siskiyous, and the Trinities, while *palmeri,* on the other hand, is a formidable, holly-like desert shrub found in the southern part of the state. *Tomentella,* the island oak, is a tree confined to some of the Channel Islands and Guadalupe Island off Baja California.

Black oaks comprise the third major group. More common in the eastern states, black oaks are represented in California by only three species, *agrifolia,* the California or coast live oak, *wislizenii,* interior live oak, and *kelloggii,* the California black oak which, as it turns golden in the fall, is our only claim to the brilliant autumn color so plentiful among oaks of the eastern hardwood forests.

These are the basic species, or at least the names, one finds in the books. Each oak tends to prefer its own specific habitat. Each bears its own botanical description. But on the face of the land, things aren't as simple as this. Two species overlap, the windblown pollen of one fertilizes the ovaries of the other, and offspring are born fit to baffle student and professor alike. Dr. Tucker knows this better than anyone. We often claimed that he could smell a hybrid oak blindfolded.

What are these hybrids and what can we learn from them? To describe them all here would offer more confusion than enlightenment, but a few examples might be in order. Our hybrid oaks fall into two categories: those which produce "mules,"

In Joshua Tree National Monument, above, J. M. Tucker and a ranger stand by a clump of desert scrub oaks and the single hybrid tree at Live Oak Tank, the only tree-sized white oak in the monument. Drawings of the leaf forms, left, show that its leaves—in outline—lie about halfway between those of one known parent, scrub oak (small leaf) and the presumed other parent, valley oak (large leaf).

On the Llano Estacado of the Texas panhandle, Milton Cavagnaro collects acorns from a creeping clone of shinnery oak. Hybrids of these oaks reveal information about past climates in the Southwest.

or sterile offspring, and those which produce fertile progeny which in turn may result in what are called hybrid swarms. We have one notable example of the former in our flora, the oracle oak. Here and there where California black oak and interior live oak grow together, an occasional instance of hybridization will occur. One species is evergreen, the other deciduous. The offspring is most often a single, isolated tree directly intermediate between the two parents in leaf form, and semi-deciduous in habit. There are reported cases of similar hybrids between black oak and the coast live oak.

Most other cases of hybridization involve swarms of individuals which exhibit a random assortment of characteristics found in both parents. For example, at some points along the southern edge of its range, the blue oak comes in contact with the desert scrub oak and the two hybridize. One can find within a few acres pure individuals of both species, big trees with tiny scrub oak leaves, little bushes with large leaves like those of the blue oak, and every variation imaginable in between. These mixed populations are the result of continual crosses and backcrosses among the parent species and their fertile hybrid offspring.

To complicate matters further, there are numerous instances of hybrid populations involving three species. A notable example can be found in the hills of Sonoma County. Stands of blue oak may grow on the rather open south-facing slope of a hill. Where these trees meet the Oregon oaks of a cooler canyon or a wooded north-facing slope, a hybrid swarm will occur; while a short walk farther on, the Oregon oaks are in turn hybridizing with the California scrub oaks of the chaparral.

The same situation occurs on a much larger geographical scale in the *chrysolepis* complex. Hybrids occur where the highest canyon oaks meet the lowest huckleberry oaks in the Sierra Nevada; and at the southeastern extremity of its range, in Arizona, canyon oak crosses with the little desert Palmer's oak. As a result of this latter genetic influence, most of the Arizona *chrysolepis* trees look a bit like *palmeri* in many respects, whereas in California *palmeri* seems to have been influenced by *chrysolepis,* even though the two species do not occur together in California at the present time.

These mixups occur in at least thirteen different combinations in this Land of the Oaks. It is a virtual circus of *Quercus!* Little wonder that Tucker, Muller, Alice Eastwood, John T. Howell, and numerous other botanists have been kept busy by the oaks these many years.

What, then, can be learned from these hybrids beyond establishing their identity? First of all, the pattern of hybridization suggests degrees of relationship between the oaks and perhaps, indirectly, something of their evolutionary development. The three subgenera were established largely on anatomical grounds, but studies of the hybrids bear out their validity as taxonomic divisions. Hybrid combinations occur within each group, but in no known case have natural hybrids occurred between them, indicating that the groups are more distantly related than the species are within them. In turn, the sterile black oak hybrids seem to imply that these oaks have diverged genetically more than those white oaks have which produce such a wild array of fertile hybrid combinations.

Equally fascinating are the clues the intergrades provide regarding past floral migrations across the land. Dr. Tucker invited me along on one of his pilgrimages to Live Oak Tank in Joshua Tree National Monument. Here, among the great wind-worn granite marbles, the patches of yucca and cactus, there is a small spring. Between the boulders there are a number of desert scrub oak bushes, and growing among them is a single, symmetrical, 30-foot oak tree. The identity of this tree has long been a mystery. It is obviously a hybrid specimen, and one could surmise from a look at the leaves and acorns alone that the *turbinella* bushes nearby represent one of the parent species.

But what and where is the other parent? By extrapolation, Dr. Tucker deduced that there is only one species which could have lent its characteristics to those of *turbinella* to produce an intermediate such as that at Live Oak Tank. The other parent, he felt, must have been a valley oak.

There are two problems inherent in this theory. Unlike some other white oaks which readily cross almost wherever their ranges overlap, hybrids between *turbinella* and *lobata* are rare, although the trees occur together in a number of places. The two species do not seem to be closely related.

Dr. Tucker has learned over the years that distantly related oaks rarely cross when both parents are abundant in the area of overlap. Pollination within each species is more successful than it is between them. Hybrids do tend to occur between such forms, however, at the extreme edge of a species' range, where the environmental conditions approach the individual's levels of tolerance. It is here, where the outermost stragglers are surrounded by a larger population of another species, that hybrids may arise.

The other more formidable problem is this: the nearest valley oak at the present time grows

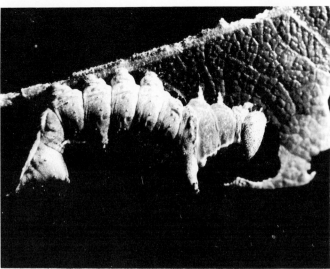

Oaks provide food and living space for many organisms. Above, old man's beard lichen hangs from an oak in the moist Coast Range. Right above, a moth caterpillar feeds on a Rocky Mountain oak leaf. Below right, acorn woodpeckers cache a future supply of acorns in the bark of a Douglas fir. Below, wasps reared from galls have given additional clues about the Rocky Mountain shinnery oak hybrids in the Navaho country.

The twisted, spreading California black oaks, below, and Oregon oaks, opposite, combined with many other tree and shrub oak species, are prime creators of the California landscape scene.

150 miles northwest of Live Oak Tank at the edge of the Mojave Desert. The possibility of long-range pollination between two distantly related species seems remote indeed. Tucker believes another explanation is more plausible.

Evidence from a variety of sources, including analyses of tree-rings, fossil pollen, and the contents of desert pack rat nests, suggests that there have been both major and minor climatic fluctuations in the Southwest during the last several thousand years. During moist periods, mesophytic plants have pushed southward; as the climate grew drier again, they retreated and were replaced with xerophytic plants from the old heartland southern deserts. Dr. Tucker feels that the tree at Live Oak Tank is a hybrid produced by the abundant desert scrub oaks and the last valley oak stragglers left behind during the most recent northward retreat of mesophytic plants. The old oaks are long ago gone, but they left behind this one contribution to the scrub oak gene pool.

On a larger scale of time the same thing has happened in the Navajo country where hybrid oaks are found. During cool glacial periods the moisture-loving Rocky Mountain oak was probably more widely distributed south of its present range and lower on the flanks of the mountains than it is now. Ancestral shinnery oaks must have been pushed far south of their present range, because the Texas Panhandle was covered with forests of pine and spruce. Tucker speculates that dry interglacial periods allowed these small creepers of the dunes to migrate northward again. At some point the ancestral shinnery oaks were divided, one population moving into the species' present range in the Texas Panhandle country, the other advancing along the west side of New Mexico's chain of mountains where introgression with Rocky Mountain oaks occurred. After numerous north-south movements, pure shinnery oak disappeared from this population. Natural conditions in the higher, cooler Navajo country were apparently more favorable for the hybrids than for this desert parent.

Little did the freight train engineer in the Llano Estacado know that, besides acorns, my father and I were gathering small clues concerning the complex migration of plants during the Pleistocene.

Some evidence supporting Dr. Tucker's explanation of the origin of the Navajo hybrids came not from the oaks themselves but from insects which inhabit them. Oaks are host to tiny wasps which, as they lay their eggs, secrete chemicals into the tissues, causing the plants to form galls. Most notable of these varied and beautiful structures are the huge "oak apples" produced on the California

108

valley oaks.

Oak gall wasps have been studied by a number of entomologists, including Dr. Kinsey before he became more interested in human sexuality, and they have long intrigued both Tucker and Muller. Gall wasps are rather sedentary insects, most often specific in their tastes, frequenting one or a select few oak species. That most gall makers found on the Navajo hybrids also occur on one or both presumed parent species does indeed suggest that the Rocky Mountain oak and the shinnery oak once occurred together.

Besides gall wasps, a fabulous array of insects, as well as their predators and parasites, are dependent on the oaks. Pick any large California live oak and study its inhabitants carefully during a full year. You will find oak moth larvae, tent caterpillars, and a variety of other butterfly and moth larvae feeding on its leaves and buds; tree hoppers and scale insects sucking juices from its twigs; and yellow jackets, ichneumon wasps, and spiders hunting their particular foods. Within the acorns themselves you will find the white grubs of the acorn weevil which, when full grown, chew

their way out and pupate in the ground. We swept enough weevil larvae from the truck during our cross-country acorn hunt to fill several buckets.

Besides the insects which the oaks harbor, imagine the squirrels, jays, deer, and woodpeckers which feast upon their acorns, the flocks of birds which feed among their twigs, and those which nest in their branches. Picture the festoons of lichens and great clumps of mistletoe hanging from them and the birds which come in the winter to feed on the pearly mistletoe berries. Think, too, of all the wood borers, termites, and fungi which inhabit their dead limbs and the creatures of the soil which thrive in the leaf litter beneath their spreading crowns, and you will know something of the importance of oaks within the larger scheme of things.

A crusty country sage once said to me, as I exuberantly reported the discovery of hybrid oaks on his property, "Young man, the oaks have been fornicating in these hills for a good many years. Why not let them breed in peace?" Apart from the knowledge gained by studying these noble and significant plants, and the joy felt from their presence, I suppose we should do just that.

CALIFORNIA'S BOTANICAL GARDENS

Elizabeth McClintock

CALIFORNIA'S coastal and valley regions have a mild climate with warm dry summers and rain during the winter. This kind of climate is not found elsewhere in North America but is similar to that of the lands around the Mediterranean Sea, Chile in South America, the Cape of Good Hope in South Africa, and southwestern Australia. The mild climate and varied topography of California have combined to give the state one of the richest native floras of the United States. The mild climate also makes it possible to grow a great variety of plants out of doors in this state which come from the temperate regions around the world. This gives to California a rich ornamental flora which is reflected in the number of its botanical gardens. In the United States as a whole there are about 100 major botanical gardens and arboretums, mostly in the eastern third of the country. Pennsylvania with 14 ranks first among the states, while California with 12 is second and New York with 10 is third. However, an important difference between botanical gardens in California and those in the eastern United States is that in California the emphasis is on plants which can be grown out of doors while in the east all but the most hardy

of plants are grown in conservatories and greenhouses.

Probably the earliest suggestion for the establishment of a botanical garden in California was made at a meeting of the California Academy of Sciences held in July of 1854. Minutes for that meeting record that "the citizens of Clinton offered to donate to the Academy a piece of ground in or near that village for the purpose of a botanical garden." A committee was appointed to consider the offer. The minutes for a meeting in the following September record that the committee reported unfavorably; apparently because the members present at that meeting believed that first things should come first, it was decided to continue to devote the efforts of the Academy to preserving and enlarging the museum collections and library and not to embark upon the establishment of a botanical garden in Alameda County.

The idea of establishing a botanical garden in California must have received further consideration within the following years, for again at a meeting of the California Academy of Sciences in 1873 Henry N. Bolander, who in 1864 had become the State Botanist, spoke of the value of botanical gardens. He did not consider the "youth

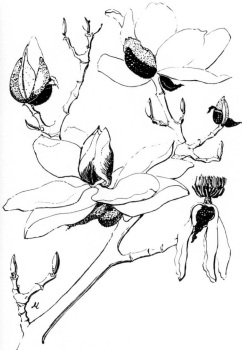

Left, a path through the Rhododendron Test Area of Strybing Arboretum under the shade of Monterey cypresses and Monterey pines. (Photo by P. H. Brydon) *Above*, the Campbell magnolia, virtually a hallmark for Strybing Arboretum, was drawn by Mary G. Means.

of our state and city sufficient excuse for the failure hitherto to do something for experimental agriculture." He mentioned what had been done in Australia, particularly Melbourne, and this led to a discussion regarding the utility of plants that had been and might be introduced into California. However, it was another 20 years, close to the end of the century, before the first botanical garden was established in the state. In 1891 a botanical garden was founded by Professor E. L. Greene on the campus of the University of California in Berkeley. This garden was devoted to native plants, reflecting the interest of Professor Greene in the flora of California. The second botanical garden to be founded is known today as the Huntington Botanical Garden. It was established in 1905 as the private garden of Henry E. Huntington on his estate in San Marino. During the period of 1925 to 1950 the other botanical

gardens in California were established.

The botanical gardens in California are situated in the two population centers of the state, the southern coastal area and the San Francisco Bay region. Since these are separated by nearly 400 miles there are minor climatic differences between them. The southern area is warmer and receives less rainfall than the northern. Therefore there are a number of plants which can be grown in one area but not in the other. The handsome pink-flowered Campbell magnolia, *Magnolia campbellii*, closely identified with the Strybing Arboretum in San Francisco where it flourishes so well, cannot be grown with equal success in southern California. However, another handsome but very different pink-flowered tree, the silk-floss tree, *Chorisia speciosa*, has been planted at the Los Angeles State and County Arboretum in Arcadia. This tree requires the

Left, an African cycad, *Encephalartos altensteinii*, from the collection of the Huntington Botanical Gardens, San Marino. (Photo courtesy Huntington Botanical Gardens)

Below, Puya alpestris, a member of the pineapple family from Chile, one of the many unusual and interesting ornamentals growing in the Strybing Arboretum of Golden Gate Park. (Photo by P. H. Brydon)

brought into the arboretum many of Mr. McLaren's earlier introductions into Golden Gate Park and in addition secured for the arboretum new plants not previously cultivated in California. Geographical sections in the Strybing Arboretum now display plants from Australia, New Zealand, the Mediterranean region, South Africa, Chile, and eastern Asia which can be grown in the San Francisco area.

The Los Angeles State and County Arboretum, founded in 1948, occupies 127 acres of land in the city of Arcadia which was originally a part of the San Gabriel Mission and later the home of E. J. Baldwin. On the land are several historical buildings, two built by Baldwin in the latter part of the last century and a third dating back to a previous owner in the early part of the century. Geographic sections comparable to those in the Strybing Arboretum feature plants from other continents, enabling visitors to become acquainted with plants from other parts of the world which can be grown in their home gardens.

Although many of the ornamentals grown in California's botanical gardens have come from other parts of the world, the cultivation of native California plants has not been neglected. Three of California's botanical gardens, the Rancho Santa Ana Botanic Garden in Claremont, the Santa Barbara Botanic Garden, and the Regional Parks Botanic Garden of Tilden Park

Below, one of several historical buildings in the Los Angeles State and County Arboretum, the Queen Anne Cottage was built by E. J. Baldwin in the 1870's. *Right,* is the lagoon with the restored Hugo Reid residence in the background. (Photos courtesy of Los Angeles State and County Arboretum)

warmer climate of southern California and so could not be grown to best advantage in the San Francisco area.

Both San Francisco's Strybing Arboretum and the Los Angeles State and County Arboretum have introduced plants into cultivation from those regions of the world having climates similar to that of California. The Strybing Arboretum occupies about 40 acres of Golden Gate Park's 1,000 acres. It was established in 1937 during the latter years of John McLaren's 50-year regime as superintendent of parks in San Francisco. John McLaren had long wanted to establish an arboretum in Golden Gate Park; Helene Strybing, who left to the City of San Francisco a sum of money for this purpose, was undoubtedly influenced by Mr. McLaren in making this bequest. Mr. McLaren, who was responsible for building a park on the sand dunes on which Golden Gate Park is situated, was interested in introducing plants which could be grown on this sandy soil. This interest was shared by Mr. Eric Walther, who was put in charge of the Strybing Arboretum at the time of its establishment. Mr. Walther

in Berkeley, are devoted entirely to the cultivation and display of these plants. The use of natives as garden subjects has sometimes been disappointing because their cultural requirements are not the same as those for introduced ornamental plants, but within recent years these three botanical gardens have done much to make information regarding the culture of native plants available to the gardening public. The Rancho Santa Ana Botanic Garden, founded in 1927, has occupied its 80-acre site in Claremont only since 1951, when it was moved there from its original site in Santa Ana Canyon. This garden was founded by Susana Bixby Bryant in memory of her father, a California pioneer. Plants displayed around the entrance area and the administration-research building demonstrate the landscape use and cultural requirements of a large number of natives having ornamental value. A special feature is a home demonstration garden which simulates various situations to be found around a dwelling in a home garden and uses native plants known to be reliable garden subjects and available in nurseries. About half of the area of the Rancho Santa Ana Botanic Garden is devoted to the development of an area for demonstrating California's plant communities, such as yellow pine forest, foothill woodland, grassland, redwood forest, and chaparral. The plant community area will be of great value in teaching botany,

ecology, and nature study in coming years. Another area at Rancho Santa Ana Botanic Garden is used for growing native plants used by the staff for research projects.

The Santa Barbara Botanic Garden has an ideal site for growing and demonstrating California native plants. Its 50-acre portion of Mission Canyon makes use of the natural streamside vegetation and chaparral covered slopes. Plantings made in the canyon were of trees and shrubs from desert and woodland areas of California. Three interesting sections feature a collection of wild lilac and buckthorn belonging to the genus *Ceanothus*, plants from the Channel Islands off the coast of southern California, and plants characteristic of the Coast Redwood plant community from the northern California coast.

The Regional Parks Botanic Garden, which dates from 1940, has a 20-acre area in Wildcat Canyon in the Berkeley hills. It contains the largest collection of California natives in the northern part of the state. These are laid out in seven major sections representing most of the plant communities and geographical areas of vegetation in California. A Guide to the Plant Species of the Regional Parks Botanic Garden enables visitors to find their way about the garden and to locate and identify the plants.

The extent of cultivation of succulent plants as a gardening hobby cannot be overestimated. This versatile group is useful both indoors and out of doors. The two outstanding collections of succulents in California are at the Huntington Botanical Gardens in San Marino and the University of California Botanical Garden in Berkeley.

Both collections were largely assembled by collecting cacti and other succulents in the wild. The Huntington collection was brought largely from Arizona and Mexico and that of the University of California in Berkeley from South America and South Africa. Since the plants of the Huntington collection were brought together originally as part of the private garden of the Huntington estate, the emphasis of this collection has been on display; while the University of California collection has been used primarily for research, with display of secondary importance.

The development of selected or "pedigreed" plants for horticultural use is being carried out at the Saratoga Horticultural Foundation in the Santa Clara Valley. The Foundation was established in 1951 as a specialized kind of botanical garden where shade trees and shrubs with ornamental potential could be grown and observed. Once the value of a particular tree or shrub has been ascertained it is propagated vegetatively so that its progeny will be uniform. Large numbers of vegetative progeny are produced and turned over to nurseries. From there the selected plants eventually reach gardens, parks, and streets. Street trees grown from such progeny are highly desirable and do not have the irregular and uneven appearance of seedling trees. Selections have been made from several native shrubs, particularly *Arctostaphylos*, the manzanitas, and *Ceanothus*, the wild lilacs and buckthorns. Trees from which valued selections have been made are the eastern sweet-gum, *Liquidambar styraciflua*, the maiden-hair tree, *Ginkgo biloba*, and the southern magnolia, *Magnolia grandiflora*. In the

Right, part of the important succulent collection at the University of California Botanical Garden. (Photo by H. G. Baker)

Below, the eastern sweet-gum, *Liquidambar styraciflua*, is one of the trees from which selected forms are being grown for street-side use by the Saratoga Horticultural Foundation. (Photo by Maunsell Van Rensselaer)

first 15 years of its existence the Saratoga Horticultural Foundation has brought to home gardens, parks, and city streets a number of useful and attractive plants.

The Eddy Arboretum of the Institute of Forest Genetics in Placerville contains a large and outstanding collection of pines and smaller collections of firs, hemlocks, cypresses, junipers, and other trees. The pines constitute probably the world's most complete collection of this genus, with about 72 species and 90 different hybrids, and have been used for breeding for timber production by the use of genetic principles. It has been the aim of the Institute to produce faster growing pines for use as lumber and for reforestation, and to combine such features as wood quality and resistance to insects and disease with rapidity of growth.

An important function of botanical gardens is the introduction into cultivation of plants from wild sources. The University of California Botanical Garden in Berkeley has sponsored eight plant collecting expeditions during the past three decades. The first of these was made in 1932 to the Himalayas of western China and Tibet under the leadership of the late Joseph F. Rock, the great explorer of the mountains and river gorges of this part of Asia. Rhododendrons, lilies, magnolias, and primulas were among the plants brought back by this expedition. The other seven University of California expeditions were to the Andes of South America. The first six of these had as a primary objective the collection of seed of all of the known South American species of *Nicotiana*, to which tobacco belongs. The study of the genus

Above left, a new species of cactus, *Browningia* sp. was collected by the Seventh University of California Expedition to the Andes and is now growing in the Botanical Garden. *Above right*, is *Nicotiana thyrsiflora*, the "lost" Andean nicotiana first discovered in Peru in 1914, rediscovered 20 years later on the First University of California Expedition to the Andes, and photographed by the Seventh Expedition. (Photos by P. C. Hutchison)

Above, an outdoor classroom in Strybing Arboretum. (Photo by P. H. Brydon) *Below,* the author in the herbarium of the California Academy of Sciences. It was stipulated by Helene Strybing in her trust to the city of San Francisco to establish a botanical garden that it be located near this institution. This close proximity has made it possible for the Arboretum to make use of the Academy's botanical facilities. (Photo by M. Giles)

Nicotiana was a major research project carried out at the University of California Botanical Garden under the direction of Emeritus Professor T. H. Goodspeed. The material collected on these expeditions was used for this project, which was completed with the publication of a monograph on this important genus. Other objectives of the expeditions to the Andes were the collection of living and pressed plants; these have added to the knowledge of the vegetation of this great mountain chain which still has large unexplored areas. Living plants of succulents and in particular those of the Cactus Family have been one of the important groups which these expeditions

have brought back. Other biological materials collected on the expeditions include seeds of many plants, birds and insects as plant pollinators, ethnobotanical material, pollen samples, and cytological material.

Another source of new plants for a botanical garden is by exchange. The University of California Botanical Garden exchanges its seed lists with about 350 scientific institutions from around the world. Such a wide circle of correspondents is of great value to students and research workers at the University who need plant materials for their studies.

The living plant collections in a botanical garden are, to be sure, a main feature and the one which attracts the largest number of visitors. However, almost all botanical gardens have another kind of plant collection, a dried collection, a *hortus siccus* as it was once called, or herbarium as it is called today. The dried pressed specimens making up a herbarium are filed in cabinets according to a systematic arrangement much as books in a library and are used for reference and research. A botanical library always supplements both living and dried collections of plants. The herbarium and botanical library of the Rancho Santa Ana Botanic Garden were the important research tools used in the preparation of *A California Flora* by Philip A. Munz, which describes all of the native plants of California. This flora by Dr. Munz is one of several important contributions to botanical science written by the staff of the Rancho Santa Ana Botanic Garden. The University of California in Berkeley supplements the many research facilities of its botanical garden with the largest herbarium in the western United States, providing important botanical research facilities for faculty and student alike.

Botanical gardens mean different things to the many visitors who walk through their gates. Some come to see the displays, and they enjoy the beauty of the plants; others to observe the plants more closely, to read their labels and ask questions of the staff or to visit the library and seek out information themselves; others to join specially conducted tours given by staff members; others to seek certain plants not to be found elsewhere. But all of these visitors, whether they be homeowners, students, professional botanists and plantsmen, or casual observers, will find something of interest which is only to be found in a botanical garden. What is it then which makes a botanical garden such a special place?

Gardens and parks also have collections of

plants, often the same ones which are in botanical gardens. But privately owned gardens and public parks have been laid out entirely for their aesthetic appeal and to add beauty to surroundings which would otherwise be drab and colorless. In addition to this, most parks provide areas for various kinds of recreational activities—playgrounds, picnic areas, paths, trails, and often a stadium for sports. Botanical gardens have aesthetic values, but are not concerned with the recreational activities placed in parks. Through their plants and displays they carry out a multitude of educational and scientific purposes. Each botanical garden has its own particular purposes, depending on the kind of organization which established and maintains it. For instance, in a botanical garden many of the ornamentals which can be grown in a given area may be displayed. These displays will acquaint the home gardener with the names of these plants, their habit of growth, and the methods of their culture. Through such displays the botanical garden serves an educational function in the community. Various kinds of teaching programs may be carried out for students of botany, horticulture, landscape architecture, and other branches of the plant sciences. Research programs may also use

the living plants in a botanical garden, thereby adding to scientific knowledge.

Arboretum is another term used for a collection of plants. Historically, it was used to designate a place for the growing of trees and other woody plants, and it was so used in Europe in the Sixteenth Century. The term has continued to be used in this way at such places as the Arnold Arboretum, Jamaica Plain, Massachusetts, and the Morton Arboretum, Lisle, Illinois, both of which have extensive collections of woody plants brought together for educational and scientific purposes. However, in recent years the term has been used synonymously with that of botanical garden, for a place where all kinds of plants are grown whether or not they are woody. In California we have the Los Angeles State and County Arboretum, Arcadia, and the Strybing Arboretum, San Francisco, which are really botanical gardens in that both have all kinds of plants. On the other hand, at the Eddy Arboretum of the Institute of Forest Genetics, Placerville, only trees are grown. However, regardless of whether the term is used for a collection of woody plants or for all kinds of plants, an arboretum is a place where plants are grown for scientific and educational purposes just as they are in a botanical garden.

A meadow in the Santa Barbara Botanic Garden with a profusion of spring wildflowers. (Photo by C. B. Jouett, courtesy Santa Barbara Botanic Garden)

THE GRIZZLY BEAR STATE

As California has become more densely populated, there have been several changes in the attitudes of people toward the state's wildlife. At first it was seen as an infinite resource, to be used at will. Toward some animals a negative attitude developed, because they made use of land—and other animals—that people wanted to use. As awareness of the limitedness of resources developed, some regions were set aside where the animals could live undisturbed, and some animals came under human management plans, so they could be used as a continuing resource. More recently it has become obvious that instead of civilization being an island in the wilderness, wilderness has become an island in civilization. Now, even many animals that are being saved for their own sake rather than as resources have come under management planning, because the islands of wilderness have become so small that, if left alone, their animals might not survive.

Despite the thoroughness of wildlife exploration and research, and the constant increase in population, the life cycles of many of California's smaller animals remain incompletely known. Wildlife biology is thus far from a closed subject, and many areas of potential research remain. Even the habitats and dwelling places of a number of animals have remained unknown, or learned only recently. One of the most notable discoveries has to do with the murrelet, until recently the only bird of North America whose nest had remained undiscovered. The discovery was finally made by a tree surgeon in 1974. "The Murrelet's Nest Discovered" (1975), was reported in the pages of *Pacific Discovery* by Steven W. Singer, Extension Instructor in Forest Ecology at the University of California in Santa Cruz, and Denzil R. Verardo, formerly Park Superintendent at Mount Tamalpias State Park.

Although some animals were reduced to extinction by predatory practices, such as market hunting, on the part of some humans, others, though reduced in numbers, have been able to make a comeback when these practices were halted. Still other animals have required even more active management, such as improving habitat or moving the animals to less-damaged habitats. Quail, once badly reduced in numbers, have within the last generation become more common. In "The California Quail" (1966), the story of the efforts to improve the quail population is told by a man who has been active in this work, rancher and conservationist Ian I. McMillan.

The California Academy of Sciences has been active in the work of saving at least one virtually-extinct species, the tule elk. A hundred years ago only one breeding pair could be found, so extensively had the animal been hunted by settlers, mountain men, and gold miners. Early in this century the Academy supervised the transfer of more than 100 descendants of this pair to 19 suitable localities throughout the state. A number of these transfers were highly successful. The life story of the animal so dramatically saved is reported, in "The Return of the Tule Elk" (1978), by Verna R. Johnston, author of the book "Sierra Nevada" and teacher of biology and natural history at San Joaquin Delta College.

One of the sadder highlights of the conservation story is that the animal that has come to be the California state emblem no longer lives here. Although there are grizzly bears in other states and countries, when California's population increased grizzlies and people found it difficult to survive together. Grizzlies lost. However, grizzlies entered into the local mythology in many ways. One, that relates to the California Academy of Sciences, has to do with the California state flag. The grizzly drawing on page 141, used for the official state flag of California, was done by *Pacific Discovery's* first editor, Don Greame Kelley. The story of the grizzlies' relation to the people of California is told, in "California's Emblem: The Grizzly Bear" (1966), by Tracy I. Storer, who was for many years Professor of Zoology at the University of California in Davis.

Still another episode in the history of man-animal relations in California has a relation to the California Academy of Sciences. During the 19th century, elephant seals were virtually exterminated. Finally only a few mating pairs remained on Guadalupe Island, off the coast of Baja California, when the Mexican government ruled that they be protected. In 1922 G Dallas Hanna of the Academy took part in the expedition that reported on their nascent population recovery. Now the animals are so numerous on California's offshore islands and mainland beaches that wildlife managers are discussing how to limit their population growth. In "Back From Extation?" (1971), Burney J. Le Boeuf, Professor of Biology at the University of California in Santa Cruz, has chronicled this recovery from near-extinction to population explosion.

THE MURRELET'S NEST DISCOVERED

Steven W. Singer and Denzil R. Verardo

The Douglas fir, in Big Basin State Park, in which the murrelet nest was found. The nest-containing limb, now removed, was opposite the goalpost-shaped limb on the left near the top. (Photograph by Denzil R. Verardo.)

ON AUGUST 7, 1974, ornithological history was made. A tree surgeon working in the Santa Cruz Mountains discovered the nest of the marbled murrelet, the only bird believed to breed in North America whose nest had never been found here. Several clues led to the belief that the marbled murrelet *(Brachyramphus marmoratus)* was a summer resident in Big Basin Redwoods State Park. The sightings which served as clues began on April 19, 1959. On that day, Park Naturalist Eleanor Pugh spotted and heard a marbled murrelet flying in the Opal Creek area of Big Basin. In July of that same year, a ranger made another sighting, verified by Pugh, in the same area. On August 18, 1960, an immature marbled murrelet was brought to Naturalist Ray Williams by campers who had found it in Campground "A." It was released in the park's reservoir where it remained for several days before it disappeared.

Not until 1973 was a marbled murrelet seen or heard again. Part of the reason for this was the absence of an expert birder in Big Basin during this period. On February 1, 1973, a rather confused scene occurred at Big Basin Park Headquarters when a camper turned in an injured bird. It was a chunky-looking, robin-sized bird colored black above and white below, with webbed feet. By this time the park staff had changed and didn't know of the murrelet sightings which had occurred thirteen years earlier. Several hours of excitement ensued as Rangers Don Patton, Ray Patton, Steve Singer, and Denzil Verardo attempted to key out the bird. Once it had been identified as a marbled murrelet, the park's natural history records revealed the previous sightings.

Four months later an injured adult murrelet was found by campers at Opal Creek and turned over to park rangers. It was now fairly well established that murrelets came inland to the redwoods for some reason—but to suggest that they nested there would still have been a bold assumption. Steve Singer, at that time an Extension Instructor at a local university, did a literature search into the ecology of the marbled murrelet for one of his classes. For the first time he learned, and related to Verardo, the mystery surrounding the nesting of the marbled murrelet.

Artist's reconstruction of baby murrelet on discovery nest. (Painting by Kenneth L. Carlson.)

The first egg of a marbled murrelet was taken from the oviduct of a bird collected off the coast of Alaska in 1897 by George Cantwell. He was told by the Indians that the bird nested "high up on the mountains in hollow trees." He searched the woods for a nest, but found nothing.

Others thought the bird nested in the Santa Cruz Mountains. One of these was ornithologist William Dawson, who camped beside Majors Creek on the slopes of Ben Lomond on May 18 and 19, 1914. On both mornings he arose with the dawn to observe groups of marbled murrelets as they flew over the forest toward the ocean. He stated his belief then, that the marbled murrelet nested in the Santa Cruz Mountains. But not until June 15, 1957, with the capture of an immature murrelet in Portola State Park, was the first search for a marbled murrelet nest in the Santa Cruz Mountains undertaken. That search disclosed no new evidence (See *Pacific Discovery*, May-June, 1972).

The winter of 1973-1974 ushered in the larg-

est snowfall in Santa Cruz Mountains' history. On January 3, one foot of snow fell at Big Basin Park Headquarters (1000 ft. elev.). For an area that receives only negligible snowfall, the result to the forest was cataclysmic. Thousands of tan oaks, live oaks, madrones, and Douglas-firs were destroyed. The park was closed to the public for three months while a clean-up of the picnic and camping areas took place. A safety-trim program in campsites was instituted to cut out limbs that would pose a hazard to park visitors.

In August, 1974, it was time for Big Basin's "J" camp to be safety-trimmed. "J" camp is a quarter mile south of Big Basin Park Headquarters, and lies about 700 feet from Blooms Creek in a virgin redwood and Douglas-fir forest. Hoyt Foster, tree trimmer for the Davey Tree Company and an expert climber of big trees, was about to make a historic climb. On August 7, he ascended a 200 foot Douglas-fir, and upon reaching the 148 foot level, noticed something very strange. He described it as a "most unusual bird. It looked like

a squashed-up porcupine, but with a beak sticking out." Although he'd seen hundreds of birds in trees before, he'd never seen one like this. His curiosity was further aroused when he saw that it had webbed feet. Foster was looking at the first marbled murrelet chick ever seen by man.

Foster tried to capture the unusual-looking chick, but it stepped backward off the branch and fell, flapping its wings vigorously, to the ground below. Unharmed by the fall, it was retrieved and turned over to Ranger Dan Friend for safekeeping. This was Ranger Friend's first encounter with a marbled murrelet, and since he didn't know what it was, he did what he would do for any orphaned bird. He began to make arrangements for someone in a nearby town to care for it. It was Verardo's day off, and the chick could easily have been given away, the tree trimmed, and the whole incident forgotten, except for a coincidence. Before the bird could be transferred elsewhere, Verardo stopped by Park Headquarters to pick up his mail. Overhearing talk of a bird found by a tree surgeon, he thought nothing of it until someone mentioned that it had webbed feet. He then made the first tentative identification of a marbled murrelet chick. He immediately notified Singer, who in turn contacted Bruce Elliott, a wildlife biologist for the Department of Fish and Game. Elliott soon took charge of the chick, and confirmed Verardo's identification.

The chick died the evening of the next day. Perhaps our inability to duplicate the food that its mother would have supplied was the cause of death. Since the downy plumage of a marbled murrelet chick had never been seen before, the chick achieved its greatest degree of scientific fame after death—as a carefully preserved specimen at the California Academy of Sciences.

Back at the park we supervised the field work necessary to document the find. Fortunately the branch had not yet been cut, so we asked the Department of Parks and Recreation to suspend trimming operations on the tree. Then we recruited Hoyt Foster to go back up, collect the eggshell fragments, and take measurements of the nest. Once this work was completed, he carefully lowered the section of limb containing the nest to the ground. The nest, limb, and eggshell fragments were then turned over to the California Academy of Sciences. A plain aluminum marker was placed high on the tree trunk at the level of the nest limb.

The nest was located close to the trunk, atop a horizontal, sixteen inch diameter limb, in an open

Top, the never-before-seen chick of the marbled murrelet. Center, head and bill. Left, newly-fledged marbled murrelet found on forest floor in Big Basin. (Photograph by Dan Friend.)

site with a southern exposure. The nest itself was merely a depression atop the moss-covered limb, surrounded by an eight-inch ring of excrement. There was no evidence that the adult bird had brought in foreign material or had, in any way, constructed a nest.

The discovery of the marbled murrelet's nest location has solved one mystery, but still another remains—how the young birds get from the forest to the sea. On several occasions immature birds have been found walking around on the forest floor, many miles inland. In fact, one month after the discovery of the marbled murrelet's nest above Campground "J," an immature marbled murrelet was found three fourths of a mile away, walking down the road in Huckleberry Campground. This bird was found on the morning of September 9, 1974, by a camper who turned it over to park staff. Since the bird was not injured, it was released into the park reservoir where Ranger Dan Friend and others intermittently observed it swimming and diving throughout most of the afternoon. On the next day, when Friend returned to make more observations, the bird could not be located. Since Singer and Verardo were both on vacation during this time, observations on the bird were very incomplete, with no attempt made to continuously follow the movements of the released bird. Such reports of immature birds being found on the ground add some credence to the theory that the young bird falls gently to the ground, waddles over to the nearest stream, and then floats downstream to the ocean.

However, if this theory is correct, one would have expected more sightings of young birds floating down coastal streams. Further doubt is cast upon it by considering the route that the Big Basin bird would have had to negotiate. The overland trek would have been 700 feet long, initially passing through dense underbrush, then crossing a state highway, and finally passing through the middle of a heavily-used campground—all during the peak of the visitor season. Upon reaching the creek, an additional eight and a half miles would have to be negotiated before it reached the ocean, and the first mile would have been through a debris-choked channel during a period of minimal water flow. The probable high degree of predation associated with a flightless trip from the nest to the sea makes this theory even more unlikely.

A more probable explanation is that the young bird flies directly from the nest to the ocean. Accidents on the wing, coupled with an inability to take flight from the ground, might explain why a number of young birds have been found walking on the forest floor. Although plausible, this theory is still unproven, since no one has seen a young marbled murrelet fly from the nest. Until that day occurs, the life cycle of this remarkable bird will remain incompletely known. ❧

Painting of adult marbled murrelet from "Birds of Western North America," paintings by Kenneth L. Carlson, text by Laurence C. Binford, copyright © 1974 by Macmillan Publishing Co., Inc.

THE CALIFORNIA QUAIL

Ian I. McMillan

ON THE historic voyage around the world of the British ship "Discovery", under the command of Captain George Vancouver, a Scot by the name of Archibald Menzies who was the ship's surgeon was also a trained naturalist. In addition to tending to the health of the ship's company the official assignment of this versatile scientist included the collecting of specimens significant of the natural resources of the regions visited.

Exploring the coast of California in the years 1792-93, the Discovery anchored at different points with surveys made of the adjacent areas on land. While the ship was at Monterey, Menzies collected quite extensively and among the specimens taken and prepared were two bird skins that would become of particular importance in the history of the new region. One of these was that of a gigantic vulture, later to be known as the California condor; the other represented a species of quail, also to be named after the state in which it was taken.

In his introduction of the latter species to the world of science, Archibald Menzies contributed more than the type specimen. The notes of his field work include items of ecological information which are of particular importance as they apply to a period of profound change throughout the main range of the California quail.

At Monterey, in December of 1792, Menzies wrote as follows: "The Thickets every where were inhabited by great variety of the featherd Tribe, many of which were also new, among these was a species of Quail of a dark lead colour beautifully speckled with black white and ferrugeneous colours with a Crest of reverted black feathers on the crown of its head, these were also met with at Port San Francisco and are common over this Country, they are equal to the common Patridge in delicacy of flavor and afforded a pleasing variety to the other luxuries with which at this time our Table abounded." Obviously, the bird noted was the California quail.

In the century following Menzies' scientific discoveries at Monterey the quail of the new region evidently continued to thrive in characteristic abundance and perhaps in even greater numbers than prior to the coming of the white man. This is somewhat surprising, for in rapid sequence throughout this period one wave after another of

Early drawing of California quail. From "Naturalist's Miscellany" by George Shaw and Frederick P. Nodder, Volume 9, London, 1797. "This bird, which is a new and hitherto undescribed species, is somewhat larger than a common quail. . . . This curious bird is a native of California, and was brought over by Mr. Archibald Menzies, who accompanied Captain Vancouver in his late expedition. The specimen from which the present figure was taken is in the British Museum."

human conquest swept over the new fabulous region, each bringing additional ecological disturbance. The era of the Spanish missions and big Ranchos with rapid build-up of great herds of livestock; the acquision of California as a new state followed by the Gold Rush and the westward spread of the American empire; the homesteading boom that peaked in the 1880's — all worked

Photographs by the author

123

Left, male California quail. Photograph by Paul J. Fair, from National Audubon Society. *Below,* female. Photograph by Allan D. Cruikshank, from National Audubon Society.

Above, in winter when predators are more active, foraging quail must remain within reach of protective cover. Thus, cover functions to control the availability of food. *Below,* except during the nesting season quail are gregarious and evidently survive best by gathering into coveys.

progressively to profoundly change the natural realm and the way of life of the California quail.

After holding up well during this first century of conquest, toward the end of that period the quail populations evidently began to suffer serious decline. In its early development this depletion was apparently rapid and extreme. In 1901 the market hunting of quail in California was made illegal. Although it took several years to become effective this early act to control hunting remains significant as one of the first public efforts toward wildlife conservation in the new region.

From the first time, evidently, that a hunter with a shotgun tried his skill on a flying California quail, the little game bird has remained a favorite among sportsmen. Together with this, there is symbolic meaning in the historic background of the species as it provided food for the pioneers and as it represented the fabulous natural abundance of a rich, new land.

In view of its superlative qualifications in the way of food and sport, it is remarkable that the California quail has grown to be held in even wider esteem in the non-hunting realm of conservation. Attractive and distinguished in appearance and behavior, sedentary in its year-round dependence on a specific local habitat and also as it readily takes up close association with humans, the little game bird has become even more popular for its non-game attributes. This common regard for the California quail was well confirmed in 1930 in the results of a popular vote taken to select a state bird.

In pointing out the progress made in matters

of managing and conserving the California quail it would be a damaging mistake to give the impression that the objectives of this work have been realized. Nothing could be more misleading. Giving all credit possible to the important gains made in matters of hunting regulations and in some work toward enhancing the ecological welfare of the quail, a continuing trend of ruinous habitat depletion must remain in front view.

To be properly informative and constructive, any review of the present status of the California quail should emphasize the fact that unbridled economic exploitation of the land operates today more extremely and extensively than ever before. And now as in past decades it is mainly through land misuse that the quail are suffering adversity and decline.

Although generally acquainted with wildlife conditions in eastern San Luis Obispo County since around 1920, for the past two decades my interest in such matters has mainly been centered in a local program of quail restoration. Participating in this project in 1946, I first liberated twelve pairs of artificially reared quail as a prospective breeding stock. Surprisingly, these pen-reared birds survived and remained in the immediate vicinity of my ranch residence to reproduce and increase. As the population grew I put into operation a corresponding program of habitat development. The planting of native shrubs as protective ground cover and the construction of artifiicial roosts with some supplemental feeding in winter was evidently effective to the point of establishing a highly localized habitat in which the original stock of 24 birds increased in six years to a covey numbering 672 birds.

On what was demonstrated in this first project I have since developed other areas on my ranch into suitable quail country. Back in the early 1920's this property, which consists of 1360 acres, was noted as a place of high quail abundance. However, shortly after that time intensive grazing practices and an increase of farming operations evidently rendered the area unfit for the sedentary game birds.

When I first moved to this ranch in 1936 there was only one small covey remaining where great numbers had flourished fifteen years before. In 1946 this remnant population was down to six birds. Since that time, with the development of favorable environment together with strict control of grazing and hunting, the quail on the same area have increased to comprise four main coveys reaching a total of around a thousand birds prior

Above, a relict quail brush *(Atriplex polycarpa),* its only remaining foliage being that which stands above the reach of sheep. This is all that remains of a once-excellent quail habitat on the east side of the Carrisa Plains in central California.

Above, this area of former quail range has been lost through conversion to grain farming. *Below,* what livestock can do to shrub cover is generally ignored in range management. Within a few months after a protective fence was removed, these pines were damaged as high as a cow can reach.

Above, on a range that supports a plentiful quail population is a relict stand of native California grasses, evidence of the value of a conservative grazing program in which quail can remain abundant. *Below,* plantings of quail brush for ground cover and evergreens for roosting shelter.

Unlike the bobwhite of the east, which roosts on the ground, the California quail generally roosts in trees or large shrubs. In winter, suitable roosting shelter may be absent. This artificial roost, made by suspending shrub branches from a tree, is used by as many as 300 quail each winter.

to the hunting season each fall. These numbers fluctuate considerably through corresponding changes in annual rate of reproduction, but otherwise they have remained generally stable for about the last ten years. Evidently an optimum density has been reached in which the natural controls which protect wild populations from overwhelming their environment now operate to prevent further increase.

Although it has been quite simple to demonstrate the limiting factors of quail abundance on my ranch, it must be pointed out that this applies only to a particular type of environment. The developed area is mainly open, rolling stockrange and cropland of deep, productive soil on which an abundance of quail food is normally produced and where water is available at different springs in the canyons. But without the previous shrub cover which was destroyed through intensive farming and grazing this food supply was no longer available for quail. Together with this, a shrinkage of suitable roosting shelter and uncontrolled hunting combined to nullify a previously ideal piece of quail country. Conversely, with a soil that was still producing suitable quail food, all that was required to re-establish the lost quail populations and even extend their previous range was to develop the necessary cover and protect it from excessive grazing while also protecting the quail from uncontrolled shooting.

Emphasis on soil productivity is included mainly because I have come to regard this factor above all others as the basis of quail abundance. Regardless of how well represented may be all the other attributes of quail country, without some areas of rich soil which are highly qualitative in their productivity the quail populations seem to remain sparse in numbers. It may be soil depletion that has caused a disappearance of quail on some ranges where the birds were formerly abundant, where the cover appears to remain suitable, and where hunting has not been a factor.

In areas where water is lacking or where additional drinking places would enhance the environment for quail, artificial watering sites have been successfully demonstrated. The Gallinaceous Guzzler introduced by the California Department of Fish and Game in the 1940's has been extensively used as a practical and efficient means of establishing a permanent supply of water for upland species. This simple device consists of a sloping concrete apron from which rainfall is drained into a partially underground storage tank. There it lasts as a year-round supply, available to the smaller species of wildlife through an opening at ground level from which a descending ramp leads to the changing water level. In addition to seeing that the natural watering sites on my ranch have remained suitable for the quail, in 1965 I installed a guzzler at a location where it seemed that a drinking site was needed.

To emphasize my claim that the California quail is in need of help today more than ever before, I might point to the main significance of what I have been able to prove on my own ranch. In the first place the quail population on the area now, would in my view compare favorably with the densities found in the days of historic abundance. It seems obvious, therefore, that destruction and deterioration of certain attributes of the early-day environment were the primary causes of the quail decline. Those causes are in operation today in growing extent and effectiveness.

Of first importance among these causes I would list the intensive, year-round grazing which in seasons of normal drought and range scarcity is destructive to certain arid-land shrubs. Of these shrubs the history of one in particular offers a good parallel to the decline of the quail. In establishing ground cover for the quail on my ranch I have mainly used a native species of *Atriplex,* commonly called "quail brush," which formerly grew extensively on the ranges of semi-arid, central California. Producing succulent and nutritious livestock

forage in years of drought when other range growth would fail, this perennial shrub, although able to thrive under optimum grazing pressure, has been extirpated on extensive areas by the excessive range practices that have grown to be customary and traditional throughout the region. Vast areas of natural quail country in being denuded of this shrub cover have been destroyed as quail range and to a great extent as livestock range.

In pointing out the continued adversity which the State Bird of California encounters at the hands of its human associate, I have done so not from any negative point of view but rather as a proposition toward positive action on this main problem of wildlife conservation. In my own experience I have found that a program of land use which includes a reasonable allowance for quail and other desirable species of wildlife can be operated without undue economic sacrifice. Ideal quail habitat can be used in livestock production, without damage, and with optimum cropping of the forage supply, if the grazing is properly managed. Quail hunting, the epitome of sport and recreation, if properly regulated and restricted, can be an additional benefit of a sound program of quail management. It therefore seems fitting to end this review with the urgent proposal that more be done to restore and protect the natural charm and abundance of California by simply giving proper care to its state bird.

California quail amid ground cover photographed by Paul J. Fair, from National Audubon Society.

THE RETURN OF THE TULE ELK

Verna R. Johnston

Photographs by the author

I T WAS a cold, pre-dawn December morning at San Luis National Wildlife Refuge. Frost lay heavy on the brown grasses. The dark trunks of willows curved upward through a thick mist. In the east the big red ball of the sun rose slowly, seemed to hang there briefly, and finally burned through onto the backs of two large tule elk bulls grazing less than one hundred yards away. They were in prime winter pelage, with thick, straw-colored coats, dark brown heads and manes, and magnificent antlers more than three feet across.

Every so often, one bull moved slowly and deliberately toward the other and lowered his antlers to the ground. The challenged bull dipped his rack in response and the two engaged horns and pushed hard, trying to shove each other backwards. Necks and heads twisted, bodies turned sideways, and vocal cords emitted high squeals as the pushing contest went on for five or ten minutes.

Then, as suddenly as it began, the sparring ended. The bulls gingerly disengaged antlers, turned away, and commenced grazing dispassionately a dozen feet apart.

It was not yet time for serious fighting. But in the highly structured life cycle of tule elk, these preliminary matches already going on among the bulls in their winter stag groups were establishing next year's peck order. Each bull was discovering, as he tested his strength against his rivals, just where he stood in the hierarchy of dominance. When the time comes, next summer, for a master bull to take charge of the harem, all the bulls in the herd will already know who is the strongest bull, who are the next ranking bulls, and so on down the line.

Then, when the bulls join the cows and the rut begins, one master bull will assume command and drive the other bulls out of the herd, charging them with a stiff-legged jog, displaying his canines and grinding his teeth. If any contend, a serious battle of strength ensues. The two bulls walk parallel to each other, about three yards apart, bugling and threatening with antlers. Suddenly they lower antlers and clash, twisting their necks from side to side, trying to catch the opponent off-balance, until one yields and runs.

Above, two prime tule elk bulls stride through the grassland of San Luis National Wildlife refuge at daybreak in winter.

Master bulls keep cows in line with the same charges and tooth-grinding, but are kept busy doing it. Cows often have ideas of their own on where to feed and they have their own hierarchy to maintain. They charge one another, with teeth grinding and a show of upper canines, and if neither gives way, both cows rear on their hind legs and flail with forelegs, boxing until one can no longer look its opponent in the eye and turns away. Such battles help to space cows in the more crowded herd of the rut.

Cows will not allow mounting until they are receptive; prior to that time, they kick or run off. So the master bull has to herd and inspect his cows at frequent intervals, along with bugling, chasing off, and intimidating the bachelor bulls that continually hang around the herd. All these demands so interrupt his feeding periods that he loses weight and within a month wears himself out.

As his strength declines, the strongest secondary bulls challenge each other and the master bull more frequently. At the master's eventual defeat, the secondary bulls split up the herd and begin the wearing-down cycle themselves. Following their decline, the tertiary bulls take control of the herd. Other opportunist bulls wait on the sidelines to mate with cows should fate give them a chance.

The grassy habitat in which this elk is bedded down is the kind of range needed to provide for the 2000 tule elk now alloted by state and federal law. Point Reyes National Seashore and San Luis Island provide extensive acreages of this habitat.

It all works according to rank in the hierarchy. In the highly social life of tule elk, the herd is the focal point of existence and rank within it the determinant of each individual's behavior. Despite the heavy fighting and herding demands of the rut, primary and secondary bulls succeed in doing over 80 percent of the breeding. With age and increased strength, younger bulls gain status in the breeding order from year to year. Old defeated master bulls often become loners in the last few years of their ten to twelve year life cycle.

The two prime bulls I was watching sparred off and on for an hour or so, but turned increasingly often to gaze alertly across the grassland toward the east. I could hear or see nothing there except willow outlines in the distance, an occasional white-tailed kite or red-tailed hawk sailing overhead, the honking of geese, the deeper trumpeting of sandhill cranes, and the mellow whistle of western meadowlarks. But the elk kept looking and listening and raising their nostrils, and soon four more bulls walked slowly into view from that direction, feeding on low herbs as they came.

Elk use all their senses in herd communication, with hearing extremely keen, sight less so, and smell probably the most highly developed sense of all. Dale McCullough, who studied tule elk for two years in the Owens Valley of eastern California, felt that elk are able to recognize each other individually solely by scent, and he learned in stalking them that they could detect the slightest contact of clothing with a bush.

Above, two bulls at San Luis Wildlife Refuge approach each other. Right, top to bottom, they lower heads and spar, disengage and strike again. They are trying, in a contest of strength, to push each other backwards. They shove and squeal, twist heads and bodies and, finally, since they prove to be evenly matched, disengage antlers and pull apart.

At very close range you can hear a virtual symphony of the small sounds that members of a herd make. Their foot bones creak with each step, stomachs rumble, bulls give a gutteral rattle, and at times teeth grind. These are the integrative signals of a herd, perhaps a din to their sensitive ears. And along with the sounds come the familiar scents of known individuals.

When an unidentified movement or sound or smell intrudes into the usual pattern, the first elk to detect it usually gives an explosive bark of alarm which brings the herd to the alert, heads high, ears out, mouths open. And if the matter is judged serious, off they run at a rocking-horse gait at speeds up to thirty miles per hour.

This same intense sensitivity to sounds and smells makes them very vulnerable and nervous on windy days when noise and scents literally bombard them. I recall one day at San Luis when the wind blew such a gale that cliff and barn swallows sat in the ruts of the dirt road to evade the blasts. That day we saw no tule elk anywhere on the refuge; they were all in the creek bottoms and swales, protected from the gusts.

But this December day was calm, and for four hours the six bulls fed and sparred and finally lay down to chew the cud with the sun warming their backs. It was like a mini-scene from the past, from the days two hundred years ago when tule elk were the dominant large mammals in the Central Valley of California, around San Francisco Bay and the Berkeley Hills, ranging north past Point Reyes, south to the Tehachapis, east into the lower Sierra Nevada foothills, and west into the coastal valleys down to Santa Barbara.

The tremendous numbers of elk that roamed these areas defied accurate description by the first explorers. Newberry (1857) wrote that the Central Valley herds rivaled the bison of the great plains and the antelope of South Africa. Audubon (1907) and Bryant (1847) reported herds of one thousand to two thousand head in the San Joaquin Valley. On Edward Bosqui's famous 110-mile walk from Stockton to Mariposa in 1850, he saw "bands of elk, deer and antelope in such numbers that they actually darkened the plains for miles." McCullough's recent intensive review of the historical literature left no question but that the elk were "extremely abundant," and that a rough estimate of half a million seemed reasonable in their heyday—but that we can never really know.

Wherever they occurred, the one common denominator always seemed to be grassland. Whether interspersed with the tule-cattail marshes of the Sacramento-San Joaquin Delta, or the river floodplains, or the drier rolling hillsides of the Coast Ranges or lower Sierra Nevada, the tule elk required open country. And there they thrived for thousands of years through periodic floods and droughts.

Of the several subspecies of elk in North America, the tule elk is the smallest, lightest col-

ored, and far and away the best adapted to drought. Its teeth, the most massive of those of the races of elk, equip it to handle tough fibrous grasses and to live a spartan existence when necessary.

The best fossil evidence indicates that North American elk (often called wapiti) originated in Asia, where very similar elk live today, and migrated across the Bering Straits land bridge in the Pleistocene around a million years ago. They spread over North America during the moist conditions of the Pleistocene; but as these mesic environments receded north, it appears highly probable that the generalized Rocky Mountain elk (*Cervus elaphus nelsoni*) remained in the Rocky Mountain area, while two offshoot populations were separated from the generalized stock by geographical barriers. One of the elk groups, living in the humid coastal areas of northern California, Oregon, and Washington, developed over time the deep brown head and mane colors, antler pattern, and large size characteristic of the Roosevelt or Olympic elk of today (*Cervus elaphus roosevelti*). The other, living in the drier California valleys, became ever more specialized for aridity as natural selection favored those better able to survive on tough grasses and over periods of drought—the tule elk (*Cervus elaphus nannodes*).

The Indian tribes of central California lived side by side with tule elk for centuries with very little impact on them. But the Mediterranean annual grasses that inadvertently arrived with the string of Spanish missions set up in California in the 1700's did start an ominous trend. The introduced annuals, not nearly as good for grazing as the native perennial bunch grasses they displaced, caused a much greater fluctuation in forage production from year to year. This, along with the vast herds of cattle and horses that were brought in by the missions and allowed to roam wild, reduced forage available for elk.

This was only the beginning of tule elk troubles. In the early 1800's, hides and tallow became the currency of Spanish California. Elk, along with cattle, were lassoed by rancheros riding their fastest horses. After being hamstrung and having their throats slit, the elk were stripped of their hides and their fat. The melted fat was poured into large hide sacks securely sewed. Both hides and tallow went to San Francisco for export at $2 per hide and 6 cents a pound for tallow, at 1841 prices.

While this activity was in full swing, the fur brigades had arrived in the Central Valley to exploit the valuable pelts of golden beaver. From Jedediah Smith's first expedition in 1827 until at

least 1843, trapping parties scoured the swamps and rivers every year. It took tremendous amounts of game to feed these hungry mountain men, and elk were easy targets. John Work led a Hudson Bay Company expedition which killed 166 elk in four days in January, 1833. His February entry for that year near the Marysville Buttes read: "395 elk, 148 deer, 17 bears and 8 antelopes have been killed in a month which is certainly a great many more than was required, but when the most of the people have ammunition and see animals, they must needs fire upon them let them be wanted or not. The animals for a considerable time back have been in general very lean, indeed they could not be expected to be otherwise being hunted without intermission."

Under the continuous hunting pressure, the elk took refuge in the marshes where hunters could not follow. But from 1838 on, another pressure plagued them—fences. What had been wide-open range now became settled ranch country, and as

cattle were brought under control, wild horses and elk became competitors for forage and were eliminated at every opportunity.

The Gold Rush brought the finishing touch. As people poured into California, the value of livestock soared. Cattle previously worth $2 for hides overnight became worth $35 for their beef. The hindquarter of a fat tule elk brought $40. More and more disillusioned miners turned to market hunting to feed the gold-hungry newcomers. In 1850 the menus of most San Francisco restaurants featured elk, antelope, and bear steaks, along with venison, wild duck and geese.

The tule elk's day in the sun as an integral part of the California scene was over. In the 1850's the elk population collapsed under the pressure of the market hunters. From the Sacramento Valley, from Point Reyes, finally from the northern San Joaquin Valley in 1863, they disappeared at the echo of a rifle. The few remaining hid in the

134

marshes of Tulare and Buena Vista Lakes in the southern San Joaquin Valley. When ditching and diking dried up these marshes in the late 1860's, this small band was again exposed to hunters and virtually wiped out.

As far as can be determined, all vanished but a single pair found in 1874-75 by a Fish and Game warden in the tule marshes of the Miller and Lux Ranch near Buttonwillow. Cattle baron Henry Miller gave his men strict orders to protect this last remnant of tule elk, saying, "they were here before we were" and offering a $500 reward for information on anyone who disturbed them. The elk prospered so dramatically that over the years they outgrew their habitat. Under the asupices of the California Academy of Sciences, 146 elk were transferred to 19 localities in the state during 1914 and 1915.

The most successful transplants went to Cache Creek in 1922 and to Owens Valley in 1933-34. The Owens Valley herd thrived in an eastern Sierran habitat of rolling sage-grass-brush terrain, not too unlike their original home in growth habit, openness, and aridity. As the numbers of elk grew, so did protests from stockmen on neighboring lands claiming elk damage to cattle fences, alfalfa fields, and cattle forage.

In response, the California Department of Fish and Game carried out a series of hunts in the 1940's through the 1960's which allowed hunters, by permit, to kill anywhere from 22 percent to 48 percent of the herds. The 1955 hunt, when hunters shot from jeeps into the herds and crippled an excessive number of elk, brought strong protests from conservationists, and when the 1960 hunt to reduce the elk to 135 animals was announced, a grassroots citizens committee, The Committee for the Preservation of Tule Elk, was formed.

Spearheaded by Beula and Tasker Edmiston, the committee rallied public support to cancel the hunt and to get a new Fish and Game policy allowing the elk to reach 250-300 animals before reduction. As other hunts were held through the early 1960's, the committee, increasingly backed by well-known biologists and champions from all parts of the world, worked to gain recognition of the tule elk's plight. The gene pool of the last wild tule elk on earth was being depleted, its finest specimens more likely to be culled in the hunts than its poorest. The tule elk needed a home, or a number of homes, where it could increase in numbers to the 2000 recommended by the International Union for the Conservation of Nature as minimum for survival in a healthy, safe condition.

Two other races of elk live in western North America. Roosevelt elk, above, occupy the coastal forests. At top, a Rocky Mountain elk bull with its antlers at the delicate, velvet-covered stage.

135

In 1964 the U.S. Department of the Interior listed the tule elk as an endangered species. In 1971 the California Legislature unanimously enacted the "Behr Bill" to restore the tule elk to that magical 2000 number before it could again be hunted. 1976 saw President Ford sign H. J. Res. 738 (McCloskey) into law, providing for federal and state cooperation to insure habitat for at least 2000 tule elk in California. The framework of the law to return tule elk to a portion of their former range is complete; implementation of the law lies ahead.

Two potential restorations are in various stages of planning and action. The National Park Service has completed and approved a plan and environmental assessment for reintroduction of tule elk to Point Reyes National Seashore. The 2600-acre designated area is bounded on one side by Tomales Bay, on another by the Pacific Ocean, and will be fenced on the two land sides. Elk can swim, but the Park Service is expecting that they will not when there is no reason to leave a favorable home territory.

Point Reyes offers choice open elk habitat, including brushy side slopes where the cows can find the privacy needed for calving. The lone calf produced hides under brush for the first few weeks, with the mother nearby, until it can run fast enough to join the herd. The Point Reyes herd will start with ten to twelve surplus animals from Tule Elk State Reserve at Tupman and will grow on its own to about 300, or whatever proves to be the carrying capacity.

Right, members of the Committee for the Preservation of Tule Elk inspect San Luis Island, near Los Banos, a potential future state park and home of tule elk. Above, committee leader Beula Edmiston, who initiates legislation related to elk preservation, monitors its progress, and alerts the committee when help is needed.

It is not yet known whether predators, such as coyotes or cougars, will be around to take occasional calves and effect normal population controls as in former days at Point Reyes. The Park Service, which manages the land, would like to see this happen; but the California Department of Fish and Game, which manages the animals, is opposed, fearing marauding on adjacent ranches. If natural predators are not a part of the Point Reyes scene, optimum capacity will arrive much sooner. Where tule elk like their habitat, they have shown themselves to be good producers. In favorable conditions cows often breed as yearlings.

A second potential home for tule elk lies waiting near Los Banos in the central San Joaquin Valley. San Luis Island represents the finest substantial piece of original San Joaquin Valley landscape still unspoiled by man, including within its boundaries native grasslands, valley woodland, oxbow lakes, vernal pools, and a heron rookery. Adjacent to San Luis National Wildlife Refuge where the recently introduced herd of tule elk that I have studied is flourishing, San Luis Island deserves to be a state park. Indeed, one and one-half million dollars of State Parks and Recreation Bond money was voted for this purpose, and legislation

Mature bull tule elk wading through creek while digging up water plants with his antlers.

Above, a group
of tule elk bulls
with their
antlers in velvet.

to secure it is on its uncertain path through the State Legislature, needing much support to avoid the pitfalls. Once again The Committee for the Preservation of Tule Elk is vigilantly monitoring its progress. (Committee address: 814 W. Markland Drive, Monterey Park, CA 91754.)

The Central Valley, original home of the largest tule elk herds, has the least preserved natural space of any of the state's landscape provinces, less than .06 percent of its 12 million acres. Among its few remaining choices, San Luis Island is the only one that could provide a 20,000-acre park encompassing an entire valley ecosystem. "I know of no other place in California where we are privileged to do this," said Howard Leach, Special Wildlife Coordinator for California Dept. of Fish and Game.

And tule elk do need space. They are versatile feeders, grazing on a wide variety of herbs and grasses, acorns and rushes—even tules and reeds in poor years. They sometimes stand erect on their hind legs to browse willows—a favorite food—and also utilize cottonwoods, wild rose, milkweed, horsetail, and locoweed, some of which are poison-

ous to cattle. Thus, given enough space, they do not abuse their habitat by specialized forage demands.

No Fish and Game manager wants a repetition of the Tupman story in which the tule elk remnant herd of the late 1800's was kept on too small a piece of pristine grassland as it came back, ate the land bare, and now has to be fed a supplementary diet of alfalfa pellets.

Tule elk at present number somewhere around 700 in California, more than half of that total in Owens Valley, the rest in smaller herds at San Luis National Wildlife Refuge, Tupman, Cache Creek, Concord, and Grizzly Island. In the former three areas where they can be observed, they draw many visitors. Something new is always visible as their annual cycle ticks on—perhaps during the calving season a cow at full speed chasing a coyote out of sight or bulls showing the interesting behavior connected with antler changes over the year. After casting antlers in March at about the same time they gain their sleek, redder, summer coat, bulls resemble cows for about a month. Their new antlers appear covered with soft tender velvet and, as bone is mineralizing under the velvet, bulls carry the rack very carefully to avoid damage. Later, when they shed the velvet over a period of five to ten days, they tear the soil and rake herbs and bushes vigorously, the velvet hanging in shreds, sometimes bloody, as it is stripped away to reveal glistening white bone beneath.

During the late summer rut, tule elk bulls go through the same thrash-urinate act that elk in all parts of the world do—thrashing the ground with their antlers while spurting urine on their underparts. And they polish antlers vigorously on posts and stumps.

The mating act is a dramatic performance. Bulls sometimes have to mount a receptive cow twenty or more times before ejaculation occurs. When it does occur, it is in one violent thrust in which the bull leaps upward, his hind feet off the ground, the momentum of his thrust forcing the cow forward—sometimes onto her knees—while the bull himself lands off balance.

As the tule elk return in numbers over the years at California parks and refuges, more and more of us will be privy to the kind of intimate glimpse into herd life that Manager Leon Littlefield had at San Luis National Wildlife Refuge recently. An elk cow on the edge of the herd made the sound that usually means "danger—fall prostrate" to its young calf. The calf did not respond. Whereupon a nearby bull walked over to the calf, placed its leg firmly on the calf's back, and pushed it flat to the ground.

Two bulls with their antlers fully developed.

Tracy I. Storer

CALIFORNIA'S EMBLEM:
THE GRIZZLY BEAR

THE pioneers of the nineteenth century who ventured to explore the vast areas beyond the Mississippi encountered many conspicuous novelties in landscape, weather, plants, and animals. Some of these were notable for size far beyond anything seen previously along the Atlantic seaboard — the great Rocky and Sierra-Cascade mountain systems, the vast interior deserts with heat and drought, forests of huge coniferous trees including giant sequoias, and a bear larger than the familiar black-coated species. This was the grizzly. It had come to the attention of the earliest missionaries in California, it gained an important place in affairs of the Spanish-Mexican era, and for half a century it continued to play a significant role in the developing American civilization. The grizzly of California is gone forever as a living animal, but its form and memory persist as an emblem on the state flag and seal, as the mascot of university athletics, as a common element in many place names, and as the motif in a rich collection of historical records and stories. Over the centuries, few persons have achieved so durable a status for posterity.

The adult grizzly is large, stout, and powerfully muscled. Compared with the better known black bear it has many conspicuous features of difference. These include the fleshy hump above the shoulders that is evident even in young individuals, the long heavy front claws that are only slightly curved, the big hind feet, the slightly concave profile of the face, and the huge 3d upper molars, always 1¼ inches or more in length. The dense coat of rather coarse hair is variable in color — whitish, pale or darker yellow or brown, or even blackish—but almost always with tips of near white on the hairs which produce the "grizzled" appearance.

Records of size for the California grizzly are few and often unreliable. Overall length of adults ranged from 6 feet 3 inches to 8 feet 10 inches and the height at shoulder from 3 to 4 feet. As to weight there are many statements, some estimates, and few facts. Often the figures are sheer "guestimates." Elsewhere it is known that growth continues for several years and males become larger than females. In California the abundance of food may have resulted in bears larger than elsewhere. Published weights of up to 1000 or 1100 pounds for a few exceptional animals may have been the maximum; statements of grizzlies that weighed 1500 pounds or over are forever suspect. Perhaps 300 to 700 pounds would have been the normal limits for adults.

The official state flag of California, designed by Don Greame Kelley after the Nahl portrait shown on opposite page.

Black bears, young or old, are good climbers and often ascend trees but the grizzly, save possibly when quite young, is strictly terrestrial. These differences give a clue to the environments used; the black bear is a creature of the forests whereas the grizzly more often seeks open places in chaparral, grasslands, or tundra.

The first record of the grizzly in California was that of Sebastian Vizcaino in December 1602 at Monterey where several "bears" were feeding at night on a stranded whale. Then for two centuries there were only vague references to the creature in North America. It first came to scientific attention in 1805 when a specimen was taken by the Lewis and Clark Expedition in the area that is now Montana. A few years later the animal was named *Ursus horribilis* by Ord, in reference to its reputed ferocious character. Additional species were described as a result of other explorations in western North America and by early in the present century many kinds of grizzlies and the related Alaska brown bears had been named. In those years it was thought that these were all distinct species. Recent scientific studies, however, have shown conclusively that grizzlies and Alaska brown bears are closely related to the European brown bear. Indeed, all of them are now considered to be members of a single species, *Ursus arctos,* that ranged originally over most of the Northern Hemisphere. The number of local races or subspecies that should be recognized is probably small but remains uncertain because the big bears are highly variable in their characteristics and museum specimens for study are relatively few except from Alaska. Brown bears in both Alaska and the Old World lack the grizzled hair tips.

In North America the grizzly was native from near the Arctic Coast of Alaska and Canada down

Female grizzly and her two cubs. The young, perhaps nine months old, show parental characteristics of the hump, long rough fur, long foreclaws, and flat forehead. Photographed by Joseph Dixon in Yellowstone Park, September, 1929.

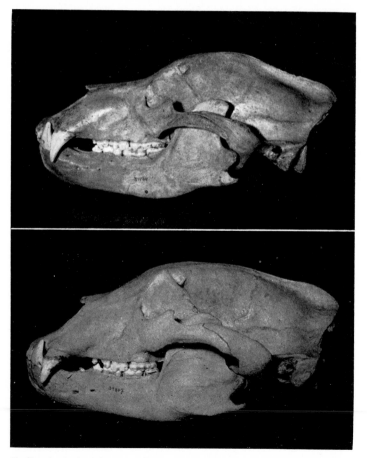

Skulls of grizzly (above) and black bears (below). The concave forehead is a distinctive grizzly characteristic. Specimens in Museum of Vertebrate Zoology, University of California at Berkeley.

to northern Mexico, and from the Pacific shores eastward to the Great Plains; but none lived in Nevada. Originally grizzlies occupied all of California except the Modoc lava plateau, the areas east of the Sierras, and the southeastern deserts. Black bears then were present in the Coast Range only down to Sonoma County and in the Sierra Nevada south to Tehachapi. Grizzlies also tenanted those areas but they alone occupied the Great Central Valley, the lowlands of southern California, and all of the foothill areas.

To visualize the grizzly in its primeval environment of a century and a half ago we must divest the California landscape of all that modern man has wrought. Gone will be the freeways and lesser roads, the cities, towns, and rural homes, the power lines, levees, and canals, the cultivated orchards and fields, and the domestic livestock. The only fires were those set by lightning or by Indians and no tree had been felled by an axe. Native plant cover prevailed everywhere. Impressive woodlands several miles in width margined all the large rivers of the lowlands. The woods were bordered by huge continuous expanses of tule marsh, beyond which were grasslands that reached to the foothills covered by chaparral or pine-oak woodland. The woods comprised many species of trees including some specimens of enormous size — valley oaks eight feet in trunk diameter, for example. Acorns from several species of oaks, fruits of a number of kinds of berries, clover, grass, palatable herbs, and various edible roots abounded.

Left, hill slope in Canada de los Osos, San Luis Obispo County, a habitat once occupied by grizzlies in California. (Photo by Lloyd P. Tevis, Jr.) *Below,* adult black bear. Distinctive features are the slightly convex forehead, absence of shoulder hump, short foreclaws same length as hind claws, and smooth-surfaced coat of uniform texture and color. Photographed by Joseph Dixon in Yosemite National Park, November, 1929.

Salmon, sturgeon, and other fishes tenanted the streams, waterfowl and lesser birds were numerous at all seasons, elk lived in the tules, deer in the woodlands and shrubbery, and antelope on the grassy plains. Through all of this ranged the grizzly, strongest of all the animals.

In structure the bears are "carnivores" — flesh eaters — but in food habits most of them are omnivorous, using a wide variety of both animal and plant materials. Practically, they are opportunists, consuming anything edible that becomes available. So it was with the California grizzly, whose diet was varied and perhaps "balanced." The list of items used in different seasons and places is long: beached whales or seals; deer, elk, and domestic livestock including many as carrion; small animals such as ground squirrels, field mice, lizards, frogs, fish live or dead, yellow jackets and their nests, other insects, larvae, and honey. In spring and early summer loose companies of grizzlies pastured like farm animals in fields of wild clover, filaree, or grasses, and dug bulbs and roots of wild plants. Later in the year they sought any and all kinds of berries — dogwood, elder, manzanita, salmonberries, huckleberries, and both wild and cultivated fruits. Throughout the lower and middle altitudes of California the most important single item of diet was of acorns from several species of oaks. Young grizzlies sometimes ascended the trees for this food and the older bears could stand on large branches close to the ground while foraging. Indians found much com-

petition from the grizzlies for this favored food and had to exercise caution when the crop was maturing and bears were present.

Temperamentally the grizzly had varied responses to events in its environment. It was dangerous and deadly when attacked or wounded by man, when come upon unexpectedly and surprised, or when a female had growing cubs. When seeking animal food it could strike down any large animal and when pitted in the fighting ring against a bull it was a violent contender. These features of behavior gave it the reputation of being a ferocious and dangerous creature. Under other circumstances, however, its manner was quite different. When grizzlies congregated to relish some desirable food

Above, Roping a bear at Santa Margarita Rancho in San Diego County. Oil painting by James Walker, about 1876, from notes made in the 1840s. The original is in the California Historical Society, San Francisco. *Right,* A natural bull-and-bear fight witnessed by J. Ross Browne, 1849.

"Return From the Bear Hunt" painted by William Hahn, 1882. M. H. de Young Memorial Museum, San Francisco. Collection of Miss Rosina Hahn.

— acorns, clover, or whale — they fed together peacefully. If approached slowly and quietly by man, a bear would ordinarily retire. There are several accounts of captive grizzlies that were completely tamed and without hazard to their keepers. In short, the grizzly had the power to be dominant but assumed that role only under selected circumstances; otherwise it was a well-behaved member of the animal community.

In regions where winter temperatures are low and snow covers the ground for several weeks or months both grizzlies and black bears have a mid-season period of inactivity. Unlike the true hibernation of bats, ground squirrels, or chipmunks, bears do not experience a profound sleep with lowering of body temperature, heartbeat, and respiration. The animals retire to a cave, tree base, or similar shelter and merely become inactive. During this period the females give birth to their young, which are proportionately far smaller than those of other large animals — about 9 inches long and 8 to 12 ounces in weight. Because of the mild climate of lowland California some grizzlies were active in all months.

On the flatlands of the Sacramento-San Joaquin Valley the big bears dug retreats down into the ground but in the hills and mountains their dens were in hillsides. The bushy chaparral of the foothills was a favored shelter at all seasons as shown by the many trails that led here and there under this extensive shrub cover. Elsewhere, in soft soils, there often were "ancestral" trails where generations of grizzlies, stepping in the same places, had made routes with a succession of deep footprints that were unsuited for use by other animals.

Over the centuries of Indian occupation the grizzly population in California probably was no greater than that found elsewhere today. The early missionaries recorded but few bears and indeed, when short of food, could not always obtain grizzly meat in any quantity. Then, during the prosperous era of Spanish and Mexican missions and rancheros, the number of free-ranging cattle multiplied enormously. Thereby a bounteous supply of food became available to the grizzlies and their numbers increased far beyond the normal carrying capacity of the land. Such was the situation in the 1830's and 1840's when the first Americans arrived and settled. In the Napa Valley early in 1831 George Yount said of the bears: "they were everywhere — upon the plains, in the valleys, and on the mountains . . . and it was not unusual to see fifty or sixty within the twenty-four hours." A decade later John Bidwell in the Sacramento Valley wrote that the grizzly was almost an hourly sight near streams and it was not uncommon to see thirty to forty a day.

The grizzly was by far the most formidable animal in the environment of most California Indians and the big bears dominated the natives who lacked weapons to deal with the creatures. Some tribes did try to kill bears and occasionally were successful and some ate its flesh. Pelts were used at times by the Indian shamans or medicine men, grizzly claws served as decorations, and myths about bears and natives were common. But the Indians had little effect on grizzly numbers.

Early in the period of Spanish occupation a few bears were used for food but such meat soon lost favor. Later, when both livestock and bears had multiplied, the grizzlies gave much trouble by killing and consuming cattle whence hides and tallow were sought for export. Efforts at destroying the bears with muskets and by roping were only moderately successful. Many persons were maimed or killed by grizzlies, yet the hazard was less than to the Indians because the white people traveled mostly on horseback.

With a supply of bears at hand, the Spaniards revived an ancient practice of their homeland, the bear-and-bull fight as social entertainment in town on Sunday afternoon. A group of mounted vaqueros would seek out and surround a wild bear. By skillful use of their reatas the animal would be stretched out, then bound, gagged, and transported on a creaking oxcart to the enclosed arena. Meanwhile a vigorous long-horned Spanish bull had been roped and tethered. One foot each of bear and bull were joined by a 20-yard leather cord to keep the two beasts near one another and the fight was on. As spectators men, women, and children were crowded on elevated seats or convenient walls or roofs overlooking the site. The gory outcome was almost always death for one participant, and sometimes both. These inhumane spectacles survived into Gold Rush days.

The early American settlers in California exhibited greater vigor than their Latin associates in many respects, including attention to the abundant grizzly population. To reduce the hazard to men and livestock several of them became noted hunters. William Gorden on Cache Creek killed nearly 50 in one year, George Nidever along the coast at different times upwards of 200, and Colin Preston claimed to have destroyed more than that number in a single year. Others shot lesser numbers and many additional bears were taken in steel or cabin traps or by set guns. The accelerated

Above, yoke of oxen pulling Samson from log trap into transport cage, near Yosemite Valley, winter of 1854-55. Adams atop cage; Stanislaus and Tuolumne, his Indian helpers, in front of cage. Woodcut drawn in New York in 1860 from description by Adams for the "New York Weekly". *Left,* Grizzly Adams and "Ben Franklin," his trained grizzly hunting companion. Drawn by Charles C. Nahl, 1860.

"Bob," a yearling Mendocino County grizzly at the Albert E. Kent home in Chicago, summer of 1869. Earliest known photographs of a California grizzly.

demands for food with the Gold Rush stimulated market hunting and grizzly meat was served together with that of deer, elk, and waterfowl.

Of all the persons who met or sought out grizzlies from the padres, vaqueros, and hunters on to early state governors, one man is pre-eminent in the literature on bears because of the extent and variety of his recorded experiences. Theodore H. Hittell's 1860 book recounts "The adventures of James Capen Adams, mountaineer and grizzly bear hunter." Stories about Grizzly Adams also appeared in contemporary newspapers, in weekly magazine articles, and several dime novels. Adams hunted and shot grizzlies, he captured both young and old individuals alive, he had a menagerie of trained bears and other animals in San Francisco during the latter 1850's, and he trained two grizzlies to be his traveling and hunting companions. All in all, his story is the greatest animal saga in California's colorful history and his exploits must be read in detail to be fully appreciated. Suffice it to say here that the amiable character of the European brown bear, an animal that has been trained and displayed over the centuries, was also present in its otherwise ferocious California relative, the grizzly.

In retrospect, it was inevitable that the grizzly had to disappear as the human population of California grew and spread. Elk, deer, mountain lions, and even black bears may exist close to or among people as demonstrated by many experiences in recent decades. Their numbers may have to be reduced at times because of damage to crops or other interests but they do not need to be exterminated. History has demonstrated that it was otherwise with the grizzly. So large and powerful an animal was a continuing menace to people and able to pilfer domestic sheep, swine, and young cattle. The grizzly could climb or rip apart any wooden fence or other protective enclosure and devour or make off with the small livestock that became its favored food. In consequence, the big bear was killed out as early as the 1860's and 1870's in some counties. In other places a few survived into early years of the present century. The trend, however, was always downward and the last known living individual was seen in Sequoia National Park during 1924. In Alaska, British Columbia, and Montana there still are enough large open spaces so that grizzlies and people may live in the same general areas. This became impossible in California — there is no *lebesraum* for grizzlies. Within a century our state's emblem, once exceptionally abundant, has joined the ranks of vanished animals.

Episodes in the history of "Monarch," the last known California grizzly. *Top,* after his capture in the mountains of southern California in 1889, he was transported by being lashed to the horse-drawn sled in the foreground, and chained to trees each night during the journey. (From a sketch in the San Francisco Examiner.) *Center,* as drawn by Ernest Thompson Seton. (From "Bears I Have Met—And Others" by Allen Kelly, Drexel Biddle, 1903.) *Bottom,* Monarch, mounted in 1911, is now at the California Academy of Sciences.

BACK FROM EXTATION?

Burney J. Le Boeuf

ON'T be alarmed if you can't find the word "extation" in the dictionary. It isn't there yet. In 1976 R. C. Banks advocated its use as a single word "to describe the status of a species whose population has been reduced to such a low level that it can no longer function as a significant part of its normal ecosystem . . . or to the point where there is considerable doubt whether the species remains extant. . . . " I will use this newly coined word as a substitute for the more cumbersome conceptions, "nearly extinct," "probably extinct," and the like.

During this century, several animal species have been virtually annihilated either directly or indirectly by human activities. The California condor, the California sea otter, the California gray whale, and the black footed ferret are just a few examples.

However, despite being reduced to a minute fraction of their former abundance, populations of some of these species have apparently recovered— at least their numbers have increased dramatically and they have begun to reinhabit their former ranges. Such has been the case with the northern

elephant seal, *Mirounga augustirostris,* an animal that has been considered an endangered species since it was brought to extation by sealers during the last century. The number of elephant seals has increased enormously during the last few decades, and their present breeding range has broadened to a point such that it is almost as extensive as it was in pre-extation days. But it would be premature to conclude that elephant seals are safe, that the population is fit and viable, that this species has come back. We must question whether any species ever fully recover from extation, from being bludgeoned to the virtual brink of extinction. A species that recovers from extation is changed; it is genetically different from the pre-extation population. Thus, the recovery of an animal population from extation cannot be viewed simply from the point of view of the number of individuals that exist and the range they occupy. This has been demonstrated for one species, the northern elephant seal, but the general argument should apply to other species that have undergone similar histories.

In 1874 Scammon noted that northern elephant seals once bred from Point Reyes to Cabo

Above, center of a densely crowded harem of elephant seals on Pilot Rock Beach, Isla de Guadalupe. All are descended from the few dozen animals that escaped the oil hunters and survived on this island. (Photograph by Burney J. Le Boeuf)

Right, Pilot Rock Beach, on Guadalupe, where one of the largest breeding aggregations of elephant seals in the world is located. (B.L.B.) Below, a most unusual habitat on Guadalupe is the marine caves just above water line. Here the rare Guadalupe fur seal breeds. (Photograph by R. S. Peterson)

San Lazaro, and that they had been abundant along the entire coast during the early part of the 19th century—before sealing began. Seals began to be exploited in the first decade of the 19th century; this activity went on at a great pace for about forty years. The oil product which was reduced from blubber was very important in industry, being considered the best oil available with the exception of that of the sperm whale. Seal oil was used in house and street lighting, for lubricating machinery, in the tanning process, and in making paint, soap, and clothing. One adult bull was reported to have brought as much as 210 gallons of oil.

Because the elephant seal was not afraid of man, it was easy prey for sealers, who killed seals of both sexes and all ages indiscriminately. Slaughter was so intensive that by 1860 elephant seals were no longer considered an important source of oil. By 1869 the species was considered to be virtually extinct ("extaille" in Banks' terminology). Ironically, this was before the northern elephant seal had been recognized as a separate species from the southern elephant seal.

During the period from 1865 to 1880, only occasional stragglers were sighted in the entire range, a few on Islas San Benito, and a few on Isla de Guadalupe. From 1884 to 1892, no elephant seals were seen anywhere, despite the fact that several museum expeditions made thorough searches for them. Finally, in 1892, Townsend and Anthony set out on a collecting expedition for the Smithsonian Institution. They saw only eight elephant seals in Baja California. All of them were in one place, a highly inaccessible, exposed beach on Isla de Guadalupe, a volcanic island 150 miles west of the Baja California mainland. The men killed seven of the seals, even though they realized that these animals represented "the last of an exceedingly rare species." This was unquestionably the nadir in the history of this species, the low point in its population history. Bartholomew and Hubbs have estimated that there may have been as few as 20 animals in the entire population in 1892, and probably no more than 100. They pointed out that the entire species has been reconstituted from this remnant population.

From 1892 until approximately 1930 the elephant seal bred only in very small numbers, only on remote Isla de Guadalupe, and for much of the time only on "Elephant Seal Beach" on the northwest side of the island. There were too few seals to attract collectors or commercial interests. In 1922, Hanna and Anthony of the joint American-Mexican expedition to Isla de Guadalupe (which the California Academy of Sciences helped organize), reported finding 264 elephant seals on the entire island. Judging that the population would again be exploited, the Mexican government granted the species immediate and complete protection. So protected, the colony began to flourish, and within a decade animals began to disperse to other places along the coast of Baja California. When animals began to appear off the coast of

southern California, the United States government followed the example of the Mexican government and granted the species protection. Elephant seals have continued this growth trend in number and range up to the present.

The following table shows when elephant seals were initially observed at the principal rookeries, when breeding began, and estimates of colony size and total population number. Colony size was estimated by doubling the number of animals censused at the peak of the breeding season. That is, I assumed that 50% of the colony, composed of the young of the previous year and non-breeding juveniles, would be at sea during the breeding season. The population size was derived by summing up all of the colony estimates. This rough and

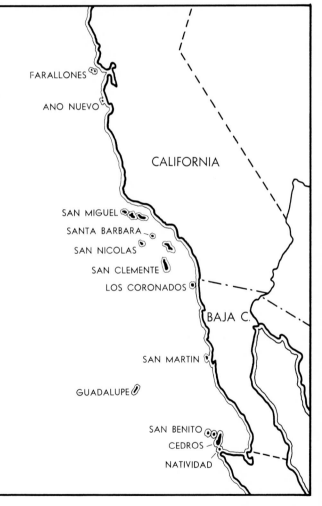

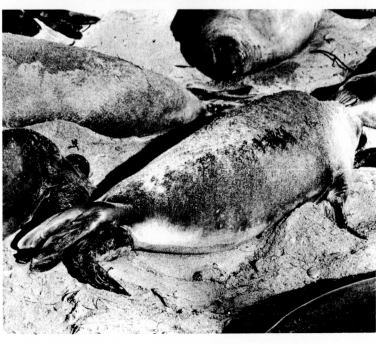

Above, northern elephant seals now breed on twelve islands along the coasts of California and Baja California. Right above, a bull seal biting a female on the neck as a prelude to mating. Right, an elephant seal pup being born. (Photographs by Ken Parker and Eugene Fisher)

most conservative estimate yielded a total of 47,-684 elephant seals in existence in 1976.

Colony	Seals initially observed	Breeding began	Breeding females at peak season	Estimated total animals
Isla de Guadalupe	—	—	4652	18,596
Islas San Benito	1918	.1930's	2382	9,238
San Miguel Island ...	1925	1930's	3842	13,980
Los Coronados	1948	1950's or later	44	152
Santa Barbara Island .	1948	late 1950's	68	252
San Nicolas Island ...	1949	last 1940's	616	2,214
Ano Nuevo Island	1955	1961	687	2,718
Southeast Farallon Island	1959	1972	60	260
Isla Cedros	1965	1960's (?)	63	274
Population totals			12,414	47,684

Bartholomew and Hubbs estimated a total population size of 13,000 seals in 1957. Thus, in less than 20 years, the total population has more than tripled in size. In addition, the number of breeding females counted at peak season gives an indication of the reproductive potential of the present population. This figure does not represent the entire population of breeding females since approximately 15% of them are at sea at the time. However, about 15% of the pups born every year die before weaning at four weeks of age, so the number of females censused at peak season yields a fair estimate of pups weaned—approximately 12,000 in 1976.

A closer look at the colonies gives another perspective on the dramatic increase in elephant seal numbers. In the present decade, four new colonies have been formed: Southeast Farallon Island in 1972, Isla Natividad between 1971 and 1975, and Isla San Martin and San Clemente Island in 1977. In addition, females gave birth on two mainland sites in recent years, the Point Reyes peninsula and Ano Nuevo Point. During the last few years, at least four major colonies doubled or tripled pup production. Pups born on Point Bennett, a rookery on the western tip of San Miguel Island, increased from 1357 in 1968 to 3711 in 1976. The San Nicolas colony increased in pup production from 218 in 1969 to approximately 737 in 1976. The Ano Nuevo Island colony produced 188 pups in 1968 and 640 in 1976. The number of pups born on Southeast Farallon Island during the years from 1972 to 1976 was 1, 2, 17, 35 and 60. Thus, the mean percentage increase in pups produced annually on these four rookeries was 12.5, 14.3, 12.5, and 25.0.

As of 1977, only two colonies seem to have reached equilibrium numbers—the mother colony on Isla de Guadalupe, and the colony on Islas San

Top, Point Bennett, the western tip of San Miguel Island, about a week before the peak of the breeding season. Elephant seal harems are all along the beach; the dark aggregations are California sea lions. (Photograph by Tom Dohl). Above, a portion of the same beach (B.L.B.)

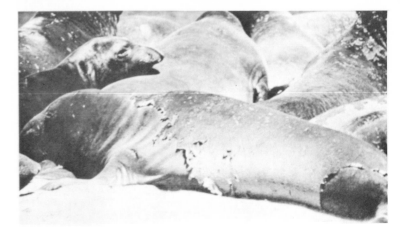

Left, in the crowded harems, bulls sometimes trample pups to death. Below, a female bites an orphan trying to steal milk from her. (K.P., E.F.) At bottom, a male molting during the summer. (B.L.B.)

Benito. Two of the smallest rookeries, Los Coronados and Santa Barbara Island, cannot accommodate many more animals because they lack suitable breeding beaches.

Obviously, the rate of increase in elephant seals since the population minimum in the last century has been extremely high. Numerically, the seals have come back from extation. However, recent evidence suggests that there was a cost incurred when their population was decimated; as a result, current generations of elephant seals may be lacking in adaptability.

Consider the fact that the thousands of seals extant all derive from a handful of ancestors, the few that lived through the carnage wrought by sealers in the last century. Various genetic phenomena characterize passing through a population bottleneck; one of the most conspicuous is a loss of genetic variability. Two principles explain the loss. The first is genetic drift, a genetic change in the population due to random phenomena rather than selection. This is simply a result of most of the population being exterminated. The extermination is presumed to be quite random and arbitrary. Many alleles, or alternate gene forms, are lost from the gene pool, and there is a great reduction in the number of heterozygotes, or animals in which genes from the two parents differ. The other factor, called the "founder principle," refers to the

Right, Islas San Benito, one of the southernmost elephant seal rookeries. (B. L. B.) Below Ano Nuevo Island shortly after the peak of the breeding season. (K. P., E. F.)

fact that the survivors of a severely depleted population contain only a small fraction of the total genetic variability of the parent population. The animals that survive extation become the founders of the future population.

One of my graduate students, Michael Bonnell, tested the elephant seal population for genetic variability. The test for genetic variation that he used is based on variation in amino acid sequences of specific proteins, as determined by gel electrophoresis. The procedure derives from the fact that proteins differing in electrical charge or molecular weight move at different rates through a gel in an electrified field. The differential movements are detected by dying the proteins. Bonnell, and Robert Selander, who did the analysis, looked for genetic variations in blood proteins, enzymes that are important in metabolism. Using seal blood samples collected at five different rookeries—Ano Nuevo Island, San Miguel Island, San Nicolas Island, Isla de Guadalupe, and Islas San Benito—they looked for polymorphisms, or different genetic forms, in 20 proteins at 23 loci. Polymorphisms are a reflection of underlying genetic differences in the loci encoding the structure of the proteins. Familiar polymorphisms are the number of different genetic forms that underlie eye color in a human population.

One measure of results is the mean number of animals in the sample having different alleles at one locus, or, to put it another way, the mean number of heterozygotes in the sample. In general, one finds 10 to 18% in vertebrates and 25 to 40% in invertebrates. Specifically, one finds an index of 15% in crickets, approximately 6% in rodents and in man, and 13 to 38% in fruit flies. Bonnell and Selander found no polymorphisms in the entire elephant seal sample that they analyzed. All proteins were monomorphic. At each genetic locus, the same two genetic forms were found in every individual that was examined. At each of the 23 loci examined, the 125 seals looked like identical twins, or rather like siblings from the same fertilized egg. The lack of polymorphisms in such a large sample, in an analysis of such a large number of proteins in this many locations, is odd, to say the least.

The southern elephant seal, *M. leonina,* the northern elephant seal's closest relative, provides a perspective on this situation. This antarctic species had a similar history of exploitation during the

last century, but its population before and after exploitation was larger in number and broader in range and it was not so severely decimated as the seals in the northern hemisphere. McDermid's analysis of southern elephant seal blood revealed approximately 3% polymorphisms, five polymorphisms among 18 proteins in 42 individuals from Macquarie Island. Genetic variation in other pinnipeds is slightly higher, ranging from 3 to 6% polymorphisms, but generally lower than in terrestrial mammals. These data suggest strongly that the extreme population reduction of the northern elephant seal was very important in bringing about the current state of impoverished genetic variability.

Several other factors may have been important in decreasing the effective population size of the northern elephant seal and in bringing about genetic fixation. One important factor was inbreeding. When the population was reduced to a few survivors, inbreeding had to occur—the animals could breed only with closely related individuals. When inbreeding occurs, recessive genes are more likely to come together in the homozygous condition and thus get exposed to selection. Many such genes are deleterious. Because of this, a condition develops which is called "inbreeding depression," a loss in fitness due to severe inbreeding. This is manifested by loss of fertility, growth anomalies, and metabolic disturbances.

Another factor relating to genetic fixation,

Top, two very young males play-fighting. (B. L. B.) Above, two adults battling. Left, a subadult male elephant seal. (K. P., E. F.)

153

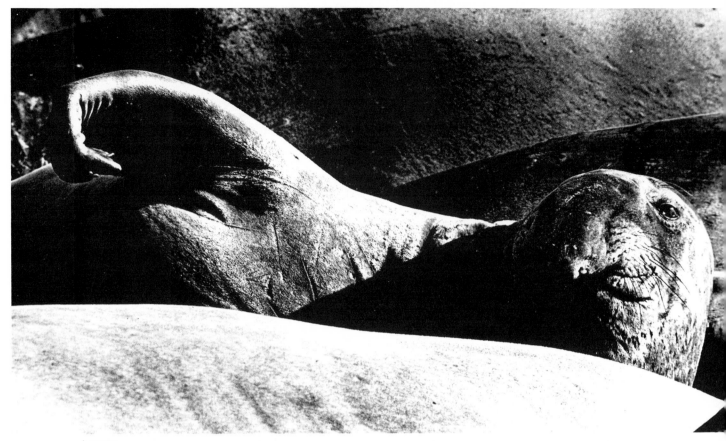

specific to northern elephant seals, is that males are extremely polygynous. A few males do most of the mating, thus intensifying the inbreeding. For example, one male may inseminate all of the females in a harem of 100 or more females, and he may monopolize breeding in this way for four or more breeding seasons, while all or most of the other males in the colony fail to mate at all. In small groups of females where there is little competition among the few males present, it is conceivable that one male could monopolize breeding even longer. This might have occurred during the period of population minimum. Such a mating system enhances inbreeding because all offspring from one year have the same father. Additionally, since females may copulate at age 2 and give birth for the first time at age 3, father-daughter matings begin to occur after a male has been dominant for 4 years in a row. If he dominates for 7 consecutive years, father-granddaughter matings would occur in the last year. Clearly, because of the manner in which elephant seals breed, inbreeding would be facilitated, particularly when population size is small. This condition, along with the population bottleneck, undoubtedly contributed to the reduction of genetic variability in the entire population which we see today.

So, there are approximately 48,000 northern elephant seals in existence today, and they breed on islands spread out over a 1,000-mile range. But relative to the southern elephant seal, other pinnipeds, and terrestrial animals, the northern elephant seal population is genetically depauparate. It lacks genetic variation. The population has recovered from extation, but apparently in a changed and genetically impoverished state.

It has long been thought that genetic variation enables a population to adapt to environmental fluctuations. G. B. Johnson recently argued that "enzyme polymorphisms (genetic variation) increase fitness by providing a means of metabolically compensating for a varying environment." That is, individuals with multiple molecular forms of an enzyme may be capable of minimizing the effect of changed reaction conditions by adapting to alternate food species. This suggests that the northern elephant seal population may not be as fit as it appears. It may not be able to adjust to a drastic change in the environment. Such a change might simply be a reduction in number of its principal prey. The seals would not have the enzymatic options to utilize different food species in the area.

Consider this possibility in relation to the radical increase in elephant seal numbers. This increase is known as a population flush. In theory, a population flush is followed by a crash. In some cases, this is due to predator-prey oscillations. The

Canadian lynx thrives on its prey, the snowshoe hare, when the latter is abundant. The following year is marked by an increase in the production of predators and a reduction in the number of prey. Bereft of its principal source of food, the lynx population crashes. Similarly, when times are propitious, lemmings overgraze arctic tundra plants and proliferate; later, when the forage becomes scarce, the rodent population plummets. These are classic examples of population cycles in a simple food chain.

Unfortunately, no one knows whether the theory applies to a high trophic level marine mammal like the elephant seal. We simply do not know the complexity of the food web in which it operates. If it feeds primarily on a single food item, like its southern congener the southern elephant seal, which feeds on squid, there could be a problem. Depletion of the principal prey stock could cause the elephant seal population to crash for lack of food unless the seals switch readily to different prey species. Johnson's argument suggests that the genetically impoverished elephant seal may have limited alternatives in this regard, that lack of genetic variability may be instrumental in bringing about a population crash.

Thus, the northern elephant seal population may not be as fit and viable as the obvious increase in numbers leads us to believe. The unusual genetic picture found in this species suggests that we withhold our optimism about the elephant seals' recovery for a while.

The broader implications of this story are obvious. Other species whose numbers have been severely reduced, species such as the California sea otter, the right whale, and the Guadalupe fur seal may also have incurred a similar reduction in genetic variability. Many research questions remain. What does it really mean for a population to lack enzyme polymorphisms? What kind of and how much genetic variation must a population possess in order to adapt to unpredictable environmental fluctuations? Why did the elephant seal recover so quickly in numbers while the Guadalupe fur seal is recovering so slowly? What is the nature of the food web in which these formerly exploited species operate? Studies aimed at answering these questions should be given high priority. ❧

Adult male elephant seal at rest. (K. P., E. F.)

ALL AROUND THE CALIFORNIA REPUBLIC

The surge of prospectors into every region of California during the Gold Rush produced a side-effect more precious than gold. The extraordinary features of the landscape of the state became known quite rapidly. It was partly as a result of this knowledge that many special geographical features were set aside for preservation while still relatively pristine. The rapid increase in population was confined largely to the coast, and the ruggedness of the mountain-desert regions did a good deal to preserve them even before enabling legislation was passed. As a result, California has a respectable proportion of its acreage maintained under one or other jurisdiction committed to taking care of it.

The term "desert" is applied to many kinds of landscapes in addition to the stereotype of barren sand dunes. Technically, it refers to a landscape where the rainfall is below a certain minimum. Many deserts are neither sandy nor barren. The Mohave Desert, in southeastern California, is an upland region of Joshua trees and quartz monzonite outcrops that, together—especially in the region set aside as Joshua Tree National Monument—provide a recreational landscape rich in the visual attractions of unusual rocks and trees with the added stimulation of wide-open vistas. In "Magnificent Desert" (1971), the enjoyable features of this region are described by George F. Jackson, whose articles on caves and landscapes appeared in many magazines throughout his writing career.

In recent years the dramatic activities of some of the volcanoes of the Cascades have obscured awareness of the beauty of these kinds of mountains. This beauty, which has caused many of them to be made into parks, derives not only from the ruggedness of the volcanic landscape, but also from the lush green richness of the plants that grow in the lava-enriched soil of their flanks. An especially fine region for hiking and camping is the land surrounding northern California's volcano, Lassen Peak. The story of this mountain and its eruptions is told, in "The Fires of Lassen" (1962), by Weldon F. Heald, who for many years was one of the most frequently published writers in *Pacific Discovery*.

Not all the special landscapes of California are large or awe-inspiring. Many unusual rock formations have a more intimate beauty, the beauty of delicacy and pattern rather than the beauty of mass and form. One such place is at Salt Point, along the northern coast. Here, an extraordinary series of geological-climatological conditions has weathered the sandstone into a fascinating assemblage of honeycomb-like designs. The same kind of lacelike patterning of the rock surface occurs in other places along the coast, and at a number of places inland, but it is at Salt Point that the water-and-wind etching reaches its peak of refinement. In "Sandstone Sculptures" (1979), the photo story of this landscape is presented by architectural designer Randall Fleming, who has taught at California State University in Hayward.

Along much of the California coast is a special geological formation on such a large scale that it is almost invisible. This is the hundred-foot terrace, a narrow belt of grassy flat land that drops off suddenly to the cliffs just behind the beach. This terrace was itself a beach before the last uplift of the land that left it stranded and permitted the waves to carve a new beach below it. The uplift has been responsible for the creation of a forest as reknowned for its tininess as the redwoods are for their height. This is the pygmy forest of the Mendocino coast, where century-old trees are no taller than bushes. In "Staircase Through Time" (1977), the blend of geology, oceanography, climatology, botany, and soil chemistry that produced this weirdly delicate forest is analyzed by Bruce Finson who, since his retirement as Editor of *Pacific Discovery*, has been devoting as much time to painting the natural world as to writing about it.

There is a portion of San Francisco that most people don't even know is there—and few will ever get a chance to visit. For it is separated from the rest of the city by about 26 miles of water. Far enough into the ocean to be just barely visible against the western horizon on a clear day are the Farallon Islands. A hundred years ago these jagged rocks were frequently visited by workers of the Farallon Egg Company and its energetic competitors, who brought many thousands of murre eggs to market in San Francisco every year. Director Leverett M. Loomis of the California Academy of Sciences recommended that the egging be halted and the islands made into a bird reservation. In "These Are the Farallons" (1967) malacologist Allyn G. Smith, who served on the staff of the Academy for many years, wrote the story of this westernmost portion of the City and County of San Francisco. (During the preparation of this volume, we were unable to make contact with any members of Mr. Smith's family, and we would appreciate hearing from any of them who see this book.)

MAGNIFICENT DESERT

George F. Jackson

Photographs by the author

SOUTHERN California's Joshua Tree National Monument is a big, uncluttered, unblighted land of great charm and contrast. Although its campgrounds are often filled, over weekends, with rock-scrambling youngsters and casual sightseers, it has much to offer the desert *aficionado,* the naturalist, the archeologist, the ecologist.

Few areas show the difference between high and low desert as favorably as does the monument, for some portions of it are in the low-lying environment of the Colorado Desert and some portions in the higher Mojave Desert. An elevation range of from 1,000 feet to almost 6,000 feet is the prime reason for its many and varied species of plants and animals.

There are plentiful evidences of prehistoric man as well as more modern Indians; and its striking geological features, its many forms of wildlife, and the variety and richness of its desert vegetation are reasons why some devotees refer to it as "the superlative desert."

Established August 10, 1936 by President Franklin D. Roosevelt, the monument was originally almost twice as large as its present 870 square miles of desert and mountains. Mining interests protested the inclusion of certain areas in the eastern portion and, in 1950, the park was reduced. Today it seems safe from further attrition except for the unthinking vandalism of some visitors.

The National Park Service has established a number of excellent self-guiding nature trails, including a recent 18-mile geological motor tour. Most of the monument remains a wilderness, little changed from its natural state. There are no telephones, electricity, or similar facilities. Visitors must bring their own water supply and firewood, although there is a water station in the central area. The number of weekend campers during the winter season is amazing, but most of them never get far away from the easy-to-reach main points of interest, which probably pleases the hikers, climbers, and those interested in other aspects of the splendid unsullied desert environment.

The plants of the region tell the story of its life zones, low desert or high desert. Up to approximately 3,000 feet, creosote bush *(Larrea tridentata)* is a low desert indicator, along with

Striking outcrops of light-gray or pinkish quartz monzonite, above, dot the north-central part of Joshua Tree National Monument. These rocks solidified perhaps 150 million years ago, when molten rock intruded into the older Pinto gneiss.

the smoke tree, the ocotillo, the palo verde tree, and the cottonwood tree. The jumping cholla cactus *(Opuntia bigelovii)* is a sort of transitional plant, occurring in both deserts. In the Cholla Cactus Garden this sharp-pointed shrub is seen to its best advantage, some specimens growing to a height of eight feet. There is a self-guiding nature trail, and informational booklets are available here.

In sharp contrast to the surrounding desert, there are oases where underground springs keep fine stands of native California fan palms *(Washingtonia filifera)* and other trees alive and green. Two of the oases may be reached by car, the others by hiking.

If there is an indicator plant for the high desert it is the Joshua tree *(Yucca brevifolia),* which normally occurs between 3,000 feet and about 4,500 feet. Higher yet are juniper, pinyon, and scrub-oak woodlands. Undoubtedly the most spectacular botanical feature of the monument, the Joshua tree sometimes grows as tall as 40 feet. It was named by pioneering Mormons who thought its strange-looking erratic branches resembled the Biblical leader Joshua lifting supplicating arms to Heaven. It is often confused with the Mojave yucca *(Yucca schidigera).* Although both plants are often found growing in proximity, the Mojave yucca prefers lower elevations. A close examination will soon show the difference between them: the Joshua tree leaves are about ten inches long with fine teeth along their edges, the leaves of the Mojave yucca are much longer and have an abundance of light-colored fibers along their edges.

Left above, the Joshua tree, for which the monument is named; and left, California palms at the oasis of 29 Palms. Above, some of the fallen boulders in the north-central region resemble fanciful animals.

To some visitors the Joshua tree seems to be good only for dramatic photographs, but for many of the desert's dwellers it is a sort of Eden in itself. It provides food, shelter, and protection for innumerable creatures, among them many species of birds, lizards, and small mammals. One of these is the rare and quite small desert night lizard *(Xantusia vigilis),* which is almost entirely dependent on the yuccas, living elsewhere with great difficulty, if at all. Usually nocturnal, this lizard has vertical pupils and no eyelids. The Joshua tree was used by Indians for a host of things: they ate the flower buds (they have a high sugar content and were often roasted and given to children as candy), also the flowers themselves, and from the ripe fruit they made an intoxicating drink. Fiber from the leaves made rope, baskets, mats, and footwear. The roots made black or red dye, medicine, and soap.

This giant among yuccas does not have annual rings, like typical trees, so it is difficult to determine its age. From February to April is has lovely, greenish-white blossoms in clusters from eight to 14 inches long, but unfortunately does not bloom each spring. When it does, however, camera enthusiasts come in droves to photograph the flowers.

The Joshua is most prevalent in the west-central part of the monument and here also are the fantastic outcrops of massive, light-grey and pinkish quartz monzonite so intriguing to visitors and rock-scramblers. Monzonite is a form of granite and originally was magma which was pushed upward toward the surface and intruded into the

This six-inch high dike, in a very remote section of the monument, runs for one-half mile over hills and through valleys.

Above, this area was a much-used Indian campground. Artifacts and mortar holes are plentiful, and the interior of the niche at the left is covered with soot from campfires. Nearby is a water source.

159

much older, overlying Pinto gneiss. Before it reached the surface it cooled and crystallized. Eventually uplifts, weathering, and erosion stripped away the top layer of gneiss, exposing the monzonite and leaving the fantastic rocky areas, boulders, and large outcrops as we see them today. This portion of the monument is the most visited, and winter weekends are likely to find all campgrounds filled. Here is the "Wonderland of Rocks," providing fine rock-sheltered camping, and "Hidden Valley," a reputed rustler's hide-out that is exactly what the name implies: a rock-enclosed, crater-like valley with a more-or-less level, forested floor. If rustlers did operate here they couldn't have found a better hiding place for themselves and their stolen cattle.

In the remote and arid Pinto Basin Wash archeologists have found evidence of extensive campgrounds of early man. Along with crudely fashioned, distinctively shaped, stone weapon points, split camel and horse bones have been found in proximity to very old fire remains. It has not been definitely established that the association is contemporary. A rough, unconfirmed date of 10,000 years has been suggested for the sites. That the artifacts are actually this old is open to question, but it has been established that they are of great antiquity. The weapon points found are too large to have been used with the bow and arrow so it is assumed that they were made for use with the atlatl, the spear thrower that preceded the bow. The spear points—thick, with rounding-convex faces, narrow shoulders, and a broad stem with concave base—have been named "Pinto Basin Points."

Today the old encampment location is in one of the last great desert valleys unblemished by man. It is not marred by even the slightest sign of civilization. Looking over it one is hard-pressed to believe that it was once a verdant valley with a sparkling stream, a lake, and stands of trees and green vegetation.

When the first white men—mostly prospectors in search of gold—ventured into what is now the monument area they found it was occupied periodically by roving bands of Serrano, Cahuilla, and Chemehuevi Indians, all members of the Shoshonean branch of the great Uto-Aztecan family. These were the peoples who left the many pictographs, petroglyphs, bedrock mortars, and the strange "spirit sticks" along an old trail that wandered from southwest to northwest through the park. The trail twisted and turned as it followed the easy contours of the land, leading from one water source to another. Then, as now, water was scarce most of the year, but the Indians had mastered the art of survival well. Their campsites were always near, but not in close proximity to, springs or natural "tanks" where pools collected after rains. Their reason for not camping too close to a water source was simply common sense, for too many humans would have frightened away any animals that came to drink, and fresh meat was not one of the Indians' daily fares.

Most of the known pictographs are concentrated in the striking outcrops of monzonite that occupy the Wonderland of Rocks area. Because this rock weathers rapidly it is thought that the drawings still visible were made in reasonably recent times, probably from 1000 to 1900 A.D. Archeologists believe that a few of the petroglyphs chiseled by the Indians may cover a broader span of time than the rock paintings and some may have been carved as long as two to six thousand years ago, thus going back almost as far as the Pinto Man era. Most, however, are not that old and are obviously of recent origin.

An unusual custom of these desert Indians was their practice of leaving "spirit sticks" at the entrances to small caves and rock shelters, apparently as spiritual guardians of items hidden in the recesses of the rock. The first archeological survey of the region was made by Mr. and Mrs. William H. Campbell and in 1931 the Southwest Museum published a monograph on their findings. Reprinted in 1963, the paper is titled "An Archeological Survey of the Twentynine Palms Region." In it Mrs. Campbell says that the sticks "were nearly always a guide to a cache and for convenience we have named them 'spirit sticks.' Their meaning was very obscure and to a large extent remains so yet, but their presence was an unfailing guide to Indian occupation." Propped vertically against ceilings, the sticks were of almost every kind of wood, usually with the upper end forked. No utilitarian purpose for the sticks was found, but they were always associated with artifacts, for "everywhere we searched for things archeological these impressive sticks grimaced at us . . . one has to be in the actual presence of the sticks to understand their impressiveness. To come upon them looming up in the half-light of a dim cave is actually startling at times. That they were used until a very recent date is evidenced by the fact that we found one or two that appear to have been chopped from the parent tree by a steel instrument, while most of them were broken off or cut with a flint knife." Modern Indians are very reluctant to talk of the sticks, or else profess no knowledge of their purpose.

The National Park Service knows of no spirit sticks remaining *in situ* in Joshua Tree National Monument today, but after long and careful searching along the old Indian trail, the writer found two small caves with what seem to be original spirit sticks in place. They were not disturbed, and the cave's location was turned over to the monument authorities.

The different kinds of wildlife and the means by which they survive in the monument's deserts and rocky outcrops are a constant surprise to many visitors. Tell the average camper that 230 species of birds have been sighted in the area, that 167 of them are permanent residents, that there are also 42 species of mammals, 36 species of reptiles, and five species of amphibians living there and he will undoubtedly be astonished. These wild creatures have so adapted to life in this desert that some of them would have difficulty in surviving elsewhere.

Probably the animals most commonly seen are the side-blotched lizard (*Uta stansburiana*) and the antelope ground squirrel (*Ammospermophilus leucurus*). Both animals are found throughout the

Indian relics. Left above, deer painted in a niche on the wall of a cave. Right above, nine-inch-deep bedrock mortar and pestle. Below left, a decorated cave about fifteen feet up a cliff. Below right, spirit sticks inside the entrance to a cave.

monument, usually around campgrounds where they have become quite tame in the presence of humans and dart around watching for discarded food scraps.

The monument's largest animal is the desert bighorn sheep *(Ovis canadansis nelsoni)*. Wary and shy, they avoid all areas of high visitor concentration. If seen they are impressive, especially the rams with their great, curved horns. They are definitely wilderness animals, but occasionally wander into areas frequented by man, possibly in search of water. Much has been written about the curiosity of the bighorn sheep, but studies have shown what seems to be curiosity actually is wariness and suspicion. The number of bighorns in the monument is not large, probably less than 500, but the herds have had protection for a number of years and have probably reached their limit of size, considering their forage resources and the water supplies available to them.

Mountain lions are reported to be scarce but the writer and his wife have positive proof that some live there, as we recently surprised a male and female near one of the remote springs. Which of the four of us were most startled is a matter of speculation. We simply saw the pair, then they were gone, bounding over high boulders. There

Many animals live in the monument. Top, a side-blotched lizard. Center, a collared lizard. This is sometimes confused with the leopard lizard; however, it is the only American lizard with two black collars. Above, one of many coyotes in the monument. Their high-pitched serenades may be heard around campgrounds. Right, squirrels are frequently seen around the campgrounds.

was no time to take photographs, except of their footprints.

Some of the desert rodents, especially the kangaroo rat and the pocket mouse, can go through an entire lifetime without ever taking a drink of water. They do this by metabolizing water from the dry seeds which are their staple food. By staying in their burrows during the day and emerging only at night they seldom encounter temperatures that would require intake of fluids. Another interesting rodent is the woodrat *(Neotoma spp.)*, better known as the pack rat, whose nests are found through the monument, from the higher elevations to the lowest. This creature is not a true rat, and as contrasted with his city cousins, which are true rats, he is very clean and does very little damage.

There are 36 species of reptiles in the monument, including the chuckawala *(Sauromalus obesus)*, largest lizard of the region, and a favorite food item of the Indians. The collared lizard *(Crotophytus collaris)* is a very handsome creature living in the rocky areas. The writer has seen both lizards frequently while hiking up the path on Ryan Mountain.

Most of the snakes are night crawlers and, normally, are seldom seen by regular visitors al-though various species occur all over the entire locality. Except for the rattlers all are harmless. Judging by the questions asked Park rangers at the seasonal campfire talks, a great many campers fear every kind of snake, especially the rattlesnakes. The latter are seldom seen around campgrounds, partly because any found by rangers are quickly transported to wilderness sections, and partly because of their secretive habits and their desire to stay as far away from man as possible. Despite innumerable hikes throughout the entire park area, the writer and his wife have never seen a rattlesnake in the monument, and one ranger-naturalist, stationed there many years, has never seen one in his many travels over the entire region. But this does not indicate that there are no rattlesnakes in the locality, it simply indicates their effectiveness in keeping out of man's sight. Miller and Stebbins in their "The Lives of Desert Animals in Joshua Tree National Monument" report five species of rattlesnakes as occurring in Joshua Tree National Monument.

The animals of this unblighted, half-million acre preserve are only one facet of its great charm. It offers something to everyone interested in our natural history and the environment in which we live. It is truly a magnificent desert. ❧

In the distance behind the spindly Joshua tree is snow-covered Mount San Gorgonia, highest mountain in southern California, at 11,845 feet. It is not in the monument, but is about 40 miles distant in this picture.

THE FIRES OF LASSEN

LASSEN PEAK is not a volcano, a geologist told me recently. It's an exceptionally large plug dome, he said. After he had carefully explained the difference, I concluded that a plug dome is simply a volcano that hasn't cleared its throat. In other words, the explosive forces have never been sufficient to blow out the solid lava in the neck. Instead, each eruption has shoved it upward, and a cone of ejected material has collected around this central plug.

Lassen, of course, is a striking exhibit of recent vulcanism. And this discussion about when is a volcano not a volcano stimulated me to learn more about California's famous fire-mountain which was in violent eruption a scant half-century ago. I found it to be a story with plenty of action, thrills and suspense.

Lassen's biography is part of a family history. It is the southernmost of the line of giant dormant volcanoes that crowns the Cascade Range for 600 miles, from northern California to the Canadian border. So the peak is one of that noble company that includes

Above, Lassen Peak from Brokentop Mountain, showing the black lava tongue which spilled down the west slope for nearly 1,000 feet in a 1915 eruption. Right, forests, lakes and meadows now occupy the caldera of ancient Mount Tehama. Looking from the south base of Lassen Peak, over Lake Helen, to Brokentop Mountain.

Weldon F. Heald

Shasta, Hood, Rainier, Baker, and a dozen others. It stands east of upper Sacramento Valley, just north of the wide gap separating the Sierra Nevada from the Cascade Range.

The first chapter of the Lassen story began some 13 million years ago, give or take a couple of million. At that time the Sierra was heaved up to approximately its present height, and the Alps and Himalayas were formed. Along the axis of the Cascades the land surface slipped a couple of hundred feet in an almost straight line. As the earth cracked and buckled, vents and fissures opened up along the entire length of the fault. Volcanic material was blown out from them in explosive eruptions, and vast streams of lava covered the surroundings in successive flows. This went on for thousands of years, and where the vents became established cones built up around them into huge volcanoes. These were the ancestors of the great Cascades peaks of today.

At the southern end of the fault was a large vent and several secondary openings which produced what geologists call the "Lassen Edifice." This was an enormous dome with gentle slopes. Known as shield volcanoes, this type is built up by quiet outpourings of highly liquid lava which spread for many miles in every direction. At its zenith the Lassen Edifice was 50 miles long from north to south and 20 to 35 miles wide, while it probably reached an altitude of at least 11,000 feet. The much eroded, laminated lava flows of this ancient sprawling mountain still form the elevated base upon which stands present-day Lassen Peak.

This vast bygone shield volcano has been named "Mount Tehama" and it reached its climax perhaps five to seven million years ago. Atop the summit dome there probably was a roughly circular cliff-lined caldera a couple of miles in diameter and several hundred feet deep. This fire-pit undoubtedly held a lava lake which periodically spilled over or broke through the rim.

But finally the plutonic forces spent themselves, the lake cooled, and the mountain stopped growing. There followed a long quiet period, lasting thousands of years. Erosion vigorously attacked the dome, channeling its slopes with canyons, breaching the great crater, and reducing its height several thousand feet.

The fires deep within the mountain still smouldered, however, and they eventually flared anew, blasting

PHOTOGRAPHS BY THE AUTHOR

Above, summit of Lassen Peak, 10,453 feet elevation.

Below, Lassen's crater is now filled with the lava plug which was pushed up some 300 feet in the 1914–1917 eruptions.

open a new crater just north of the former caldera rim. This was the infant Lassen Peak. It was then a true volcano and must have been an unusually active one, because the dip of the early lava flows indicate it reached a height of some 12,000 feet in a relatively short time. But once again the subterranean forces weakened and the new volcano either collapsed in a gigantic eruption or was afterwards greatly decimated by erosion. For when the present phase of activity began in recent times, the crater rim was not more than 8,500 feet elevation.

The story of the modern Lassen Peak is one featuring both fire and ice. About two million years ago world climate became cooler and precipitation increased. This was the Ice Age when enormous glaciers ebbed and flowed across the land at least four times. California was too far south to be covered by continuous ice sheets, but tremendous mountain and valley glaciers developed in the Sierra, and the higher parts of the Lassen area supported icefields up to 1,000 feet thick. Glaciers are master sculptors and their grinding action greatly modified the topography by widening and deepening the valleys and planing off the rough edges.

Early in the Glacial period the Lassen vent became active again. But this time the pent-up gases beneath were never powerful enough to blast out the stiff lava neck of the old volcano. Each eruption, however, pushed the plug upward into or above the crater, often several hundred feet at a time. Between eruptions the exposed hardened lava disintegrated and spread outward as talus slopes. These, together with ash, pumice, and cinders blown out from around the plug built up a rather steep-sided cone which is the modern Lassen Peak, 10,453 feet elevation.

Possibly the geologist was being a bit technical when he said that this is not a volcano. But he's correct if we regard it as a special type. Vulcanologist Howel Williams'[*] cross-section of the Lassen area graphically illustrates the difference. The base of the mountain is about two miles across, while the disintegrated lava plug above the throat of the original crater is more than a mile in diameter, and tapers to the summit, over 2,000 feet above. In fact, the lava core forms at least 80 per cent of the entire cone. There are also several other nearby plug domes, such as 9,211-foot Eagle Peak to the south, pushed up during the same period, only on a much smaller scale. Obviously their formation differs greatly from that of conventional volcanoes. The latter are built up by lava flows and ejections from their central craters. Shattered remnants of prehistoric Mount Tehama still stand in a semicircle, three miles across, just south of Lassen Peak. Highest is cliff-guarded Brokentop Mountain, 9,232 feet elevation.

[*] Professor of Geology, University of California, Berkeley.

After a tremendous eruption about 230 years ago, construction work stopped. When first sighted by Captain Arguello's expedition in 1820, and named San José, the mountain was in peaceful repose. In the early 1840's Yankee settlers called it Lassen's Butte, after the famed Danish pioneer, Peter Lassen. Later the name became Mount Lassen and finally officially Lassen Peak.

The area was considered such an outstanding example of recent vulcanism that in 1907 President Roosevelt created Lassen Peak and Cinder Cone national monuments to preserve the most striking phenomena. Cinder Cone is 10 miles northeast of the peak and is an almost perfect small modern volcano, 600 feet high, which was active as late as 1851.

That might have been the end of the story, but Nature had one more surprise punch left. On May 30, 1914, Lassen Peak suddenly burst into violent eruption. The mountain shook and rumbled. The crater belched a mushrooming cloud of smoke, 20,000 feet high, accompanied by explosive ejection of ash, rock, and superheated gases. For three years Lassen Peak was the only active volcano in the United States, and altogether some 300 separate eruptions occurred before the outburst spent itself in 1917. These spectacular pyrotechnics attracted wide attention and the area, including the two former national monuments, was set aside by Congress in 1916 as Lassen Volcanic National Park.

Top, Lassen Peak as seen from Kings Creek Meadows. Lower photo, the devastated area on the north slope of Lassen Peak seventeen years after the explosive eruptions of May 1915. Vegetation has advanced greatly in the last few years.

Today the mountain sleeps once more, but around its flanks are groups of hissing steam vents, bubbling mud pots, boiling lakes, miniature geysers, and other dramatic indications that deep down the fires of Lassen still burn. There are also 120 ancient and recently active craters. The park's 163 square miles comprise not only the varied volcanic exhibits but an outdoor recreation area of rare beauty. There are evergreen forests, lush wildflower meadows, and cascading streams and waterfalls. The western section of the park is traversed by the paved 38-mile Lassen Peak Loop. The road is scenic and revealing, and almost without leaving the family car one can clearly read the dramatic life story of the 13-million-year-old prodigy of vulcanism.

The 1914–1917 eruptions of Lassen Peak have been called, "The final spasm of an old and moribund volcano." Perhaps so. Nobody knows. In the past, flareups have occurred about every 65 years— 1720, 1785, 1850 and 1914. Will there be another outbreak around 1980? At any rate, twenty years from now this remarkably persistent California volcano—or plug dome—will bear watching.

Top, boiling lake in Bumpas Hell, Lassen Volcanic National Park. Lower photo, Bumpas Hell, high on the southeast slope of Lassen Peak, is a 10-acre area of mud springs, boiling pools and hissing steam vents.

A steam vent or fumerole on the south slope of Lassen Peak.

Right, Brokentop Mountain, 9,236 feet altitude, is a ragged remnant of the great prehistoric Mount Tehama, ancestor of Lassen Peak.

SANDSTONE SCULPTURES

Photo Story by Randall Fleming

APPROXIMATELY fifty million years ago, during the Eocene epoch, the sandstones that are now visible at Salt Point State Park were deposited. The continuing interaction of the sandstones and the sea on this portion of the Sonoma coast has produced a sculpture-scape worthy of its fifty-million-year heritage.

The formations appear to be the work of a possessed sculptor with unlimited energy. Large sections of sandstone define room-sized spaces along the headlands. Within these rooms toadstool-like concretions stand on sandstone pedestals, and softer sandstones are carved into smooth, sensuous shapes. Spreading among the sandstones are honeycombed fretworks, appearing as the petroglyphs of a silent culture.

Whether a sculptor be human or otherwise, form is in part determined by the material and the tools used to shape the material. The Salt Point forms are determined by the characteristics of the sandstone plus the carving action of wind and sea.

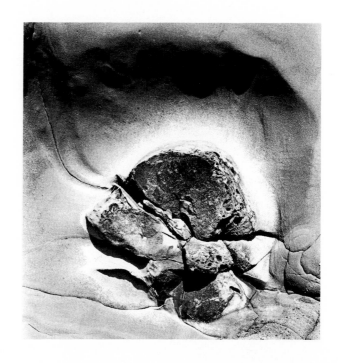

At Salt Point, California is an extensive beach-frontage of extraordinarily-eroded sandstone. Left, in the foreground are the honeycomb-fretworks of differentially-eroded *tafoni*. Top, a partially exposed concretion. Above, concretions on pedestals.

Left, sensuously-eroded striations of thin strata of sandstone. Below, two examples of *tafoni,* the softer parts scoured out by water and windborne sand to leave the hard ridges standing out boldly.

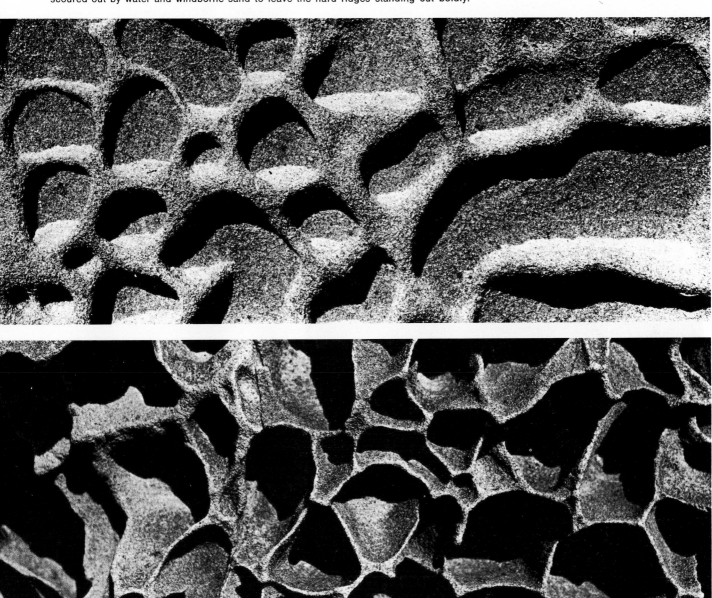

Salt Point has a mix of sandstones with varying hardness. The softer sandstone erodes readily, yielding soft, rounded, undulating forms. The harder sandstones offer greater resistance to weathering. It is this differential weathering at the point of interaction between the harder and softer sandstones that has created many of the exceptional forms at Salt Point.

The process of differential weathering has created the concretion-topped pedestal formations. The concretions were originally formed within the sandstone mass. Mineralized solutions chemically precipitated within the rock, often forming around a nucleus that differed from the enclosing body. This created a formation harder than the surrounding sandstone. As the sandstone was eroded, the concretion was exposed. The concretion's greater resistance to weathering shielded the sandstone beneath the concretion, thus creating the pedestals.

Perhaps the most intriguing forms at Salt Point are the honeycomb-like fretworks or *tafoni.* These forms are also more difficult to explain. Most likely the fretworks represent a mix of processes, including those of differential weathering,

The variations in deposition, cementation, and erosion of the sandstone produce a great variety of shapes, textures, and sculptures at Salt Point. Left above, layers of sandstone. Left, honeycomb weathering. Above, monumental sculpture.

preferential cementation along a system of intersecting fractures, salt crystallization, and wind erosion. Sandstone consists of cemented sand grains. As with concretions, some bodies are cemented harder than others. The carving action of the wind and sea removes the more weakly cemented sand grains, leaving behind a network of more toughly mineralized calcareous sandstone. Also, the crystallization of salts evaporated from the sea water can exert sufficient pressure to loosen sand grains. Once a pit begins to form, wind-powered sand grains scour out the pits, furthering the development of the fretworks.

The harder and softer sandstones were also critical in determining the fate of the Salt Point formations at the hands of man. At the turn of the century, the harder Salt Point sandstone was quarried, and shipped to San Francisco to be used as building stone. Fortunately the softer and more sculptural sandstones were not disturbed, and remain to be enjoyed today. ❧

STAIRCASE THROUGH TIME

Bruce Finson

Photographs by the author

ALTHOUGH a forest is often considered to be the ultimate development of tree growth, many of the most distinctive trees of California do not invariably grow in dense, impenetrable forests. Sequoias often develop in parklike groves, with shady esplanades among the trees. Monterey cypresses grow naturally only in a few isolated patches at Point Lobos. And a number of California oaks do not form close associations at all, but exist as individual trees scattered across a savanna landscape, surrounded by meadowlike expanses of sunny grassland. By contrast, several endemic California trees that together do constitute a forest have such an unusual growth habit that their community is not usually regarded as a forest at all. The trees are simply too small to be readily perceived as anything so landscape-encompassing as forest. These trees, pygmy cypress, Bolander pine, and dwarfed bishop pine — along with several shrubs and herbaceous plants largely of the heath family —make up the strange and lovely "pygmy forest" of the Mendocino coast. It is one of the smallest genuine forests in the world.

The pygmy forest is an unsettling place to visit. It certainly does not look like a forest. Nor does it appear as a copse of saplings, small though the trees may be. The place has its own distinctive and somewhat eerie atmosphere. The majority of trees are no more than five or six feet tall, over-topped here and there by an occasional forest giant of ten or twelve feet. In some sections of the forest the trees are no more than knee-high. Yet they are fully mature trees, with cones and catkins hanging from their limbs. Their trunks and branches are gnarled and twisted, their bark split and weathered and half-hidden beneath lichens of many shapes and colors, their branches misty with hanging moss. These trees look old, worn, mysterious. Their ancient aspect, together with their diminutive size, gives the walker in these woods the feeling of having suddenly stepped through a dimensional discontinuity, and come out among the primal wildness of a radically smaller world.

Although the pygmy forest is a quiet place, it is not at all gentle or restful. The trees are stiff-branched, and look as if they would stand tensely

Above, morning fog enhances the mysterious quality of the ancient pygmy forest of Mendocino, where groves of tiny conifers have been growing in an unchanged climax association for possibly half a million years.

against any breeze. The ground is hard, sparsely covered with mosses, streaked whitely with mineral salts. There is little of obvious aesthetic appeal here. One does not wander blithely through these woods, or rest quietly beneath the boles. One stands and wonders, and feels the strangeness of all things. As with many more-or-less barren places, it is easy, here, to wonder not only how this forest came to be, but how anything organic comes to be, in the midst of the deathy mineral world. To stand in such a place and look about is like suddenly discovering oneself at the farthest edge of life, having unaccountably been granted a rare opportunity to look beyond.

And yet, for all its strangeness, the pygmy forest is not at all abnormal. It is perfectly normal for its ecological situation. True, the combination of small size with mature appearance is so odd as to seem the result of special conditions preventing normal growth. Yet the strangest thing about the pygmy forest is not simply that it is normal, but that these tiny trees constitute a climax forest, and are the inevitable result of an orderly evolutionary sequence. This sequence includes a series of co-evolutionary changes in the soil and the plants, mutually interacting under the persistent dominating influence of heavy annual rainfall and continually rising land. The result of these influences is a climax forest so anomalous as to be spectacular —if the diminutive can be said to be spectacular. Here is a climax forest that is the utter opposite of

Left, the flat seaside grassland, seen here across the mouth of Jughandle Creek, is the first of the series of marine terraces. About 100 feet in elevation and roughly 100,000 years old, it represents the first stage in the evolution of the pygmy forest landscape. The present fifth terrace looked like this 400,000 years ago. (Photograph by Barbara J. Blubaugh.) Above, below the first terrace, visible from the beach, is the bedrock of the pygmy forest, graywacke sand stone of the Franciscan formation.

177

Above, looking up from the first terrace—grassland—toward the second—bishop pine forest. The cliff that formed the front of the second terrace 200,000 years ago has been eroded to a gentle slope. Right, salal is one of several plants of the region common on the pygmy forest floor. Far right, a stand of mature, though short (six feet) pygmy cypresses, a primary tree of the pygmy forest. These trees, though thinner than a person's wrist at the base, are forest venerables perhaps a century old

the tall and lavish growth that is the usual state attained by woody plant succession. Such a reversion from the usual botanical procession provokes inquiry as to its occasion.

The extraordinary aspect of the pygmy forest is most thoroughly comprehended in terms of the geology of the region. Thus, the story of the trees' dwarfing begins not among these stunted, sickly-looking saplings that barely cover a mineral-clogged substrate, but 500 feet below and half a million years ago, down on the Mendocino coast at a time when the pygmy forest terrain was rugged ocean beach devoid not only of trees but even

grass. The Mendocino coast is a remote and dramatic place—windy and cloudswept and rainy, and lonely with the special loneliness found only at the edge of a continent fronting half a world of ocean. Here, round and forested mountains rise gently, close to the sea. Pacific winds, heavy with moisture drawn up from the ocean into dark clouds, push against the tree-covered hills and drop their rain. Under these dense downpours, rock erodes quickly into soil and forests grow thickly. Short quick rivers drain lush canyons and run siltily down to the surf.

Behind the narrow beaches low cliffs rise.

Atop the cliffs, long narrow meadows run along the coast like beaches of sand. And the meadows are indeed beaches—or were. They are fossil beaches, remnants of a time when the land was lower in relation to the sea. These fossil beaches stretch intermittently for hundreds of miles. Together, they are known as the "hundred-foot-terrace." Along the Mendocino coast, several such terraces—each behind the next—form a giant staircase on the land, with risers (old beach cliffs) of perhaps a hundred feet, and treads (old beaches) a quarter to a half mile wide. These terraces stretch back and up, and back and up again,

to the pygmy forest and beyond. Such a series of progressively older marine terraces is evidence that again and again the surf has carved into the coast to form beaches, and again and again the land has risen to strand those beaches.

Each of these terraces is older, by some hundred thousand years, than the one below it. On any one terrace the soil is more thoroughly modified, by weathering and plant decomposition, than on the terrace below, until, at the pygmy forest, a stable condition is attained. Along with the changes in the soil from one terrace to the next, the plant life changes also. The first terrace is covered with coastal grassland. On the second is the regional forest of redwoods and bishop pines. And on the higher terraces, pygmy forest grows.

Although any plant community is perfectly adapted to its physical environment (or it wouldn't be there), it is not always obvious how the vegetation and the landscape have developed in relation to each other. But here on the Mendocino coast, the plant succession from terrace to terrace is more obviously linked with the geological succession than in many other watersheds. On this series of wave-cut terraces the story of land and the story of life cohere as a single ecological unit.

The land is sandstone. It is the same gray sandstone that occurs all along the California coast. It was formed from Sierra Nevada granite, eroded and washed down to the sea bottom, then again congealed into rock. Since this sandstone was formed, the edge of the land has risen slowly but repeatedly as the continent of North America pushed west and overrode the Pacific seabed. At any moment during the past million years, the exact line of meeting between land and sea has been the result of this recurrent uplift, combined with the falling and rising of the sea during glacial and interglacial eras.

Whenever the glaciers melted the sea would rise more quickly than the land was uplifting, and the slowly rising surf would carve into the land, creating a gently sloping underwater terrace and a narrow sandy beach backed by a low cliff. (This is exactly the process that is occurring at the present time along not only the Mendocino coast but also much of California.) During the next glaciation the sea level would slowly fall, and the retreating waves would deposit sandstone-based gravel and sand on the emerging terrace to depth of 20 or 30 feet. Had the land not been uplifting, the ocean would then have covered the beach terrace again during the next interglacial sea-rise. But the land continued its upthrust, carrying the gravel-covered terrace high above the waves, and exposing yet another portion of itself to the terrace-biting action of the next interglacial-rising sea.

The giant staircase thus formed consists of almost-level terraces, up to a half-mile wide, just barely sloping toward the sea, separated by slopes that are the eroded remnants of beachback cliffs about a hundred feet high. The terraces are covered with sandstone-derived soils of differing ages and degrees of development. Along the seaward edge of each terrace, just behind its frontage cliff, are dunes formed by the shore-breeze when that terrace was the one just above the beach. The bedrock of the terraces is solid sandstone. This impenetrable foundation blocks deep drainage from the heavy coastal rainfall. As a result, each winter the water table rises. The soil and the tree roots are soaked for months. All winter long the water oozes sluggishly across the barely sloping rock, steadily leaching the soil of soluble nutrients. On the first terrace the proportion of feldspar to quartz in the soil is the same as that of the parent materials, about 18% feldspar—rich in plant nutrients—in a matrix of quartz. But on the upper terraces, where the pygmy forest lives, the feldspar has been dissolved and washed away. The soil is almost totally drained of its original nutrients.

On this geological base has occurred the plant succession that produced the pygmy forest. The fifth terrace is half a million years old, and well-leached, and each lower terrace is about 100,000 years younger. To examine the terrace-by-terrace sequence of soils and plant communities is like entering a doorway in time through which one can descend, step by 100-millenium step, into the ancient landscape. All that is necessary, to see what the pygmy forest landscape was like half a million years ago, is to walk three miles west, 500 feet down, and half a million years into the past.

From the edge of the first terrace one can look down at the beach and watch the sea as it carves the next terrace-to-be. Much of the beach is not sandy but rocky—flat, platelike layers of stratified sandstone. Wherever the surf has abraded the sandstone down to a lower layer there are tidepools rich with anemones, urchins, and starfish. At the seaward edge of the layered rock are dense growths of barnacles and algae. Toward the rear of the beach, sections of the older beach landscape of the first terrace have already been detached by erosion. Atop these, in the little pockets of soil still remaining, grow bright-blooming succulents. The entire beach is a terrace-in-genesis. Someday, perhaps few or many thousands of years hence, the

The conditions of the pygmy forest habitat produce unusual forms. Left, dwarfed bishop pine showing dieback of main trunk with harmful gall formation and secondary trunks. Left below, rhododendron with cluster-like malformation of upper branches. As with the dieback shown at left, this results from constant nutritional deficiency. Below left, the cones of the pygmy cypress are often overgrown with lichens. Right, the dwarfed Bolander pine, like the pygmy cypress, is an endemic form of a tree common in the region (B.J.B.).

rising land or the glacially-falling sea, or a combination, will lift up this beach and expose the wave-hidden extension of the terrace beyond the surf. The retreating sea will blanket the bedrock beneath sand and gravel. Eventually this beach will become the first marine terrace, similar in appearance to the present first, or hundred-foot, terrace.

That terrace, now, is covered with tall grasses and many kinds of coastal wildflowers. It is like a prairie, but a seaside prairie. The soil, as can be seen where its profile is exposed along the cliff, is dark and rich. It has had a hundred thousand years to develop from a feldspar-quartz beach gravel

Above left, the floor of the forest, with standing pool of rainwater that remains for months every winter, soaking the roots of the trees. The hardpan below the surface makes rapid drainage impossible. Right, a leaf-litter tray used in measuring the sparse biomass productivity of this limited habitat. This was one of a series of experiments conducted under the supervision of pedologist Hans Jenny of the University of California, whose researches were responsible for the present understanding of the rock-soil-plant-climate relationships of the forest.

into a soil made fertile by the decomposition of thousands of generations of grasses and soil-enriching, nitrogen-fixing lupines. The soil is rich and the rainfall lavish. And yet few trees grow here. For the soil is rich with one mineral too many. Onshore breezes have deposited salt-laden spray enough to make the soil inhospitable to any but the salt-tolerant plants that have evolved in this saline biosphere. Yet eventually, as this terrace moves upward, and farther from the waves, the heavy coastal rains will leach the salt out of the soil, and this land will become like the present second terrace, a hundred feet higher and half a mile farther from the sea.

The second terrace, another hundred thousand years older, is well forested with redwoods and Douglas firs. The trees grow well on the rich soil formed earlier by the grasses and legumes, soil now cleansed of its salt. The roots of these trees are able to withstand the wintertime soaking of the high water table. But the leaching action of this slowly draining groundwater is continuing. Toward the rear of this terrace, and on the old beachcliff slope leading to the third terrace, the steady leaching has already begun to impoverish the soil, and the redwoods and douglas firs are gradually being replaced by bishop pine, which can survive on a sparser supply of soil nutrients than the other trees require. As the leaching and the rising of the land continue, the second terrace will become more and more like the third, in soil composition and plant growth.

On the third, fourth, and fifth terraces is pygmy forest. The soil, having suffered another one to three hundred thousand years of rainwater leaching, is severely denuded both of the original nutrients contributed by the feldspar, and those deposited by decaying plants. On these terraces the ratio of feldspar to quartz in the soil is only one to a hundred, in contrast to the eighteen to a hundred of the beach gravels and the bedrock from which the soil was formed. As this soil was stripped of its minerals, the vegetation changed. Some trees, such as the bishop pine, developed dwarfed varieties that could come to maturity, and produce viable seeds, when only five to ten feet tall and no thicker than one's wrist. Many of these little trees, although short enough to see over, are a century old. They are twisted and gnarled both from age and from the effects of chronic malnutrition. Still other trees of the pygmy forest are kinds that have evolved here, on this soil. These, the pygmy cypress and the Bolander pine, are the primary trees of the pygmy forest. They developed from ancestors that produced seedlings able to survive, and pass on their survival capabilities, on this highly acid, mineral-deficient soil.

Conditions for growth in the pygmy forest, the conditions that pushed plant evolution toward the puny, are severe and limiting to an extreme. Several soil factors have coalesced to produce conditions conducive to rapid evolution of new sub-

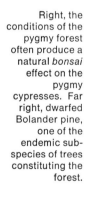

Right, the conditions of the pygmy forest often produce a natural *bonsai* effect on the pygmy cypresses. Far right, dwarfed Bolander pine, one of the endemic subspecies of trees constituting the forest.

species, dwarfing of other trees and shrubs, and elimination of tall-growing trees. First is the leaching regime that has produced a soil severely deficient in potassium, calcium, magnesium, and phosphorus. So extreme is this situation that the forest growth is not only small, but sparse. Perhaps a fourth of the ground surface is bare, and much of the rest is covered with mosses and lichens. The land cannot support a denser growth. In fact, there is so little surplus organic matter in the soil that before there can be new growth, older vegetation must die and decay.

The next condition contributing to the endemic dwarfism is the extremely acid condition of the soil, resulting from millenia of decay of acid-rich pine needles and heath-plant leaves. Different kinds of plants require different pH balances in the soil; so, as the soil gradually becomes more acid, plants requiring more alkaline soil are replaced by acid-tolerant ones.

This extremely acid condition has been responsible for another limiting factor—the impenetrable hardpan that underlays the pygmy forest about a foot below the surface. The acid-tolerant plants produce chemicals that leach the surface soil of its iron and carry it below. There it becomes cemented to the quartz grains to form a hard layer that plant roots cannot penetrate. Thus, with only the upper foot of soil available to their roots, the plants cannot obtain the nutrients that have been washed down to the deeper soil layers, and are limited to the surface supply for their food.

And the final limiting condition—the perched water table that floods the roots for months—results directly from the existence of this hardpan. Rainwater diffuses through hardpan extremely slowly. Much of the water thus remains close to the surface, even forming standing pools, and for months each year soaks the plant roots in an acid-water bath.

These conditions and interactions of soil, climate, and vegetation have produced an ecosystem that is utterly stringent and spartan—but stable. Land and life are here in final balance. In the absence of new geologic or climatic upheavals, further changes are unlikely. No new or migrant species of plants will have much chance to replace those that have evolved here. Although the pygmy pines and cypresses look anything but thriving, they are successfully occupying this terrain. More than that, they are actually the maximum vegetation that can maintain itself on this soil, in this climate. The trees, and their associated shrubs and herbs, maintain soil conditions that favor continued reproduction of their kinds, rather than replacement with other species. Thus the pygmy forest, runty and sickly though it looks, is classified as a climax forest, the final stage of a particular sequence in plant succession. And it has maintained itself in this steady-state condition for a long time. The plant-and-soil association on these Mendocino marine terraces produces pygmy forest as early as the third terrace, and the pygmy forest then maintains itself on the fourth and even the fifth terrace. Thus, the pygmy forest of the fifth terrace is truly ancient. Here the trees have evolved, and endured, for more than a quarter-million years in one of the most intractable of environments.

The evolution of the trees into their present emdemic, dwarfed forms could not have occurred without a parallel evolution of the soil into conditions that not only permitted, but even promoted, this evolution. Nor could the soil have evolved as it did without a corresponding evolution in the landscape on which that soil is based and from which it has developed. And the evolution of the landscape itself is further based on a large-scale evolutionary process of the entire planet. This is the interminably slow, yet sempiternally incessant, clash of tectonic plates that repeatedly joins continents together and rends them asunder, continually modifying the geologic and climatic conditions within which life evolves.

The pygmy forest is thus a superbly elegant example of the foundations, processes, and results of evolution. It is an ongoing natural laboratory of the interaction between organic and inorganic that conditions all existence. Contrary to first appearance, it is not aberrant at all, but is the inevitable result of a coherent developmental process including many mutually-interacting natural forces. And for all its grim and grizzled appearance, the pygmy forest has a harshly haunting appeal that is enhanced by awareness of the conditions within which it has developed and endured. ❧

This beautifully-contorted specimen of pygmy cypress, less than two feet tall, is one of many such fascinating trees to be seen in the pygmy forest. Several areas of pygmy forest still grow along the Mendocino Coast; one of the most completely preserved has been designated Jughandle State Reserve. Located a few miles south of Fort Bragg, it contains virtually an entire water-shed, including a complete sequence of five marine terraces.

THESE
ARE
THE
FARALLONS

Allyn G. Smith

ON CLEAR days from almost any high vantage point in the San Francisco Bay area, a small group of islands can be seen by looking due west. These are the Farallon Islands — "farallon" being an old Spanish nautical term for any jutting rock or ocean cliff of importance to navigation. Few who have seen these islands know that they are an offshore portion of the City and County of San Francisco, presently under the jurisdiction of the United States Coast Guard.

The Farallons have a fascinating history beginning early in the nineteenth century. For well over a hundred and fifty years these small, barren, almost forbidding chunks of granite played a significant part in the commercial life of the San Francisco Bay area. They play a different but equally important role today, being directly on the shipping lanes to Pacific ports.

There are seven main islands in the Farallon group. Largest, and the only inhabited one, is the Southeast Farallon, on which the lighthouse and much navigational and weather recording equipment is located. This island is about 27 miles west of Point Bonita and is roughly a mile long and half a mile wide. The Southeast Farallon is at times almost two islands, the eastern portion being cut by a deep surge channel subject to heavy wave action at high tide although passable on foot when the tide is low. The tallest point, on which the lighthouse has been built, is 350 feet above mean sea level. A Coast Guard station is located on a flat area toward the south end. There are no major docks or piers. Landings are made in small tenders operating from Coast Guard supply ships anchored offshore. When the weather is stormy and the waves are high, landing is a hazardous experience.

Top, air view of the Southeast Farallon. (Call-Bulletin photo, courtesy of San Francisco Public Library.)

Above, sketch of just-completed lighthouse by Lieutenant W. P. Trowbridge. (From an 1855 U. S. Coast Survey Report.)

Some early accounts of the Farallons say they
are volcanic, but they have since been learned to
be an outcrop of an immense dike of granite. On
the Southeast Farallon three wave-cut terraces are
evident, the ones at the upper levels accompanied
by ancient sea-caves, indicating a considerable uplift of the island in relatively recent geologic
time. At the present sea level new caves are being
excavated, some of them quite large. For details
of the geology of the Farallons the reader is referred to Dr. G Dallas Hanna's account in the
"Geologic Guidebook of the San Francisco Bay
Area", published in 1951 by the California Division of Mines as Bulletin 154. This report was
prepared by Dr. Hanna shortly after he and I spent
a week on the Southeast Farallon in May of 1949,
exploring its geology and natural history.

In early accounts, the complete lack of fresh
water on the island is generally inferred. This is
not strictly correct. In the *Overland Monthly* for
September of 1892, Charles S. Green states:
There is, I believe, but one spring on the Farallon—
a mineral spring in a little bight on the north side,
within a few feet of the breakers. The water has a
slightly yellowish color, such as would be given a glass
of clear water by adding a teaspoonful of strong tea.
Its taste is very pleasant, slightly acid, and a little

puckery. It requires no analysis to show that there
is iron in it, and there is an entire absence of suggestion of sulphur. The effect is mildly aperient, and
the dwellers on the island prize it highly. They say
one can drink it in unlimited quantities in hot weather
without the distress that rainwater causes.

We looked for this spring and finally located
it; the flow was quite small. It was in the middle
of an area where sea lions had been hauling up
onto the beach for some time, leaving such a mess
that tasting a sample of the spring water offered
little attraction, even to an inquiring scientist. Rainwater no doubt furnished an occasional source for
the early sealers and bird-eggers but this had to be
supplemented, as it is today, with an assured supply
from the mainland coupled with adequate tank
storage on the island. In addition, the Coast Guard
long ago poured concrete aprons on some of the
accessible slopes to channel and store rainwater for
emergency use.

The Southeast Farallon is probably the only
island in the group where vegetation of any kind
can find a foothold. Even so, there are no native
trees or shrubs. In discussing the botany of the
island in 1892, J. W. Blankenship listed as native
only ten low-growing plants, a rare fern, an abundant moss, and four species of lichen. He also

listed seventeen introduced plants, some of which were well established and others localized only in gardens. This latter list has no doubt been much enlarged since. The most striking plant we noted in the spring of 1949 was the Farallon weed (*Baeria maritima*), which grew in thick stands two to four feet high in favorable locations. According to reports, this plant was used by older Farallon inhabitants as "greens" and as a salad constituent. It is the primary mainstay of the introduced, bothersome rabbit population.

Writing in 1858, George Davidson, navigation expert, boundary surveyer, and later President of the California Academy of Sciences, attributed the discovery of the Farallons to Ferrelo in 1543. However, Henry R. Wagner stated in his 1928 account of Spanish voyages along the northwest coast of America that there was no direct evidence for this belief. Thus the real discoverer of the Farallons is not certainly known.

In June, 1578, Sir Francis Drake and some of his crew of the *Golden Hinde* landed on the Southeast Farallon, the first men to set foot there. After careening and refitting his ship in Drake's Bay or vicinity, he set sail for England, stopping at the island, as his journal says, to take "such provision as might competently serve our turne for awhile." He reported that the island had a "plentiful and great store of seals and birds", of which he no doubt killed some for fresh meat to be used during his long voyage. Drake named the group "The Islands of Saint James", the first name to be bestowed on them.

Drake's name was never accepted. Neither was Vizcayno's name, the "Isle Hendida", for what was probably the Southeast Farallon. The most appropriate name, a shortened version of which we now use, is reported to have been given by Juan Francisco Bodega y Quadra in 1775. He called them "Los Farallones de los Frayles" — the Headlands of the Friars — in honor of the Spanish padres who founded Mission Dolores in San Francisco.

Perhaps the first human use of the Farallons was as navigational aids. But about the beginning of the nineteenth century they began to assume commercial importance. Russia had at this time formed the Russian-American Fur Company, which dominated the fur trade in the north. The sea otter, whose beautiful fur was in great demand in Russia and China, was being hunted actively and with considerable profit by the Russians. Native Kodiak islanders, or Aleuts, were employed for this because they were particularly adept at spearing sea otters from their two-place kayaks. Fur seals were also discovered on the Farallons, and were killed by the tens of thousands by hunters stationed on the islands.

There seems little doubt about the great size of the original Farallon fur seal herd, but within a space of thirty years it was completely exterminated. The species of fur seal that occupied the islands has never been determined. Neither the skin nor the skeleton of a Farallon fur seal is preserved in any museum, so far as is known. The seal might have been the northern species now

Left, South Landing and Sugar Loaf. The prominent arch is a remnant of an ancient, uplifted sea-cave. *Above,* Landing operation, South Landing. A winch lifts the small tender 50 feet up onto a concrete platform. (Call-Bulletin photo, courtesy of San Francisco Public Library.)

Top, an egger being attacked by birds. *(Harpers Magazine,* April, 1874.) *Above,* early photo of eggers on the Farallons. *Below,* California murre eggs—on bare rock—and Brandt cormorant eggs in a nest of seaweed. (Photos by O. J. Heinemann from his photo collection at the California Academy of Sciences.)

protected on the Pribilof Islands; it might have been the Guadalupe fur seal; or it might have been a different species or subspecies. Adele Ogden, in her research into the Pacific coast fur industry, says the Farallon fur seals were smaller and blacker than the Alaskan fur seals, with coarser fur that made them less valuable. During our visit in 1949 we hoped to verify this indication that they might have been a separate species, but our results were not conclusive. While we were able to collect many skulls, teeth, and various other bones from an old killing field buried under several inches of decomposed granite soil near one of the present buildings, expert examination indicated that these were the remains of young sea lions.

No one knows how many sea otters were killed for their fur around the Farallons. Once they were thought to have been completely exterminated, as none had been seen for many years. However, discovery of a small herd off the Monterey coast a few years ago, and the subsequent increase in their numbers under strict protection, has been a source of good news to conservationists. The story of the sea otter almost but not quite parallels that of the passenger pigeon, but with a happier conclusion. It is well told by Adele Ogden in "The California Sea-Otter Trade, 1784-1848", published by the University of California press in 1941.

The destruction of the once great herds of fur seals and sea otters and the departure of the Russians closed a significant era in Farallon history. Soon, however, the islands became the center for another profitable industry. The Farallons have been noted for rookeries of sea birds since Sir Francis Drake's visit in 1578. Principal among the birds nesting on the Farallons is the California Murre (once called a guillemot). The murre is a handsome bird, about the size of a large duck, mostly black with a white breast. It sits erect, usually with its beak pointed upward. Its egg is large for the size of the bird, being almost as large as an egg of a goose or turkey. The egg is olive-greenish, variously blotched, and tapers toward one end. If dislodged from its position on a narrow ledge it rolls in a tight circle without falling off.

In the gold-rush days, hen's eggs were in short supply and were expensive. It was not long before some enterprising individual discovered that a fresh murre egg rivalled a hen's egg in quality. By 1850 the robbing of the murres' nesting ledges on the Farallons for the San Francisco market had become well organized. Almost from the beginning the industry was dominated by the Farallon Egg Company. However, there was soon an egg

Above, portion of a Brandt cormorant rookery on the Southeast Farallon. *Left,* a mother Farallon cormorant. *Right,* the western gull, a dominant Farallon resident. (Photos by Paul J. Fair.) *Below,* a group of tufted puffins (sea-parrots) with a California murre. *Bottom,* California murres on a Farallon ledge, with a western gull looking on for an opportunity to dine on their eggs. (O.J.H.)

The Farallon Light, which warns ships approaching the Golden Gate away from the dangerous, rocky islands. (O.J.H.)

war. The profit was too great not to cause keen competition. Highjackings of small boats bound from the Farallons with cargoes of murre eggs were frequent. The conflict grew so intense that guns were used and lives were threatened. Finally the U.S. Government had to step in to keep the peace.

Although the toll of the nine years of operations prior to 1873 had averaged 25,000 dozen murre eggs, it fell off thereafter to 15,000 dozen. Fearing the effect of the depredations on the murre rookeries Leverett M. Loomis, then Director of the California Academy of Sciences, visited the island in 1896 and found that the egg production had been reduced to 7645 dozen. He realized the murres were in danger of extinction. The alarm he raised led to federal action. In the following year the traffic in eggs was forbidden and the islands were placed under the jurisdiction of the Lighthouse Board, a branch of the Treasury Department. And on February 27 ,1909, an executive order by President Taft made the islands a bird reservation. In 1918 jurisdiction over the islands was transferred to the Department of Agriculture.

Summarizing this story in his book, "Birds of California", W. Leon Dawson states:
The infamous egg traffic is a thing of the past, but the Farallon rookeries have never recovered. Birds, which in fifty years had been called upon to furnish the market some twelve million fresh eggs, were not

able, in spite of protection, to cope with new foes nor to stand up under the onslaughts of an ancient enemy, the sea gull, himself a notable beneficiary of protection.

When I visited the Southeast Farallon in 1911, for two weeks, I found about twenty thousand California Murres terrorized by about four thousand Western Gulls. . . . The case would not be so bad on an uninhabited island, for the Murres en masse are proof against the assaults of the gulls even. But the Southeast Farallon supports an increasing population of government employees, lighthouse keepers, weather men, wireless operators, etc., and these poor exiles have to stretch their legs once in a while. At the approach of a human the apprehensive Murres edge away, and the gulls swoop down to clean the uncovered eggs and to urge the Murres to further flight.

When Dr. Hanna and I were on the Southeast Farallon in May, 1949, the murres had only just begun to arrive for nesting so we saw only a few of them during our week on the island. From what we were told by the Coast Guard people at that time we are inclined to support Dawson's observations as still reflecting the situation, even after nearly forty years of protection.

At the present time the Farallons are of use as a combined Coast Guard, lighthouse, and weather station. The Farallon Light is one of the principal ones on the Pacific coast, the first one mariners look for on approaching San Francisco by sea.

The lighthouse, completed in 1855, is now powered by electricity furnished by large diesel-electric generators, one in use, the second as a spare, and a third for the rare emergency in the event the other two fail. However, a light alone is not enough, as the vicinity of the Farallons is the source of most of San Francisco's fog. The first fog siren was a steam-locomotive whistle powered by waves forcing air into a blow-hole. The present fog siren is a modern diaphone producing a well-known, low-pitched moan that can be heard for miles.

Although the murre rookeries have not regained their former population, there are still many birds, of several kinds, on the Farallons. Of the night birds the small Cassin auklet, somewhat larger than a quail, is the noisiest. It has a nerve-shattering cry somewhat like the loud creaking of very rusty gate-hinges. The South Farallon is also the nesting ground for thousands of petrels. They come in at dusk; some evenings the air seemed full of them. Small slate-colored birds, they often flew close to our faces like giant fluttering moths. Their call is a soft, drawn-out twitter. The nights were full of their voices, frequently giving the impression of a pet store full of chattering parakeets, magnified many times over. Another bird we saw often in our ramblings over the island during the days was the oyster-catcher, with its brilliant red beak, chisel shaped for prying limpets off the rocks for food.

Rabbits are the only prevalent land mammal on the Southeast Farallon although a few hoary bats have been collected there. Rabbits were introduced many years ago; no one knows when, or by whom. In 1949 the rabbits were present but not numerous, probably the result of a poison campaign several years before. It would not be surprising, however, to find that rats and mice also had been introduced.

There are not many insects on the Farallons, except for kelp flies that are present at times in uncounted millions; often these are a real nuisance. We collected what insects we could find and, although the catch was small, we found a click-beetle that proved to be a new species. We saw no red ants but did find that the bodies of dissicated pelicans and cormorants harbored quantities of large ticks. Fortunately these were not the kind that bothers people.

There are no snakes on the Southeast Farallon, but a species of spotted salamander lives there. We had hoped to find some of these but failed in spite of a careful search.

Mollusks are plentiful. Both the red and the black abalones are large and abundant. Many shells of the Alaskan abalone were washed ashore on the few sand beaches and into the surge channels, indicating a sizable quantity of this deep-water species. Owl limpets, now quite scarce on the mainland because of overcollecting, are abundant and large. We had not seen so many and such fine ones in years. Low tide uncovers many tide pools, some small and others quite large.

Rarely had we seen more colorful ones, their bottoms covered with brilliant mats of red and purple sponges and their accompanying invertebrate inhabitants — sea urchins, shrimps, nudibranchs, and shelled gastropods, both living and occupied by hermit crabs.

There are two land mollusks. The common European brown snail, a mainland garden pest, has been introduced but evidently is not too successful in the environment of salty fog. It was a bit surprising to find them on the open ground, looking dead and bleached, only to pick them up and find them alive. The other land mollusk is a large greenish yellow slug of a species common on the mainland. These were about in the grassy areas early on foggy mornings. Standing in one spot near a small fresh-water reservoir, I counted more than fifty. It is not known whether their presence on the island antedates human habitation.

In addition to the evaluation of animal populations, one special result of our geological exploration was the discovery of a most unusual phosphate mineral new to the Western hemisphere. Dr. Hanna has reported on this discovery in the Division of Mines Geologic Handbook for 1951:

On the north shore of the west end of the island (Indian Head), and just across a low divide from 'Shell Beach', there is a huge sea cave extending eastward under a steep cliff. To the south there is a smaller one extending at nearly right angles. The latter is not very large and has, just inside the entrance, a tide pool as brilliantly colored with marine life as one might expect in the tropics. Farther inside, the floor of the cave can be reached, but not without some danger if a heavy sea is running. The place was visited twice, and both times the floor was wet with salt spray. At high tide water drips slowly from the roof but leaves no deposit there. On the wet floor small,

A bull sea lion on the rocky Farallon shore. (O.J.H.)

A narrow-gauge railroad connects the landings. (Photo by G Dallas Hanna.)

191

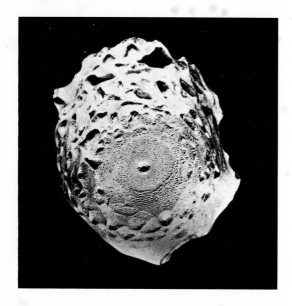

San Francisco, but it turned out to be of poor commercial quality. However, we did find these guano areas to be interesting collecting grounds for deep-water shells. These are eaten by fish, which the cormorants catch by deep diving and bring to their nests as food for their fledglings. The cormorants are good providers, bringing in more fish than their youngsters can eat. The leftovers eventually disintegrate, leaving the shell contents of their stomachs on the surface. We found a new gastropod species on this garbage-guano heap.

Our visit to the Farallons proved profitable in many ways — the first geological survey of the islands, an opportunity to evaluate wildlife populations, discovery of new gastropod and beetle species, and discovery of a rare mineral. Our work was aided by the Coast Guard employees who, with their families now stationed on the Southeast Farallon, are an efficient and hardy people, living happily on one of the most desolate and barren places on earth. Nordhoff, in his 1874 article in *Harper's,* expresses this quality of the Farallons very well:

Except the rock of Tristan d'Acunha in the Southern Atlantic Ocean, I have never seen an inhabited spot which seemed so utterly desolate, so entirely separated from the world, whose people appeared to me to have such a slender hold on mankind. Yet for their solace they know that a powerful government watches over their welfare, and — that, thirty miles away, there are lights and music and laughter and singing, as well as crowds, and all the anxieties and annoyances incidental to what we are pleased to call civilization.

These, then, are the Farallons.

Right, minervite, a rare phosphate mineral from a Farallon sea-cave. (G D.H.) *Below,* the Southeast Farallon at sunset. (U.S. Coast Guard photo.)

flower-like stalagmites about two inches in diameter and two inches high have formed. These have beautiful, wavy, scalloped cups on the outside and in the center of the cone there is a slight crater-like depression. They are minervite, a phosphate not heretofore recorded from California.

So far as is known, minervite, which was discovered in Italy under much the same conditions described above, has not been found anywhere else in the world other than these two places.

The guano which is partly responsible for the formation of the minervite is extensive about the cormorant rookeries. Some years ago there was an attempt to gather, bag, and sell it for fertilizer in